Do Robins Cough?

*

Do Robins Cough?

*

BEVERLY PEBERDY

ORION

Acknowledgement

With thanks to Mrs Barbara Herne for
permission to reprint her photographs.

Copyright © Beverly Peberdy 1996

All rights reserved

The right of Beverly Peberdy to be identified as the author
of this work has been asserted by her in accordance
with the Copyright, Designs and Patents Act 1988.

First published in 1996 by
Orion
An imprint of Orion Books Ltd
Orion House, 5 Upper St Martin's Lane
London WC2H 9EA

A CIP catalogue record for this book
is available from the British Library

ISBN: 0 75280 175 9

Filmset by Selwood Systems, Midsomer Norton
Printed and bound in Great Britain by
Butler & Tanner Ltd, Frome and London

Dedications

*

My love, gratitude and admiration go to John, my husband, and Russell, my son. Without their tolerance, support, understanding and love none of this would have been possible. I am indebted to them both and dedicate this book to them.

I should also like to dedicate this book to the children, the poor, the elderly and the handicapped of the world, those who are not wanted or loved, but some of whom Mother Teresa and her Sisters devote their lives and faith in God to helping.

I should particularly like to thank Andrew Crofts, who helped me put the book together.

I should also like to thank my editor, Caroline Oakley, for her help, encouragement and most of all her patience!

Acknowledgements

*

Working as I do in the voluntary world, I am constantly indebted to the many people who sacrifice their time, give freely of their expertise and help with donations.

Some of the people to whom I owe the most thanks do appear in the pages of this book, having somehow become inextricably enmeshed in the story. There are many others, however, to whom equal thanks are due but if I was to list all their names here the reader would soon become bored with such a saintly roll call.

I only hope that everyone whom I have been in contact with since I set out on this adventure in 1991 knows just how grateful I am for everything they have done and given and that those whose names did not make it through to the final draft of the book will understand and forgive me.

Contents

✳

CHAPTER ONE

Arrival in Hell

*

*I*t was early February 1991 and I felt like we were going out on an SAS mission as we six new recruits from the Romanian Orphanage Trust set off from the hotel in Bacau. There were no windows in the sides of the van and those at the back were thick with sludge spun up from under the wheels. We caught glimpses of the spectacular scenery through the windscreen, over the shoulders of the driver and his two colleagues in the front. They were talking to one another and ignoring us as we were bumped and tossed about in the back. There were no seats, just wooden benches bolted to the metal sides. There was nothing to hold on to so the two Irish girls and I linked arms and tried to stabilise ourselves but we still kept being bounced off the seats, landing painfully on the floor and hitting our backs on the benches. I felt dizzy with travel sickness and prayed that I would make it to Ungerini without showing myself up by having to ask them to stop and let me out.

Every time the van's wheels crashed into the potholes that dotted the roads, hidden beneath the snow, our heads banged agonisingly against the roof. Despite the discomfort, I still felt excited at the prospect of finally approaching our destination; at making a start on improving the lives of the pathetic little figures I'd seen on TV.

We kept on climbing up the snowy mountains, our wheels often spinning on the compacted ice. We passed through tiny villages made up of wooden cottages painted pretty pastel colours, overtaking carts pulled by horses and oxen. Everyone who saw us waved and children ran along beside us as, over an hour after leaving Bacau, we came into the village of Ungerini and made our way to the Orphanage for Irrecuperables.

The van slid to a halt in front of some gates set in a long, breeze-block wall. The driver sounded the horn and climbed out. He came round the back and opened the doors so that we could get out into the wet, muddy snow. I took deep gulps of the crisp fresh air, hoping to quell my nausea and soothe my nerves.

'Can't take the van in there because of the snow,' the driver explained. 'We'd never ever get out again. We have to walk down.'

Summoned by the van's horn, an unshaven security guard stumbled out. He was wearing a cossack hat and was wrapped in a huge sheepskin which he must have been using as a blanket in his tiny sentry hut. He had a rough complexion and his fingers, protruding from soiled mittens, were black with grime. He fumbled for what seemed like an age with a jangling bunch of keys before starting to struggle with the rusted padlock, at the same time babbling in Romanian, which none of us could understand. Eventually he pulled open the forbidding gates and we walked in through the sludge, passing under the wrought-iron sign bearing the legend IRRECUPERABLE HOSPITAL.

They were just like the gates I had seen on bleak, grainy, black and white documentaries about death camps and a feeling of dread and depression mixed in with the travel sickness and nervous tension which was already churning inside me. But nothing that I had seen on the television, or been told by the people of the Romanian Orphanage Trust who had sent us out from England, could have prepared me for the horrors we were about to see.

The sludge turned to thick, churned-up mud as we made our way down the hill into a big courtyard. The building's light brown walls stretched up around us, the windows all rusting and barred, the glass black with dirt and lined with grey net curtains. Behind the building I could see a beautiful little Orthodox church. I heard a tapping noise and looked up. A small face was peering out through a piece of clean glass and I saw a hand wave. I waved back.

The guard shuffled along with us to a pair of metal doors and unlocked them with another key-jangling performance. Once he had conquered the lock he threw open both doors in a gesture of welcome and the blast of putrid air made me step back in shock.

2

It was like a great heat hitting us and I retched involuntarily at the smell of rotting food, urine and excrement, mixed up like some giant, steaming compost heap.

Inside everything was grey, gloomy and wet. A couple of small, shadowy figures darted across the passage from one of the rooms, pursued by the shouts of angry women. The floors and walls were all running with water and there were no windows. As the doors banged shut behind us, the key crunching in the lock, it took several moments for my eyes to adjust to the darkness and even then I was only able to see a few feet ahead. Somewhere, far down the high windowless corridor, one light bulb emitted some feeble rays. The cold and damp made me shiver but the worst thing of all was the noise. Frantic, distorted folk music blared deafeningly from invisible speakers but even that wasn't loud enough to cover the manic screaming and moaning which seemed to come from every side. It wasn't like listening to human voices; it was like a tide of misery washing over us. I felt completely lost and trapped.

A girl with mad, darting eyes, who looked to be about twelve, came running down the corridor and leapt onto one of the drivers, wrapping her legs round his waist and hanging there a few moments before leaping onto another person, like a monkey swinging through the trees. She was pulling at their hair and clothes and wanting to touch everything in an agitated manner. They laughed and talked to her, calling her Wilma. It looked odd because she was so big and it was as if they were treating her like a pet. I hoped she wouldn't latch onto me because I didn't know how I would get her off.

What on earth am I doing here? Why aren't I back home, safe and warm and free, instead of being locked inside a bedlam where I don't speak the language or understand anything that's going on? I thought. It was like being transported back to the Dark Ages and then being left to fend for myself in a foreign land.

The existing team members who'd collected us from Bacau were still chattering amongst themselves, according us the occasional word. They led us down the passage and through a set of doors covered in net curtains into a chaotic room which had some natural light coming in. There were shelves of supplies like powdered milk, baby creams, talcum powder and boxes of toys. 'This is the team room,' someone told us, 'where we store

3

all our things. We have to go and meet Madam Augustina now, the Director.'

We went down another wet, dark corridor with Wilma still attached to one of us and were shown into an outer office where there was a typist and three other office staff. There were more dirty net curtains over the windows, cutting out the light, and a traditional kiln in the corner pumped heat out into the room, filling it with the smell of coal and making my eyes smart. I was wearing all my thermal underwear because outside there was a – 20 degree wind-chill factor. Now, in my three pairs of socks and heavy boots, I felt faint from the overpowering heat.

The staff were all smoking. They seemed to be talking a lot but not actually doing anything. There was one man and three women all wearing the sleeveless sheepskin jackets and head scarves that I assumed must be traditional for the area. There was a telephone and a couple of old-fashioned, pre-war typewriters, filing cabinets and a few bedraggled pot plants. A threadbare carpet covered the floor. The office women shrieked an order at Wilma who leapt off the person she was clinging to and scurried away.

Taking no notice of the office staff, our guides waited as one of the women knocked at the door of an inner office to announce our arrival. Something was said from inside and the woman went back to her desk, avoiding our gaze as we continued to stand, waiting, until a commanding voice on the other side of the door shouted for the woman to bring us through and we were ushered into the even more intense heat of Madam Augustina's office.

As we came in the Director of Ungerini stood up from behind a huge old carved desk, covered in paperwork, and gave us the first friendly greeting we had had since arriving in Romania. She was a big woman with a heavy face and just the slightest twinkle in her eyes. She wore a jumper and cardigan, thick woolly tights and a mighty pair of boots. She strode across the threadbare, maroon paisley carpet and embraced each of us in turn. When it came to my turn she hugged me to her, holding my shoulders in her huge hands and kissing me hard on both cheeks. But she didn't release me as I expected and I realised that she was repositioning her face and was going to kiss me on the mouth. I tried to pull back but it was too late and she pressed her lips against mine and forced her tongue deep into my mouth. I gagged, unable to breathe. There was an overwhelming taste of stale garlic, coffee and tobacco and the terrible kiss seemed to last forever. I wondered if this was a normal local custom! When she finally let me go I panted for breath but there was no relief to be had from the thick, close, smoky air.

Madam Augustina shouted for chairs to be brought in which caused a frenetic burst of activity from her underlings. She seemed very concerned about my comfort and insisted that I sat down next to her. When we were finally seated nothing else happened and we all sat staring at one another, smiling nervously. It was obvious that none of the team had learnt any Romanian and Madam certainly didn't know any English. Eventually she broke the awkward silence with more shrieks, this time demanding that coffee be brought.

As we sat, more members of the existing British team arrived, as well as a girl called Dana who was to be our translator. More chairs had to be found. Dana was fabulously attractive with a melancholy face framed by black hair and enlivened by sparkling dark eyes. Having a means of communication eased the embarrassment for us but it was obvious that there was a set etiquette to how the conversation should proceed. We weren't expected to speak first; we had to wait for Madam Augustina to say something and for it to be translated by Dana and we could then respond. A great performance was made of serving coffee off the formal tray which was brought in from the outer office, accompanied by a proud announcement that this was 'finest Nescafé'.

As we drank the hot, viscous, sweet coffee and Madam smoked endless cigarettes, she asked each of us in turn what we did in Britain. The telephone rang once and she screamed an order down it before slamming it back on its cradle.

A little girl with a squint was brought in by an unsmiling carer and shown to us. I was surprised by how healthy she appeared and that she was comparatively well dressed. She went very readily to Madam Augustina without any show of apprehension. The Director pinched the child's face in a friendly manner and made a fuss of her. The carer, who was dressed like the peasants we had seen in the villages on our travels from Bucharest, stood, her eyes modestly cast to the ground, until she was told to take the child away again.

The whole welcoming ritual took an hour and a half and I was becoming impatient to see the rest of the children and the home itself. Madam Augustina talked to us almost apologetically about the conditions in the home and explained how they wanted to improve things but that money was only just starting to get through to them. Within this building were 186 mentally and physically handicapped children between the ages of three and eighteen and a staff of 142.

At my interview in England the ROT had explained that under the old political regime every orphan in the country was given a five-minute test at the age of three. If they failed they were considered to be of no worth to their country and were sent to places like Ungerini to live amongst the mentally ill or disabled and the hopelessly crippled.

Madam Augustina explained that before the fall of the dictatorship there had been no money to pay the wages of the carers. Now, she said, things were getting better and there were no children dying any more. She seemed very proud of this fact. She said they were trying to train the staff to do their jobs better but it was hard because there weren't enough of them to be able to take the necessary time away from their daily duties. She hoped that with our help they would be able to do more for the children.

She told us that the interview was now over and that we would be taken to look around the home. The British team and Dana took us back out into the cold, damp corridor. Opposite the door a sink had a tap permanently running into it. 'That is the only place to get fresh water,' we were told. 'If you need water for anything, this is where you come.'

We came into a big hallway and once more we could hear screaming from behind another pair of double doors. We turned right and went down a flight of stairs to the laundry. As we approached, the smell of excrement grew stronger until it overwhelmed us. It seemed to reach right to the top of my nostrils, so strong that I knew I would never be able to forget it. I could feel it seeping into my clothes and feared that I would never get rid of it.

There were about eight women working in the freezing laundry, dunking sheets and clothes covered in faeces into a bath of icy cold, chlorinated water, beating them down into the scummy brown soup with brooms and then throwing them out onto the ground where other women threw more cold water over them. The resulting swill was sloshing all around the floor and over our feet on its way towards the central drain. I watched it going over my canvas boots with sheepskin linings which had seemed so practical when I set out from England, wondering if it would soak in and make them unwearable. The women were then picking the laundry up, gigantic piles of it, and pushing it into two industrial-sized old washing machines. There was no sign of any soap powder and once the washing had been turned around a few times they hauled it back onto the floor and wrung it out by hand. Everything was then carried downstairs in giant containers to hang on hot pipes to dry. I was amazed by the strength of the women. When there was no more room on the pipes they took the rest outside but, as Dana explained, 'It freezes very quickly at this time of year.'

The women had been calling out to one another as we came in but became silent and apprehensive as we stood watching them working. There was only one small window which let hardly any light into this damp, cold hell-hole. Their hands were red, raw and painful looking. I couldn't believe how bad these working conditions were. If this is how the women helpers are treated, I thought, what happens to the children?

'Every load of washing has to have a treatment of chlorine,' Dana explained, 'to kill the germs. The children are all diseased and this prevents the diseases spreading.'

I tried to hide my horror from Dana because I didn't want to embarrass her. I wondered what she imagined we were thinking as we watched this filthy, primitive ritual. She showed no sign of emotion as she explained to us what was happening and then led us up, past the ground floor doors and all the screaming and up to the first floor to Salon One which contained about fifteen children. There we were introduced to Jenny, an immaculately neat and rather nervous English lady, the wife of a merchant banker whose children had all grown up. She told us that she had been an SRN before marrying. Her clothes were so perfect she seemed almost surreal amongst the horrors of the room, her scarf tidily held round her neck with a pretty pin.

'Jenny is in charge of this room,' Dana explained. 'Up here are the smaller and the most severely handicapped children, the ones that need constant nursing.'

I was shocked by how dark the room was because of the filthy glass in the windows and the net curtains caked in dirt. There was no light on. The terrible, loud folk music was crashing through a loudspeaker, jangling my nerves. Another coal-fired kiln seemed to be keeping the room at a comfortable temperature until I realised that I was wearing lots of thermal layers; the children were lying in thin, filthy rags in their cots on bare, apparently wet, linoleum. The children themselves were also dirty, covered in a mixture of dried milk and snot. Many of them were damp with urine and faeces.

'How old are these children?' I asked, trying to make conversation and distract myself from the smell.

'They range,' Jenny said, 'from three to fourteen.'

'Three to fourteen?' I was puzzled because they all looked like babies to me. I went over to one of the cots which held an infant girl and I looked at her more closely. The most startling thing about this baby was her teeth – they were adult teeth. I realised that this tiny scrap of humanity must be at least twelve years old but she couldn't have weighed much more than an average newborn baby in Britain.

The most unsettling thing of all was that these children weren't screaming like the ones we had heard downstairs – although a couple were moaning softly and continuously to themselves. They didn't seem to be reacting to us in any way at all; seemed unaware that we had even come into the room. As I went to each cot and reached out to touch them they cowered away, like frightened puppies expecting a blow. Many of them were rocking constantly and rhythmically from side to side. A couple were on all fours, widthways across their cots, bashing their heads against the bars without stopping. When I got closer and my eyes had accustomed themselves to the gloom I could see that they had bald, red stripes across their shaved heads from where they had worn the hair away with this rhythmical banging. Neither Jenny nor the Romanian carers seemed to be making any effort to stop them damaging themselves. I wondered if there might be a reason for this – if perhaps they did worse things to themselves if this bizarre comforting was stopped. I made a mental note to ask someone whether I should try to prevent it once I started work.

The Romanian carer in the room was called Lucia, a dark haired, middle-aged woman with almost black flashing eyes. She seemed more spirited and friendly than the other workers, making a big fuss of us and watching us rather slyly as we took in the scene, as if calculating whether we were going to give her any trouble. She made a big show of grabbing one of the children and hugging it to her but I saw the child flinch away, as if unused to so much attention. It was impossible to tell whether it was a boy or a girl because of the shaved head. She put the child on the floor and made it walk around for us. The child looked so frightened I decided I would try to go much more slowly and gently with whichever children I was given to look after.

Apart from the cots there was nothing else in the room in the way of furniture or toys. Everything was perfectly tidy. The few cots that weren't being used had cushions placed symmetrically in them but there was nothing for the children to look at. At the end of the room I could see a pile of lovely continental quilts with gaily coloured, embroidered satin covers. They were neatly piled up and seemed incongruous beside the rags that the children had with them in the cots.

'Why don't they use them?' I asked Jenny.

'They are frightened of the children soiling them,' she explained.

As we went from room to room I became more and more puzzled by the lack of toys and activities for the children. I couldn't imagine how they were kept occupied all day. In the upstairs rooms were some hundred children, many still in the rusting cots that had been their prisons throughout the years of oppression. They were nearly all lying very still on cold, wet lino with only thin rags for cover, staring into space, waiting to die. Many had their legs curled up to their chests. What on earth could I do to help such pitiful creatures? I asked myself.

In some of the rooms the children had grown too big to be contained in their cots and were free to move about. These children were making more noise and several of them ran up and started hitting us as we came in. They were small enough not to be intimidating. 'This is the bad boys' room,' Dana explained as we went into a room with about ten active boys who leapt off their beds onto us. I was beginning to notice some gruesome deformities amongst the mass of bodies milling around us. There were legs pointing in all directions, some with feet going completely backwards. Others had missing limbs. None of the boys was dressed in more than flimsy, soiled pyjamas and many had nothing on their lower halves at all. My own clothes were becoming drenched with urine where the children had clung onto me. Their noses were all running and caked and the slime was transferring itself to my clothes. All their eyes were red and sore-looking. There were scabs on their shaven heads and I wondered if they had been cut by the razors or beaten, or whether they had

9

done it to themselves. Many of them were constantly squabbling, scratching, slapping and biting. Their skins were pale beneath the patterns of scabs and sores and they all looked anaemic. The greyish pallor of their skins was almost more alarming than the angry-looking scars and smears of blood from more recent wounds. I just wanted to put them all into warm, soapy baths to try to cleanse and soothe their sores.

Some of the women carers seemed quite proud of the children in their rooms, telling us who they all were. I couldn't believe I would ever be able to learn all the unfamiliar names that I was being told, or be able to remember which children they belonged to in the swirling hubbub around us. Every so often the women would scream even louder than the children to try to bring some order to their rooms, adding even more nervous tension to the already hysterical atmosphere.

The more active children all wanted to touch my hair. They seemed fascinated by it, stroking it and making strange, trance-like moans. A couple of them took a firm grip and had to have their fingers prised open to release me. I had tied it back in a pony-tail that morning as the other British teamworkers had instructed us to do, to try to avoid catching nits and lice, but one of the children had wrenched the little tie out and run off with it. One of the women tried to chase him and recover it but it disappeared and wasn't seen again. All the children who came up to us sniffed us like dogs, pushing their snuffling, caked and slimy noses against our hands and faces and necks and hair. As they leapt in and out of my arms I hoped they wouldn't bite me or head butt me in their excitement. I had noticed that even the calmer ones seemed to occasionally lose control of themselves and attack the nearest person.

I had so many questions I wanted to ask but everyone seemed too busy or preoccupied to answer them. I couldn't understand how the women carers could bear to keep the children in the state they were in. What sort of callous monsters could they be, not to see what needed doing in order to make the children more comfortable? They seemed to be behaving like concentration camp warders rather than 'carers'. I noticed that there were Norwegian Red Cross nurses in some of the rooms, all dressed in immaculate white uniforms. They were working very quietly and purposefully and didn't stop to talk to us apart from saying hallo, giving us friendly grins and going straight back to the small groups of children they were working with. No one in our group explained their presence to us or even signified that they had noticed them.

There were three older children, including Wilma, who, I was told, lived downstairs, but who seemed to be allowed more freedom than the others and kept darting in and out of the rooms we were being shown. The little children appeared to be frightened of Wilma who was able to talk and used the skill to be rude to the women, screaming at them what sounded like abuse while they tried to send her away. Another of the bigger girls was called Valentina. She looked different from the others because she had longer hair and better clothes. Her hair was in a short, boyish cut and she was proudly wearing a British school cap and blazer with britches. I noticed she had pierced ears which surprised me. She was also rude and shouted at everyone in a deep, masculine voice.

She looked like a thin, pale, eight-year-old schoolboy but had strangely grown-up facial features and her deep, slow voice made me think she might have a hearing problem. I wondered why they hadn't found such an energetic girl anything constructive to do. She put her face very close to mine and then bellowed a word which I was told meant 'foreigner'.

There were other British workers in some of the rooms. They took little notice of us, just nodding a greeting and then getting on with their work. In one of the rooms an Englishman in his twenties called Mark introduced himself. He was tall and slim with long blond hair that was beginning to thin. He had a very posh voice and seemed tense. He had a tendency to giggle: an attractive, chesty laugh. I noticed he was very tactile and gentle with the children. He seemed friendly, talking to the woman carer in his room and working together with her. I made a note to get to know him as soon as I had a chance and to learn as much as possible from him.

'Now we're going downstairs to see the older children,' we were told, after half an hour or so. 'In some of the rooms they are quite violent. You need to be careful. Don't go too far in.'

'Do you go downstairs much?' I asked Jenny as we made our way down.

'Oh no, not since I first arrived. The little ones need me more . . . Do be careful, my dear,' and she gave me a nervous little smile.

I felt very apprehensive as we descended the stairs and crossed the hall, hearing the manic screams and shouts and unpredictable banging noises coming from behind the doors we were now, finally, heading for. Our guides opened the doors into a black corridor and turned into the first room.

'This is where the children eat,' someone told us. 'They've finished their lunch now.'

As we stepped into the dark, forbidding room I stumbled on the uneven floor. Glancing down I saw that I was wading through ageing food debris. I looked around and realised that the walls and ceiling were also plastered in food. I tried to look more closely to see what it was and it appeared mainly to be soup with lumps of bread and fat in it. There were also sharp bones sticking out from the slush on the floor, which seemed dangerous for the children. There were only four tables in the room and no chairs, which I thought was odd. The tables might once have had melamine on the surfaces but that had all flaked off long ago, leaving bare, cracked wood and rusty metal legs. It occurred to me that virtually no new furniture or fittings could have come into Ungerini since the outbreak of the Second World War. Time had stood still for half a century. I couldn't understand why so much of the food had been discarded when the children I had seen looked so hungry and malnourished. Two women workers were coming in with more buckets of cold water, throwing it down on the floor to sweep the waste food away towards an open hole in the corner. I didn't move quickly enough and a tidal wave of mush came over the top of my ankle boots.

We went back into the pitch black corridor and I felt utterly disorientated. It reminded me of an amusement ride where you pay to be scared out of your wits, not knowing what is going to happen, unable to see where you are going. And all the time there was this manic and unnerving noise. Our guides pushed open another set of double doors, letting out a little light and we were met with a cacophony of mad screams. Just as the doors opened I was able to see about fifteen large children sitting on two beds before they leapt to their feet and ran towards us. The rest of the beds were neatly made with worn blankets, like in a hospital.

The large, round woman carer in this room seemed almost kind to the children, bringing them forward to meet us and then gently scolding them if they became too clinging or too rough. They seemed to be comfortable with her and I began to revise the sweeping judgements I had made about the staff upstairs.

Our guides then took us from room to room, showing us more and more of these children sitting in the same bleak surroundings. We were told there were eighty-six of these older children in the downstairs section. The same thing happened in each room. They became very over-excited when we entered, many of them appearing anxious, rocking manically back and forth, chewing on their hands. I noticed that some of them had developed extra flaps of flesh on their thumb joints, others seemed to have torn open their own flesh. All the women had big, thick sticks to protect themselves.

Apart from a few exceptions like Valentina, all the children wore an assortment of thin, filthy, torn and unsuitable clothes, none of them buttoned or zipped, so that their private parts were permanently on display and they had to yank up their trousers all the time. None of them had socks, shoes or underwear. Their feet were blue with cold. Some wore only pyjama tops and hugged their legs to their chests as if trying to make themselves as small as possible. Many of the older girls' breasts were exposed as well as their genitalia. Some of the boys were quite mature and several of them were masturbating feverishly, which made them look even more threatening. Again I wondered if it was a good thing to let them do this; would they become so excited they might rape another child, or did it help them let off some of their pent-up frustrations? My mind was working in overdrive. I found such uninhibited sexual behaviour embarrassing in front of the men in the team. The children's lack of modesty didn't seem to concern either them or the workers; they didn't even appear to be aware of it, which made it seem even more dehumanising. We could see that some of the girls were menstruating. How must it feel, I wondered, to live so wretchedly; to be so cold, filthy and hungry with no privacy or dignity, no attention or love? I felt over-whelmingly sad. I was appalled just to see them so neglected – what must it be like to have to endure these conditions? I felt like an intruder, barging in on their misery. Many of the faces were devoid of expression or emotion, staring anywhere rather than make eye contact with us.

In one room there was a big boy, mature enough to have pubic hair, sitting on a very small baby's potty. He watched us for a few seconds when we came in and then jumped off the potty, leaving a painful red ring around his bottom, and leapt onto Nellie, a tall, strong nurse who had come out in the same team as me. He was making an agitated grunting noise, clinging so tightly that no one could get him loose. Eventually Nellie and the carer managed to tear him off and sit him back down on the tiny potty. I was very impressed by how calm Nellie remained. I couldn't have coped.

Many of the children were lost in strangely ritualistic behaviour, similar to the little ones banging their heads on the cots upstairs. One boy was holding a piece of string up in front of his face and staring at it intently, just flicking it back and forth. Another would walk a few steps and then bend as if to pick something up, straighten up and repeat the process. Others were staring at their hands or swinging their heads from side to side as if doing permanent exercises. Some of them were doing it so fast I imagined their necks must be agony by the end of the day. Others just sat staring ahead of them.

The deformities were as bad as upstairs but more frightening because of their size. There were children whose legs had knee joints the wrong way round or of different lengths, cleft palates and hair lips, squints, club feet, heads two or three times too big for the bodies that supported them and teeth that protruded in unexpected directions. There were a lot of 'floor children' shuffling themselves around on their bottoms or on all fours like dogs, and some who were on their feet but were obviously spastic. And then there were other children who appeared normal apart from their shaved heads and dirty conditions.

Just like upstairs, none of the rooms had anything for the children to do, look at or even sit on and often the beds were packed so close together that there wasn't even room for them to play on the floor or to fit in a chair. In many rooms the floors were wet with urine and all the children were huddled together on just two beds. When one of them wet themselves the puddles ran along the lino covering the mattress, saturating each child as they spread. How could anything ever come to any good here? What could I possibly do to even begin to alleviate this suffering? The sights were so terrible and the despondency so overpowering that it felt like drowning – as if a tidal wave of misery had swept over us and spoiled everything and everyone in its path.

In one room I saw two naked girls hunched together beneath a bed.

'What are they doing under there?' I asked.

'They're blind girls,' Dana said, as if that explained it. I wondered if they were down there to keep themselves out of the way of the more violent children. I felt like a spectator at a particularly poorly run zoo, viewing badly treated, bored and filthy animals.

In one of the downstairs rooms a carer had a bowl of thick soup and a spoon and was feeding all fifteen children from it, giving each a mouthful in turn. I couldn't understand how they could let the children share a spoon when it was so obvious that so many of them had colds and mouth sores, let alone more serious diseases. I wondered why they didn't let them feed themselves. The soup also seemed to be burning the children because it was so hot and I wondered why they didn't let it cool down first. I could see there were chunks of bread in the bowl which had gone soggy and I thought it was a pity they hadn't given the children the bread separately so that they could have had something to chew on. I assumed there must be a reason for doing it that way. Just as there must be a reason for the dining room with no chairs.

Finally we came to a room which Dana told us was for the big, completely mad boys. 'Be careful,' we were warned. 'They can be spiteful in here.'

The strong-looking carer in this room had a large lump of wood beside her chair for protection. There were about ten boys in the room who became highly agitated as we entered and began milling towards us. By this point I was genuinely scared of what might come next. One of them was howling like a wolf and others were shouting and screaming, most of them doing ritualistic acts like flicking their fingers in front of their faces. Two of the boys started to fight, snapping, snarling and biting at one another. The woman screamed at them and whacked the lump of wood down on the side of the bed to make them stop. They separated and slunk away from one another, growling.

From the far end of the room one of the bigger boys started to trampoline down towards us across the beds. As he reached the final bed he stared straight into my face and I knew that he was going to hit me. Before I could avoid him he launched himself off the bed and punched me in the eye with all his considerable strength. He caught me on the eyebrow and I had never felt pain like it. Stars exploded in my head and the air was knocked out of my body as I fell backwards. Everyone rushed round me asking if I was all right. I tried to sound blasé and brave and staggered from the room, my head splitting with pain.

'What did I do to upset him?' I wanted to know.

'It's not you,' one of the team assured me, 'it's just that we have broken into their routine and it disorientates them. We were intruding into Marius's lair.'

'Marius, is that his name?' I asked.

'He's one of the brighter ones,' one of the team explained. 'They give him medication, but not in a controlled fashion, so he's either completely out of it or aggressive.'

I thought I was going to have to admit my mistake and go home. I was the wrong person in the wrong place, too frightened to be useful and unable to achieve anything because I had no experience or training to back me up. My eye was throbbing painfully.

But the worst was yet to come. Once I had stopped seeing stars we continued our tour with a visit to the 'bathrooms'. Virtually no light came in through the tightly closed and filthy windows but as my eyes adjusted to the gloom I could see the wood was rotting on the walls. There were two dirty baths in the far corner with a dividing wall between them and the rest of the room.

Along one wall were a line of about ten overflowing babies' potties. There were also four Western-style white toilet bowls in doorless cubicles which were not plumbed in but were nevertheless being used. They were full to the brim with excrement. There was no paper or anything else with which to wipe or clean the children or the room.

'They empty the toilets out every so often by hand,' our guides explained.

The concentrated stench was so overpowering that I found it hard to get air into my lungs. It was like breathing clouds of poisonous chemicals and my head felt as if it was splitting. It was the most hideous odour I had ever encountered and it made me feel dizzy with nausea. It permeated everything – my clothes, my hair, my nose. I could feel myself getting hot and panic gripped me as I struggled to appear calm. Drawing breath was becoming a problem. The contents of the pots and lavatory bowls had flooded out over the floors so that not only were we wading through it in our shoes but the floor children had to shuffle through it on their hands and bottoms, soaking it up into their clothes. Those that could walk were coming in and out in bare feet. We were skidding around on the wet floors as if in some ridiculous nightmare and I was terribly afraid I was going to slip and land in all the muck. I felt selfish to be having such thoughts because everything was so much worse for the children. Surely, I reasoned to myself, the plumbing should have been the first thing to be put right in a place where sickness and disease were rife. To my relief we were shown some other toilets for our use: two holes in the ground with a tub of water to tip down after. I looked around for some comforting toilet tissue but there wasn't even an old newspaper. It wasn't good but it was better than the children had.

As the misery of Ungerini Irrecuperable Orphanage soaked into me, I wondered how the children could have survived at all. Not only was there dreadful physical deprivation but a lack of any sort of human contact. There was a total absence of emotion; no stimulation, no touching, no conversation – just the barking of orders and the screaming of abuse. The children were herded like cattle, prodded, pushed, fed, watered and then returned to their prisons. I couldn't believe that hell could be any more frightening or wretched than this place.

From bathrooms we moved on to the kitchens, past women peeling potatoes with knives, sitting on low kitchen stools with their massive legs wide apart and their thick, full-length knickers on display. It occurred to me that a few simple potato scrapers would have made a big difference to their lives. They were being very wasteful, cutting great chunks out and discarding them, and once they had finished peeling they just put the potatoes on the floor so that they then had to pick them up and put them into a pot in a separate operation. It all seemed like a tremendous waste of energy to me.

One of the women gave me a sweet smile as we went past into the main kitchen where they had a massive, central cooking range. It was being run on petrol which made the air smutty and everyone had red eyes. Wafer-thin metal sheets had been placed haphazardly across the flames with huge cauldrons of food boiling up on top – they didn't smell too bad after what we had just experienced. My first thought was that if the metal sheets gave way they would have a major disaster on their hands and then I wondered how they ever managed to lift these enormous pots. There were a lot of bones and other unrecognisable pieces of meat being dropped into the mixture. There were six men eating round a table on the other side of the room. I assumed they were workers and I noticed that they had some fairly decent looking meat on their plates. It looked like they got the best bits.

'There is no running hot water here,' Dana explained to us, 'so if they need it they have to boil it up for themselves.'

I noticed all the dirty feeding bottles from the children's rooms upstairs were standing around on the floor waiting to be washed in cold water. I was stunned by the lack of hygiene all around the building and then I thought that in some perverse way it might help to make the children resistant to everyday germs. The children who were still alive in Ungerini must be exceptionally strong in order to have survived all the various cross-infections that must be travelling around between the bedrooms, the lavatories and the kitchens, let alone all the other hardships they endured.

By the end of the tour all six of us had become strangely silent, each of us lost in our own thoughts as to how we were going to be able to cope with working here. Some of us had started to cough from the smoky, damp air.

'We'll stop for lunch now,' our guide told us and we headed back to the team room.

I couldn't eat, not only because of nausea. Adrenalin was rushing through me as my mind raced over all I had seen and I tried to work out what on earth I could do to help these people. The established team was talking quite happily amongst themselves whilst we newcomers kept fairly quiet. Three or four of the children stood outside the door, watching us handing round our packed lunches which had been made up at the hotel from food shipped out for our use from Britain. There was bread, cheese, meat, fruit and cups of instant coffee.

One boy had been allowed into the room. He was introduced to us as Lucien and we were told he was seventeen, although he was very tiny and propelled himself around the home on a skateboard. He had horribly deformed arms and legs which went in all different directions. He reminded me of E.T. and seemed to be a favourite of the British volunteers. They were feeding him bits and pieces of chocolate, sitting him on a bench. One of the Irish girls remarked sadly that he looked like an organ grinder's monkey. I couldn't understand how they could do that in front of the other children who were being given nothing. As time passed more and more expressionless little faces joined the crowd outside, their noses pressed up against the window, watching Lucien with envy.

In the afternoon I noticed that the Red Cross nurses had got

18

very small groups of the bigger children dressed and were taking them outside for walks, which I thought looked like a wonderful idea – the first positive thing I'd seen all day. Our British guides still didn't make any mention of these other, quiet helpers. It was all very odd.

At the end of that first day I felt physically and emotionally drained. We drove back to the hotel with the other British team members in silence. My head was pounding. My clothes stank and felt squelchy with the children's bodily excretions. Mark, the friendly blond chap, made me a cup of tea with huge lumps of powdered milk floating around in it and it went down like pure nectar. I shared a room with Nellie at first because the other two girls did not like her smoking and, although I shared their feelings, I wanted to diffuse at least one of the tensions amongst us. After the first two weeks we were each given our own rooms. There was no hot water so Nellie and I had cold showers and then dunked our clothes into a bath full of cold water. I lay on the bed for about an hour clutching Tough Ted, my teddy, trying to make sense of it all. How could they keep the children like this? How could I change things to make it better for them? Would the staff listen to me and help?

'I thought you were brilliant with that boy who latched onto you,' I told Nellie. 'I don't know what I would do if he did it to me.'

'Old Potty Man?' she laughed. She was a trained nurse and had worked with the mentally ill before. 'Don't worry, Bev. If he jumps on you I'll get him off.'

One by one, other members of the team I had travelled out with came into our room and we began to talk, to run over what we had seen and heard while I made coffee. The team that was already out there was also staying in the hotel but they were on the other side of the building and seemed otherwise occupied until we all met downstairs, in the ornately carved hotel dining room, to eat a basic meal of chicken and chips. The old hands were laughing and joking about the standard of the food but I didn't think we were going to starve. That evening I was told by our team leader that I had been allocated Salon One where Jenny had been working and where all the most severely handicapped and the children who were expected to die were put. They said they felt that there my lack of experience would do the least amount of harm – to me or the children. Their deaths were seen as inevitable so I wouldn't be able to do anything to worsen that prognosis!

For some reason that first evening we had all smartened ourselves up for dinner. I had even put on some earrings. It was a bizarre, surreal experience, sipping local champagne so rough it gave you a headache before you felt drunk, and making small talk in the shabby grandeur of the hotel dinning room after having seen such terrible sights. The waiters in their old-fashioned uniforms had even managed to resurrect some elegant old champagne glasses for us. I felt like I was an onlooker, watching the strange scene from outside myself. There were about sixteen of us round the table and everyone seemed to be very negative, complaining about the children, the carers, Madam Augustina, the Romanians, the hotel, the food. I looked across at the other table which was occupied by the Norwegian Red Cross team who seemed to be having a much jollier time than us. An elderly woman amongst them caught my eye and gave me the sweetest of smiles across the room. I was later to learn that her name was Dr Kari; she had suffered as a girl at the hands of the Nazis in Oslo. There was no one else in our section of the dining room, the local Romanians having to eat in the outside area.

Although I had planned an early night I couldn't get to sleep. I wondered if I could ever clear those awful recurring images from my mind. Would I ever breathe again without being sickened by the smells which seemed to have invaded my body despite having scrubbed myself raw and liberally sprayed myself with precious perfume. It was only weeks since the whole adventure had begun but it felt like years. In one day I had seen more suffering and horror than most of us see in our whole lives. It was two in the morning before I finally sank into a fitful sleep.

CHAPTER TWO

Leaving an Ordinary Life

*

I would be the first to admit that by the age of forty I had started to lead a fairly humdrum life. Coming from a large, drama-ridden family I had deliberately opted for a quiet, rather ordinary adulthood. During the day I worked as a secretary in the computer department of Abbey National. The people I worked for were extremely nice and conditions were excellent but the job was not an exciting one and I got more satisfaction from chatting to the various people who came to me with their problems than I did from the job itself. I've always found that people like using me as a sort of agony aunt. I was a bit older than most of the others in the office, with a very stable home life and plenty of time on my hands to listen to their woes and give them the sympathy they felt they needed. In the evening I went home to my tidy house, my kind and loving husband, John, my stepson Russell, whom I had brought up as my own for twenty years, and my two border collies, Misty and Moss.

It was a secure and happy life and I honestly didn't believe that I had the ability or desire to achieve anything more. At least, most of the time I thought that. Just occasionally, however, I had harboured little fantasies of going out into the world and doing something that would 'make a difference' to the lives of others less fortunate. Sometimes I would express this desire to John but his reaction was always the same: 'You need qualifications for that sort of work,' he would say gently. 'No one would take on someone of your age with no medical or teaching background.'

I supposed he must be right, I certainly didn't feel confident enough to stick my neck out and apply for anything without his support and I never had the nerve to give up my much needed salary in order to go and get the qualifications that I lacked. So I stayed in my rut, like millions of other people, thinking about doing great and good things in the world, then getting on with everyday life.

At the end of 1990 I heard about the fall of President Nicolae Ceauçescu. Like everyone else in Britain, John and I started reading all the articles which were appearing about Romania in the newspapers. To begin with it sounded like just another tale of an old tyrant brought down by his own greed and the corruption of those around him, but I felt excited by it and all my sympathies were with the revolutionaries who had brought about his downfall. Gradually, as the Western news teams moved into the newly liberated country, the full horror of what had been happening under his rule was revealed. The Western world had witnessed nothing like it for nearly fifty years. We had grown used to seeing images of war and starvation and natural disasters – earthquakes and floods – on our screens, but this was something else entirely. As the cameras and journalists entered the orphanages and madhouses of Romania, we were shown as shocking a picture of man's inhumanity to man as at the liberation of the concentration camps at the end of the Second World War. There were the same threatening buildings and inmates who looked like dead-eyed skeletons, imprisoned in the most horrifying conditions of neglect. This time there wasn't even the excuse of a war; these children had never done anything to hurt anyone and had been completely unable to defend themselves – they simply hadn't fitted their leader's vision for the future of his country.

As I watched these pictures, I felt that familiar twinge of longing to do something to help but what could someone as unqualified as me possibly do? Months later Romania was brought to our attention again. *Blue Peter*, the children's television programme, had started raising money for the area and telling some of the stories of the children trapped in the institutions. My sister Suzy's children had mentioned this to us, so John and I made a point of watching the programme with our tea when we got home from work. We were moved and shocked. The more I found out about the country and its people the more I felt that I was somehow destined to be involved with Romania.

*   *   *

About a week before Christmas 1990, I was sitting reading my boss's *Daily Telegraph* one lunchtime, munching on something from the company sandwich and salad bar, when I spotted an advertisement placed by the Romanian Orphanage Trust. It asked for volunteers to go out to an orphanage for physically and mentally handicapped children and help some of the children get a little closer to leading normal lives. This was exactly the opportunity I'd been looking for. Somehow I felt that the ad was talking just to me, that this was how I was going to get to do something to help. But then my heart sank. They were looking for qualified nurses, doctors, teachers and physiotherapists. I felt desperately disappointed but remembered what a Scotsman once said to me: 'If you don't ask, you don't get.' So, with a mixture of excitement and trepidation, preparing myself for the inevitable disappointment of rejection, I telephoned the number in the advertisement.

'I'm afraid I don't have any medical or teaching qualifications,' I confessed to the rather grand voice on the other end of the telephone, burbling on to cover my nervousness, 'but I am good at organising things and getting things done, and I enjoy the company of children and I work hard.' I was desperately trying to think of what other attributes might endear me to her but I was running out. 'I'm good at following instructions, not prickly or anything. I'm a good team member. I'm not expecting to be a star.' I could hear myself going on and on but I couldn't stop.

The woman sounded unsure as to whether I would be considered. I felt that if I could just win her over I would have passed the first obstacle. 'I think they really need people with specific skills for helping sick children,' she told me, not unkindly, 'but I would be happy to send you an application form anyway so you can see what you think.' I felt childishly excited to receive even this much encouragement.

When I got home and told John what I had done, as casually as I could manage, his reaction was just as I would have expected. 'Don't get your hopes up too high, Bev,' he warned me. 'I don't want you to be disappointed. They're looking for doctors and nurses and childcare experts – people like that.'

I knew he was right, but I still couldn't suppress a surge of excitement when the envelope arrived a few days later. I tore it open and started to read. Not only did I have none of the professional qualifications they were asking for, I didn't even have the right amateur skills. Could I paint? Only in the most childish manner. Could I drive a car? No. Could I play a musical instrument? No. There wasn't a single question that I could answer positively. Was I really such a failure? Did I really have so little to offer? On top of everything else they were asking for people to stay in Romania for at least one month, in order to give the children some continuity, and I knew that my bank manager was not going to take kindly to the idea of me being unpaid for that long, even if the Abbey National allowed me the time off work.

I pushed the form into a drawer and decided, with a heavy heart, to forget it.

That evening we watched Anneka Rice on television, answering a challenge to refurbish an orphanage in Siret, Romania. John set the video to record in case we were interrupted by the telephone. The terrible state of the children made us cry.

'What could you possibly do to help children like that?' John asked, his eyes still full of tears. 'Where would you start in such a hopeless situation?'

'I don't know; perhaps they just need a little love and attention,' I said. I wasn't going to give up that easily. I stared at the drawer where the form was for what seemed like ages, feeling desperate, and then dismissed once more the thought that I might be able to do something, when I remembered all the things I couldn't do.

I don't normally have trouble sleeping, but at two in the morning I found myself still awake, images of the orphans circling round in my head. How could it possibly be that I had nothing to offer those poor children? I could wash and feed them, help them to dress, play games with them, take them out in the fresh air, talk to them, cuddle them. I could scrub walls and floors and wield a paintbrush just like Anneka. Weren't any of those things needed before the specialists moved in? I slid out of bed, careful not to wake John and crept downstairs.

I can't think properly if I'm cold, so I pulled a sleeping bag out of a cupboard and wrapped myself up in it as I replayed the programme. The dogs watched with puzzlement as I turned off the television and sat down at the kitchen table to re-read the application form. Misty, unsettled by my strange behaviour, climbed up onto my lap and I had to rest the form on her back. After a few minutes I got out a pen and started to write down what I could do. I could sing, well enough to get others going, and I might not be able to draw for toffee but I could use bright colours in paintings. In one of the boxes I wrote: 'Please, please read the attached sheet.' I then took a clean piece of paper and told them why I thought I might have something to offer the unfortunate orphans of Romania. I told them that I was always jolly and willing to tackle any jobs I was given and that I made gallant attempts to be supportive in difficult situations; that I was good at working as a team member and at doing what I was asked.

The next day I posted the form off, one minute preparing myself for the possibility that I would not hear another thing, the next moment planning exactly what I would do when they accepted me. I could take lots of beach balls – they wouldn't weigh too much in my luggage and are brightly coloured. Playing catch would teach the children co-ordination and would liven them up for the day. I could take bubble-mixture out with me. All children love bubbles and it would be fun for them to chase them around and pop them. I warned myself that all these plans would probably come to nothing, but something deep inside my head wouldn't take no for an answer. I was so confident that I actually rang a temp, a lovely Jamaican girl called Gloria who'd sat in for me at Abbey National before.

'Would you be free for a month if I was to go to Romania?' I asked.

She said she would be and I made her promise she wouldn't tell anyone until it was confirmed. Knowing Gloria would cover for me was a great relief because I knew she was good at the job and I wouldn't be leaving my bosses in the lurch. I was working as a secretary to two of the managers in the computer department, both of whom I liked very much. I wanted to be ready to counter any arguments they might put forward against my going and to leave them with someone who would look after them. When I told John that I had sent off the form he seemed rather proud, which surprised and pleased me, although he still kept counselling pessimism.

Impatient for an answer, I rang the grand but helpful lady again. Felicity MacPherson was a volunteer who worked from home so I was always able to get straight through to her, but felt guilty about bothering her so often. 'I've filled in the form and posted it,' I told her, 'but I'm worried you won't think I'm qualified enough. I'm sure I'm too old as well.'

'Don't worry,' she tried to calm me as I babbled on, 'I really don't think your age will be a handicap. It might even be a positive advantage because of all the life experience you've had.'

All through Christmas I kept dreaming of what might happen, and then telling myself not to be so foolish. The holiday seemed to delay things intolerably and I didn't receive a confirmation of receipt of my application for nearly three weeks. But at least I hadn't been rejected out of hand. I didn't find the letter until late in the day and even though it was well after work hours I rang Felicity MacPherson again. The poor woman was about to have her dinner, but she told me that the Consultant Paediatrician, Dr Judith Darmady, was going to look at all the applications which hadn't been rejected the following weekend. I was so excited I could feel a wave of hysteria coming on and had to take the dogs for a walk to try to get rid of some surplus energy!

The papers were full of the impending war with Saddam Hussein over the next few days, which put me in a reflective and sombre mood, worrying about the troops lining up out there and their poor families waiting at home. Then, on 15 January, Felicity rang. She invited me to go for an interview the following Tuesday. I think John was even more amazed than I was, but he still kept telling me not to get my hopes up because they were probably seeing hundreds of people. I was overjoyed, but a little nervous; I hoped Dr Darmady would feel my enthusiasm would make up for my inexperience.

'I think I'd better give you a lift down there,' John suggested. 'I don't trust you to get there on your own. God knows how you'll find your way to the foothills of the Carpathian Mountains.'

I was grateful for this offer; it would take a lot of the strain out of the ordeal for me to have him along and not have to worry about travel arrangements. John always took care of all the practicalities when we went on holiday simply because he enjoyed that sort of thing and I didn't. I did wonder how I would manage in a strange country, so far from home, without him. We arrived far too early, but I didn't mind, and we sat in the car chatting nervously.

'I won't come in with you,' John said. 'I'll wait in the car and listen to the news about the Gulf.'

At last the appointed time arrived and I joined a bunch of other waiting hopefuls. Most of them seemed to be professionals – teachers or music specialists – or had experience working with handicapped children.

'My name's Fiona,' an intense, smiling young woman of about eighteen, with cascades of hair, introduced herself. 'Call me Fee.' I thought I talked a lot but even I couldn't get a word in edgeways as she chattered nervously on as we waited our turn. She told me all about heavy carriage driving which was her hobby, and her flute playing. She told me she was a committed Christian. Oh well, I thought, someone has to be! She was very friendly and jolly and I admired her for volunteering for something like this when she was still so young. She told me her mother ran a home for people with mental and physical handicaps and that she had helped out all her life.

Another woman told me that she was a teacher and had played hockey for England. She asked me what I did. I told her. 'Oh,' she said after a long pause, 'do you think that your experience as a secretary in the Systems Department of the Abbey National will prove useful to the orphans?'

I wished I could think of a smart answer, but I couldn't because she had voiced exactly the doubts which had been gnawing away in my head for the past month.

At last I went in to meet Felicity MacPherson and was introduced to Dr Darmady, a warm, lively woman with sparkling eyes who explained all aspects of life and work in the orphanage, good and bad.

'Do you still want to go?' she asked at the end.

'Oh, absolutely,' I assured her.

'There is quite likely to be violence from some of the bigger children,' she warned me. 'How would you handle that?'

I have been afraid of violence, since childhood. My father had a drink problem and a temper and often took his frustration out on my mother. His rages were very frightening and I only plucked up the courage to interfere once. He fixed me with such a look that I scuttled away, never daring to challenge him again.

'I think,' I chose my words carefully, 'that if they know I'm not going to hurt them and that they have nothing to fear, then they won't want to hurt me.'

'The women working there will be unfriendly, unhelpful and definitely unco-operative,' she continued, not commenting on my answers, 'completely deaf to new ideas. How will you handle them?'

'The worse they are the more cheerful and persuasive I will be,' I assured her, 'until the results speak for themselves.'

Dr Darmady nodded, still without commenting. I dare say she thought I was being rather optimistic. After we had talked for a while I mentioned that John was waiting in the car and she suggested I invite him in. I suppose they wanted to see how supportive he was being and whether he was likely to put pressure on me not to go. Normally John is the most confident man going, able to talk to anyone and everyone, but he was so worried about saying something that would spoil my chances at the last moment that he behaved as if he was applying for the job himself.

I noticed both Dr Darmady and Felicity were talking about 'when' I went out to Romania, but I didn't have the nerve to stop them and ask if it meant I'd got the job. Eventually I summoned up the courage to ask and they said, 'Yes, we need you urgently. Can you fly out in two weeks' time and stay for three months?'

I leapt up, grabbed the doctor's hand, shook it vigorously, kissed her on the cheek, gave her an enormous hug and then did the same to Felicity. I thoroughly embarrassed myself.

'Well,' Dr Darmady recovered from her surprise and gave a broad smile, 'those children can look forward to lots of warmth, touching and hugs from you, can't they, Bev?'

When we got outside John and I just fell into each other's arms, our eyes full of tears. We didn't say anything; we just hugged and hugged. The one factor that we still couldn't predict was the reaction of the Abbey National to the news that I was going for three months (it eventually turned into four and a half months). I could take the first month out of my annual holiday, but what about the rest?

'They may not agree to let you go, Bev,' John warned, still reluctant to believe that things were actually going so well.

'No,' I agreed, 'I know.' The idea worried me because I didn't feel confident about leaving and having no job to come back to. It would be enough of a culture shock to be travelling alone to a foreign country, without losing all my security blankets at home. John was working hard to set up his own direct marketing company and although it was doing well it was still a small business, vulnerable to the whims of a few clients. Knowing that at least one of us had a salary coming in each month gave us both a lot of comfort, and my working for Abbey National meant that we had a special deal on our mortgage that we didn't feel we could give up. I've never been good at managing money, always spending it as soon as I have it and never saving anything, and with plenty of debts to credit card companies there was nothing stored away to cover months without a salary.

'Two weeks really isn't enough time for you to get yourself sorted out,' John continued.

'No, it isn't,' I agreed, staring out the window at the passing winter scenery. I knew that everything he was saying was true but in my heart I knew that I had to go to Romania now, whatever happened, and I rather wished that he would stop looking at the potential obstacles and concentrate on the fact that I had been accepted. We didn't allow our doubts to deter us from planning exactly what I would need to take with me on the trip. I thought it would be better to take lots of layers to keep warm, rather than very thick clothes, and John volunteered his two rugby shirts. I would have to spend out on a good coat and some boots and thermal underwear – what a sight that was going to be! Funds were too low to buy much more; I would just have to make do with what I had.

I was very nervous when I went into work the day after the interview and went straight to my boss, Peter Lazard. I told him what I wanted to do, holding my breath as I waited for him to tell me it was impossible.

'That's wonderful,' he said. 'I admire you so much. Leave it with me and I'll go to Personnel for you and sort it out with them. I'm sure it will be fine.'

I couldn't believe that it was going to be that easy. He went off to do battle and I waited nervously for the response. When he came back he told me that initially the personnel people had grumbled about 'setting precedents' but that he had pointed out that not many people were likely to want to pack up and head for Romania at a moment's notice and they had agreed.

I had rather hoped that I wouldn't have to tell anyone else about what I was doing. I didn't want to draw attention to myself; it would sound rather like showing off to announce that I was going to Romania to help orphans. By now it felt so natural for me to be going that it didn't seem anything out of the ordinary or worthy of special attention – I was just going. But I couldn't keep it a secret for long. A female manager I had always been rather in awe of stalked over and told me she couldn't decide whether I was 'mad or wonderful', and another woman, Janet Stevens, who worked in the management training department, gave me a ring with a wooden crucifix on it. 'You won't understand the significance now,' she said, 'but you will when you get there. You will never be the same person again.' Being an atheist I didn't put much store by her words, but I took the ring and I appreciated the gesture.

The next two weeks were a whirlwind of activity. I never got more than a few hours' sleep each night as I charged through the house cleaning out cupboards, mending clothes that had been awaiting my attention for months, washing and ironing everything I could find. I even tidied up the garden – in January! I was taking on an expedition mentality – getting everything and everyone organised. I was up at five every morning to arrive at work early so that I could get up to date with my filing – something I have never been good at – and prepare everything for an impending office move.

I went to see our family doctor, Dr Prisk, at the Central Milton Keynes Health Centre a few days later about injections and he gave me stern warnings about the risks of getting AIDS from the children. I told him that I had read up on this and would be taking proper precautions. Almost as a throwaway comment he added, rather wickedly I thought, 'Oh, and of course there is the risk of AIDS from promiscuity.'

'Doctor,' I said, 'you would only have to see me in my thermal underwear to know that there's little risk of promiscuity.'

I went to the local library and John went to the Romanian embassy looking for background information on the country, but there seemed to be virtually nothing available beyond market and population trends. The Romanian Orphanage Trust, which was organising and financing my trip, sent me a little material but it was obvious that no one in the West knew much about what had been going on in the area since the last war.

At the same time I wrote letters to anyone I could think of, asking for donations or help for the project. Amongst others, I wrote to Roy Castle. He sent a very nice letter back, enclosing £25 and apologising for not being able to spare more, but explaining that he received so many requests that it was impossible to respond to them all. He told me that he wanted me to spend the money on getting myself a pair of warm boots rather than on anything for the children. I ignored the final instruction. (I wrote to him on my return, and we struck up a friendship. He was greatly cheered to have positive news of the children he had helped.)

I did have to buy some clothing for myself and I headed to C & A for most of it. When I asked for advice the girls behind the counter thought I was going skiing. When I explained what I was doing they brought out more and more stuff they thought I would need and I had to admit that I was on a very limited budget. They then talked amongst themselves and came back to say that they would like to donate their own staff discounts and vouchers. I was very touched by the gesture and grateful for the extra layers I was able to afford.

My sister Karen, who has a sort of siege mentality, believing you should always bulk buy in case of emergencies, also gave me a lot of sensible stuff. I had cause to be very grateful on the cold nights in the hotel with only a sheet and blanket on the bed.

All sorts of people at work and in the family rallied round to help raise money and collect extra things which I could take with me for the children. I found it all very encouraging but deeply embarrassing. On a trip to the office loo I discovered colleagues had posted a notice on the board opposite announcing, 'Bev Peberdy is going to an orphanage in Romania – please can you help?' I had known that some of the girls were fund-raising but I hadn't realised it would be so public. I shot into the loo, my face brick red and pulsating with embarrassment. It was then I really began to panic. Had I bitten off more than I could possibly chew? Was I going to be taking the place of someone who would be of some specific use to those poor children? I was racked by nerves and self-doubt. One minute it seemed like a great adventure, the next like a ludicrous act of self-delusion.

John was astonished that not only had I been invited to go but that I was actually going to go through with it. But not for a moment did he try to talk me out of it. One evening shortly after the 'loo' incident he told me what some of his clients had said about me going and I was surprised I cropped up in his conversation at work.

'You told them about me?' I asked.

'Of course,' he said. 'I'm really proud of you. They were very impressed.' I felt very touched.

John was more than willing to help me get everything together for the trip and to look after the house and dogs while I was away. There was only one stipulation: 'Do not,' he warned me, 'on any account, come back with a baby or a toddler!' We both roared with laughter at the very thought. Although we loved our smaller nieces and nephews coming to visit, we were always relieved when we had the house back to ourselves. Taking on a small child full-time was unthinkable.

When we first got married I had hoped that we would have children but it never happened. John wasn't too upset because he had already had Russell (by his first wife) and after a while I had talked myself into thinking that perhaps bringing up a stepson from the age of four was as much as I wanted to do on the maternal front. John was already divorced when we started going out, so there has never been any animosity between Edna, his ex-wife, and me. She was always very co-operative about John having regular access to Russell and we saw him either in London at John's parents or he came to us for weekends. He had his own little bedroom in our tiny flat and was very much part of our family, if only part-time. After we had been married for about a year, Edna decided that Russell would have a better life with us and I found myself the full-time mother of a six year old. Of course, Russell still saw his mum whenever it was possible. I stopped pining and settled for enjoying the freedoms that came as Russell grew up.

My biggest worry about going to Romania, to be honest, was whether poor old Misty and Moss would get enough attention without me around. Joy, my sister-in-law, promised to walk them in the woods regularly.

'I couldn't do what you are doing,' she told me, 'but I can provide you with support back here at home.'

By the time I was due to leave England I had accrued boxes and boxes of toys, paints and other materials which I thought would help with the job. I had been to the medical department at work and they had stocked me up with surgical gloves and syringes. *Blue Peter* heard, I assume via the Romanian Orphanage Trust, that I was going and asked me to take out the posters which their viewers had made for the orphans. I was happy to agree, not realising quite how many parcels there were going to be.

John and I went to meet the rest of the group in the evening on Wednesday, 6 February, three days before we were due to depart. I had been told by Felicity MacPherson that I had been appointed 'wave leader', which meant that I was to be in charge of the half dozen people who would be flying out from Heathrow with me. I protested that I would much rather be just a team member. I had no ambitions towards leadership but she said they had thought about it carefully. She promised that as soon as we reached Romania I could hand over responsibility to the existing team leader, a nurse working full-time at Ungerini. The team was an eccentric and interesting bunch of characters, all endowed with exactly the sorts of qualifications I so obviously lacked. Coming from such diverse backgrounds I wouldn't have expected the team to be the best of friends in normal life but I assumed that, united by a common cause, we would manage to cover our differences and work together.

As the time to leave drew nearer it became increasingly obvious that I was not going to be able to get everything into my luggage. Thankfully, Russell, a seasoned camper and traveller, came to the rescue and repacked for me. Then it was the morning of departure and time to say goodbye to Moss and Misty, to the house, to comfort, to security and, though I didn't realise it at the time, my whole way of life.

When it was time to say goodbye to John at the airport, I wept, feeling a terrible wave of panic sweeping over me. Anyone watching would have thought we were going to be apart for years. How would I manage without him, without his company and support? We had never been away without each other in twenty years of marriage and he had looked after every practical arrangement we had ever made. How could I possibly get this group of people all the way to Romania without him? As I went through the departure gate, I glanced back and, through a blur of tears, took one last look at my beloved John. Then all too quickly he was gone and I was on my own.

CHAPTER THREE

Culture Shocks

*

I felt my first task would be to keep the group's spirits up through a thirteen-hour flight delay. We were all heading for a foreign land and had virtually nothing in common.

Roger had trained as a barrister but had recently been looking after adults with very special needs. He turned out to be wonderful with the children, but not so good at communicating with his colleagues. Roger was particularly skilful with the most difficult and unattractive children. Whereas there was a temptation for all of us to work hardest with the children who were the most normal, he always struck a chord with the ones with the most problems. There was a little Down's Syndrome boy, Andrei, in Salon One who always lay on his back. Roger became a particular friend to him and we would get him up and put him in a corner seat, from which he would survey the room like an old judge, blowing bubbles with his spittle all the time.

There were two Irish girls; Jacqui, a feisty young psychologist and Diane, a beautiful, six-foot physiotherapist who had already done three months in Romania and was fluent in the language. I was sure she would have been much better than me as wave leader.

Matthew was a very handsome and personable nurse who specialised in looking after old people, and there was another nurse named Catherine, and who preferred to be called Nellie. She had cared for mental patients and, being immensely strong, did more than her fair share of carrying our cases around.

And then there was me, a secretary and seemingly the most placid personality in the group – just wishing that someone would turn up and take responsibility and tell me what to do next. I could tell immediately that I was going to get on with the two Irish girls (before long I was calling them the 'Two Irish Tarts' or 'Tits' for short, and they referred to me as 'The Old Bag').

By the time we boarded the aircraft I was already getting to know some of my fellow travellers. They weren't turning out to be how I had imagined charity workers to be. I had imagined that all women charity workers and volunteers would be crosses between Anneka Rice and Esther Rantzen, and that the men would be somewhere between Philip Schofield and Dr Finlay. I imagined they would be problem-free, existing solely to carry out admirable works. Their saintly endeavours would require vast amounts of energy, expertise and self-sufficiency, which they would all have in abundance. They would all be incredibly pro-active rather than reactive. It came as a surprise, and something of a relief, to find out that they were human just like the rest of us!

I suppose if I had thought more deeply about why people might give up everything – job, home, family – I would have realised that there would be people who were looking for a way to escape from their own personal problems. After all, I had been looking for a way to enliven my own existence.

The moment we stepped into the TAROM plane we knew that we were moving into a very different culture. No one working for this national airline was worried about things like courtesy and customer service. 'Sit over there!' the stewardess shrieked at us. The plane was horribly hot and a familiar feeling of nausea began to well up inside me, despite the travel-sickness tablets. Roger begged to be allowed to sit next to me. I was rather surprised, expecting him to want to sit with one or other of the attractive Irish girls. Then I realised that he was so terrified of flying he was looking for a comforting presence rather than flirtation and he had been fooled by my outward appearance of calm. I did my best to offer him gentle encouragement. He was red hot to the touch and sweating profusely as he held my arm in a grip of steel with one hand and threw back drinks with the other. I thought he was very brave to volunteer to put himself through such an ordeal.

Around us was a group of about twenty Baptists who had had the Bible translated into Romanian and were heading out to 'spread the word'. They talked a great deal about how we should be 'letting Jesus into our hearts'. I was actually more worried about keeping my food down. I warned them that I was an atheist and unlikely to be satisfactory material for conversion.

'You can't be an atheist,' they insisted, 'if you are going out to Romania to do God's work.'

I couldn't quite see why only Christians were allowed to help other people and why they should have the monopoly on caring, but I didn't feel up to a heated debate and I was fairly certain that nothing I could say would change their opinions anyway. In the coming months I would meet a lot of people with strong religious convictions, some of whom were doing very good practical work indeed, and some of whom were concentrating on getting as many converts as possible to their particular sects without actually doing anything to help improve the quality of life in Romania … it takes all sorts.

I was feeling worse and worse as the plane grew hotter and circled for what seemed like an age before landing at Bucharest. Roger said that even though he was otherwise occupied with his fear of flying, he did notice that I had gone more colours of green than he knew existed. It seemed that the flight would never end and I was beginning to wish I had never heard of Romania. Eventually we descended onto the tarmac and were directed onto a bus which took us swaying and bumping over to the terminal building.

Because of the delay in London we had arrived in the early hours of the morning. There only seemed to be one light on in the whole airport and there were a number of bored looking soldiers hanging around the concourse with rifles and machine guns and worn-out uniforms. A greeter from the Romanian Orphanage Trust had come out to the airport to collect us but had failed to bring the necessary documents so we were unable to clear customs. After the seemingly interminable flight, this was the last straw and some of our team were ready to go home, saying, 'Do they want our f. . . . . . help or not?'

Realising that this was the moment when a 'wave leader' should be taking control I put on my most confident face, willed my hands to stop shaking and handed the officials my Romanian Orphanage Trust letter of acceptance which ran to six pages. The letter was in English and looked very official. They looked at it suspiciously and then took it away for about forty-five minutes and pretended to read it. I know they only pretended because when they gave it back they spoke to me in French, obviously having been unable to discern what language the letter was in. Anyway, it seemed to do the trick and we were let through. I was astounded that I had actually taken charge and succeeded in achieving something already but I was nervous that the other team members would think I was pushing myself forward. I waited for somebody to decide what would happen about getting the luggage out to the waiting van but no one seemed to be making any suggestions, so I tentatively suggested that perhaps we should organise ourselves into shifts with two people standing guard outside to make sure the luggage wasn't stolen from the van while the others took turns to ferry the cases out. I alone had 103 kilos of luggage so I could see that I had to do something to get things moving. Russell had rather unkindly but honestly pointed out when repacking for me that it was lucky airlines did not take a passenger's body weight into account when setting weight limits, otherwise I would have been lucky to get on board with a carrier bag.

After carrying out almost the last load I tried to go back in for the rest. A soldier shoved me in the ribs with his rifle, barring my way. I felt breathless with a mixture of pain from the blow and sudden fear, and I was desperate to spend a penny but could find nowhere to go. By this point I felt close to tears and couldn't face going back into the airport. The others brought the last pieces out and we climbed into the van with relief. Diane and Jacqui were also desperate for a pee by then and our agony was intensified as the brakeless van which picked us up bumped and crashed into town over the potholes.

The hotel in Bucharest must once have been a rather elegant old establishment but was now decidedly faded. Our driver dropped us off in reception and disappeared. There was a note telling us our room numbers and saying that the next leg of our journey would be delayed because the van in Bacau had broken down, but there was no number for us to call to find out the details of when it would be fixed.

We had to haul our luggage up seven floors by hand because the lifts weren't working. The lift woman was very apologetic and helpful, making a big show of beating the dust out of the chairs on each floor as we sat down to catch our breath before attempting the next flight of stairs. I gave her a bar of chocolate to thank her and she was overwhelmed with gratitude, returning the favour with some undrinkably grainy, sweet coffee which she made a great fuss of presenting to us. Having got ourselves into a complete muck sweat humping the luggage, we discovered that there was no running water, hot or cold, at that time of day, most times of day in fact, and no food or drink available.

John had given me a case which he'd told me not to open until we arrived. Retreating to my hotel room hungry, thirsty and, like everyone else, increasingly desperate I found that he had packed half a dozen meals and soft drinks. The whole group fell on this bounty gleefully! Everyone happily tucked in, while I wondered how I was going to manage three months without John. He had slipped in a card telling me how much he loved me and how proud he was of me and there was also a note from Russell. Boy, did I feel homesick.

On the evening of the following day we met in the dining room a group of volunteers from the Romanian Orphanage Trust who were on their way back to England. They were very depressed and negative about everything they had experienced, believing it had been a complete waste of time. The more they moaned and complained about the authorities, the conditions, the workers and the children the lower our team spirit was sinking. When they had gone I tried to revive everyone by saying that perhaps they had just had bad luck – our experience would probably be completely different. Deep in the pit of my stomach I was beginning to feel that I might have misjudged just how bad things were going to be at Ungerini, even though these volunteers had worked elsewhere. I had imagined spending afternoons with the children doing simple crafts, drawing and such and taking them for walks in the countryside, but the picture these people painted was altogether greyer and more depressing. The worst part for me was the fact that these volunteers had ended up with their spirits broken. I assumed they must have come out with dreams like mine and I worried that I might end up as disillusioned as them; that I wouldn't be able to do anything useful or help the children at all.

No messages arrived for us the next morning and we had no idea how to contact the existing team at Ungerini who were supposed to be coming to fetch us. To begin with we hung around the hotel waiting, but that seemed like a complete waste of time, so we left a message with reception for anyone who called or came looking for us to please leave us a number or address and set off to see a bit of Bucharest. Diane knew her way around and spoke enough of the language to take taxis and talk to the locals. This allowed us to acclimatise ourselves to this country that had been through such devastating times and about which the rest of us knew next to nothing.

I was shocked by just how little food there seemed to be available. We visited a huge covered market and found it almost bare of produce; some ancient yellow apples on one table, a few yoghurts or pickled cabbages on another, each stall manned by a dead-eyed peasant man or woman wrapped in layer upon layer of shabby grey clothing. I began to realise just how deep the poverty of the ordinary people had become. All the best food, we were told, was exported to bring in dollars. Stopping at restaurants we were surprised by the size of the menus but soon learnt that virtually nothing listed was actually available. The trick was to ask what they had and then choose from the three or four items offered. The food would then arrive in whatever order suited the kitchens. Potatoes, for instance, might arrive way before or after the omelette they were supposed to be accompanying.

The whole city seemed as grey and drab as the peasants in the market. No one looked up or smiled as they bustled about their business and an air of depression hung over everyone. Most people walked along the pavements with their heads down and if you caught their eye or smiled at them they would look away and hurry past. Some were more enterprising and would latch onto us, offering to exchange our dollars for local currency. While Diane haggled with them to get the best rates their eyes were always moving furtively as if expecting police officials to appear at any moment and reprimand them for speaking to foreigners, an activity that had been strictly prohibited by the previous regime. There was an air of oppression everywhere.

One beautiful gypsy child, who looked no more than three years old, latched onto me and begged for some chewing gum or chocolate whilst quite skilfully attempting to go through my pockets. I was horrified to see she had only plastic summer sandals on her bare feet. Her little hands were blue with cold and as she stared directly into my eyes with a beaming smile her teeth chattered with the cold. She had a brightly coloured but grimy scarf on and a full, flared skirt, an exact miniature copy of her mother who stood nearby, watching nervously.

Wherever petrol was sold there would be queues of cars, mostly rickety, bald-tyred little Dacias – the poor quality of the fuel was obvious from the way the cars kangarooed around the potholed, cobbled streets, giving off noxious dark fumes. There was an occasional Mercedes, but they nearly always had diplomatic flags on their bonnets. Most of the taxis were Dacias and although there were enough of us to fit into two cars they nearly always managed to squash us all into one. The drivers ran round the cars to let us out because the door handles were missing, or leant across us, reeking of garlic, to let us out. Many of them had to hold the doors shut with pieces of string as they drove along.

Everyone seemed to be afraid of the police and the officers we saw did appear very threatening, always heavily armed and swaggering along the pavements, forcing other pedestrians into the road. We stopped to ask one policeman for some directions and he indicated that the information would cost us five cigarettes. As with chocolate, we used cigarettes as currency and never got the whole packet out or the whole lot went.

Many of finest avenues of this once elegant city had been bulldozed to make way for massive prison-like complexes of apartments for the family and friends of the Ceaucescus. But it was still possible to see some beautiful buildings hidden beneath the grime of pollution and neglect. Many rural villages had been flattened in just the same way in order to move the people into the towns where they could work in factories and help to fulfil the President's dream of turning Romania into an industrial power.

We could clearly see bullet holes in many of the buildings which had been badly damaged in the weeks of turmoil surrounding the fall of Ceaucescu. As we found people who were willing to stop and chat we learnt much more about the background to the rebellion and the terrible years of repression which had preceded it. Many civilians were still armed and we often heard sporadic gunfire at night.

On our way back to the hotel, gazing up at the beautiful old buildings with their balconies and bomb damage, we came into a square full of chanting crowds with placards. From the flags on the building they were picketing we assumed it was a government department. The protesters spotted us and came over to talk. Everyone in Romania seems to think that all foreigners have some sort of influence on world events. Diane told us that they were from a part of the country which had been annexed by Russia and they were demanding that the new authorities ask for it back. We felt very nervous about being seen talking to these people in case we were accused of indulging in political activities and thrown out of the country before we even got to the orphanage. As we tried to move through them towards our hotel there was a screeching of brakes and tyres as the police arrived in force, distracting the picketers enough for us to walk quietly away. Glancing back over our shoulders we saw the crowd dispersing under the terrifying gaze of the law.

The atmosphere never lost its tension but these were the early signs of people regaining their courage. Later that day we passed a church and, hearing some lovely singing coming from inside, ventured in. It was an Orthodox service with everyone standing and the beautiful, icon-decorated church was packed with worshippers.

We paid a visit to the Graveyard of the Martyrs, where two thousand of the people who had been shot or beaten to death in the revolution were buried. We lit candles and laid flowers on some of the huge graves which bore pictures of the dead. Word spread that we were there and several Romanian women came up and kissed us, thanking us for taking the time to visit the bodies of their sons, brothers and husbands. It was very moving to see places we had seen on the news coming to life.

Diane took us to visit Ceauçescu's Palace, the biggest building I have ever seen. It was designed like a gigantic modern Hyatt Hotel but with entrances on each corner leading directly underground which were big enough to take tanks and other armoured vehicles. We bribed two sets of guards with bars of chocolate, which they wrapped up carefully to take home to their children before letting us past. They took us in to show us just the smallest part of this colossal mansion and I have never seen such opulence. There were fabulous mosaic floors and marble walls, hand-carved staircases, crystal chandeliers and completely over-the-top gold-plated bathrooms.

'They say these are not the best areas of the palace,' Diane told us, 'that there is much more. They say there's another whole complex underground with passages leading all over the city, some of which they haven't even been able to trace yet. No one has been able to count how many rooms there are.' It was an extraordinary contrast to the life of the people outside, especially since it now stood empty and unused, waiting for some foreign investor to take an interest and think of a way of utilising it.

The enforced waiting revealed more of the various characters within the group and I was surprised by my own ability to mediate between them and to make decisions, even at a very basic level. It was a side of my character which I had forgotten existed and reminded me of my earlier life.

My father had been away a lot of the time when I was a child, working as a foreign correspondent for Reuters. Because of his drinking it was rather a relief when he went off on his trips to exotic-sounding places like Africa. Mum was always a very gentle and sweet person. The eight of us lived happily in Wimbledon, south London. In my youth I had an ambition to be an actress but both my parents told me, very sensibly, that I should get some business training first so that I would have something to fall back on if the acting didn't work out. While I was on the business course my mother died of a coronary thrombosis and Dad just fell to pieces. My youngest brother was still only five and that meant that someone had to be around to help get him to and from school and generally provide some support. As the oldest girl I could see that was my responsibility and I was quite happy to take it on. Living with my father, a sometimes difficult man, and being responsible for the family when he was away taught me to deal with practical problems very pragmatically. It didn't seem sensible to think any more about taking up acting and so I started working as a secretary. I went to work at Philips, the electronics company, and that was where I met John who was newly divorced.

Once my responsibilities at home were finished (after two years my father married Margaret, a very attractive and lively divorcee with three children – making us a family of eleven in all), John and I married and decided that we would have more to talk about if we didn't work for the same company. So I moved on to work as PA to Professor E.M.L. Beale, FRS, Technical Director of a very large computer company, Scicon, President of the Royal Statistical Society, Chairman of the Mathematical Programming Society, Visiting Professor at Imperial College etc, etc, etc. It was an extremely exciting, rewarding and fulfilling job which taught me many of the organisational skills which I realised were res-urrecting themselves. After I had been with him for sixteen glorious years Martin Beale died, but John and I remain great friends with his widow Betty and his family. Betty has been one of the people encouraging me to write this book. When Scicon moved to Milton Keynes we moved too and John and I settled into our comfortable life. Years later I was rediscovering those old powers of diplomacy and mediation.

After two days of sight-seeing in Bucharest a Romanian driver arrived for us and we were taken out to Bacau, a six-hour drive away in a battered old van with no brakes and not enough seats – Jacqui sat on my lap all the way. As we set out our spirits were high. I stared out of the windows, wide-eyed with wonder and curiosity at everything we passed. There were very few cars on the roads but many horses and oxen pulling carts being driven by peasants. The scenery was rural with primitive little villages dotted along the sides of the road, as I imagine it must have been in Britain a hundred years ago. Each village had a well that the residents went to for all their water, carrying it back home in any way they could. It all seemed a million miles away from the President's extraordinarily luxurious modern palace in the capital.

Diane had got up early and managed to buy us some pastries from a patisserie, which we ate as we went along, but we had nothing to drink. The bumpy roads made us all want to relieve ourselves within a couple of hours and the driver pulled up at a public lavatory next to a beer house. This was our first experience of the plumbing that lay ahead and none of us were able to bear the smell long enough even to step inside. We decided that it would be better to resort to the bushes, despite the freezing temperatures. A few miles further down the road the driver stopped at a corn field and we all got out for a much needed steaming pee! Necessity was beginning to melt some of our inhibitions.

I had been given an SAS survival kit to bring out, complete with water purifying tablets, but they tasted so foul I hadn't bothered to make up any drinking water for the journey. We were all nervous about drinking untreated water but soon became too thirsty to care and when someone suggested stopping at a village well we all agreed. The driver found one and helped us to pull up an ancient bucket full of icy cold water. I didn't fancy the look of the rusty cup attached to it and used my hands to scoop the water up. It tasted good and I was later told that most well water was actually a lot cleaner than some of the tap water we drink in England.

Bacau was a shock after passing through so much beautiful countryside. It is an unwelcoming industrial city with a population of 180,000. It boasts some surprisingly modern additions like an Olympic stadium, a concert hall and public swimming pool. I rather liked the idea of the swimming pool and wondered if we might be allowed to take groups of children for therapy and exercise that would be fun too. Clouds of smoke and chemicals from the factories settled over the buildings, making them seem even more dismal than their architects had intended. The pollution hung in the air, making all of us cough.

We were shown to the Hotel Dumbrava, a rather average establishment, where we were told we would have to share until enough rooms became free for us to have a room each. Initially we would be in the old part of the hotel, which was meant for locals, rather than the modern part where foreigners usually stayed. In fact, the old part was much nicer, with old-fashioned wooden floors and ornate carvings. I shared a room with Nellie; our room had a little hallway with a double wardrobe. The main room had twin beds, each with sheets and one blanket, and a balcony. I was worried that someone would think I was a dollar-rich visitor and break into the room.

During the months to come drunken Russians would often bang on our doors in the night, shouting demands that we couldn't understand, so I always slept with the hall light on and my torch handy in case of power cuts. It was at night that I missed John most: someone to chat to; someone warm, to cuddle up to. Each room had its own bathroom, although the water only worked at certain times of the day, and there was a 'team room' where we could all meet and make cups of tea or coffee. There were also a great many cockroaches and we were warned not to leave anything in the rooms because if the maids ever showed up they would steal whatever they could find. One day, when I had managed to get hold of a prized bottle of Fanta to take my blood pressure pills with, I went to drink direct from the bottle on getting back to the room and nearly gagged on the sudden smell of garlic. I realised that the maid must have had a swig from this precious bottle earlier and I couldn't face it any more.

We were now twenty kilometres from Ungerini and I couldn't wait to get there, to meet the children and begin to help them.

The waiting since that first day when I knew for sure I was coming seemed so prolonged that I couldn't bear the thought of any more delays now that we were so close.

CHAPTER FOUR

Making a Start

*

*T*he night after our initial visit to Ungerini I woke many times, my head full of images of sad, empty eyes, suffocating smells and blood-curdling sounds. Everything seemed grey and dark and I couldn't imagine ever thinking in colour again. All life seemed to me to have been drawn from the children we had seen. I could only guess at the hardships they had had to suffer, the experiences that had left them bedraggled, unwashed, unloved and seemingly hopeless.

When I finally gave up trying to sleep and got up I felt a mixture of dread and excitement. I couldn't wait to get working, but I was terrified by the feeling of not knowing where to begin. What could I possibly do amidst such scenes of despair? Jenny, who was in charge of Salon One, had been out there for six weeks and I was relieved to be working with her as she had been one of the friendliest and most welcoming people the previous day. Without a mentor I wouldn't have known where to start.

Breakfast at the hotel was erratic, with the food arriving in a rather strange sequence, but there was plenty of it, with lots of camomile tea, and I felt okay in myself as we set off once more on the hour-long commute up the slippery mountains.

When we arrived, Jenny took me to the team room and showed me the things we needed to take upstairs with us. She took some Sudocrem for sores and rashes, and some rough, unscented talcum powder to help keep the children dry once they had been cleaned up a little. She also took a few toys.

'I lock them back in here at night,' she explained, 'otherwise the women take them home and you never see them again.' I felt like a new girl on my first day at school as I tagged along behind her, watching everything she did, hanging on her every word, full of naïve, eager questions.

'I try to change and clean up all the children each morning,' she told me, 'and get the ones that don't become hysterical at the prospect out of their cots at some stage, although we don't always have time to get to all of them.'

Lucia was on duty in the room again, dressed in the same thick white coat with a white scarf tied around her head and under her chin, giving her a rather Middle-Eastern look. I noticed that she had the most appallingly worn footwear, with newspapers covering the holes in her shoes. I wondered how far she had had to walk in the snow like that in order to get to work. Lucia liked to talk a lot, rabbiting away at us in Romanian, regardless of whether we understood what she was saying, but she didn't seem to be doing very much actual work.

'Please don't hesitate to tell me exactly what you want me to do,' I told Jenny. 'I won't be at all offended because I have no experience at this and I just want to make myself as useful as possible.'

'Don't worry,' she said sweetly and comfortingly, 'whatever you can do for these children will be good.'

We started work on cleaning up the ones Jenny pointed out to me. I noticed that she was concentrating on the ones who were the most advanced and the easiest to handle, but it was still taking a long time to change and dress each child and I could soon see that it would never be possible for her to get round to everyone. I began to see how the weaker and more difficult children became left further and further behind as the staff tried to share their time and efforts around as best they could.

It was hard to dress them because there weren't many clothes available. No child had anything of their own so we had to search anew each day for everything, right down to socks – complete pairs of which were a rare find at Ungerini. When you could find some they never came with matching partners and were either for babies or grandads, with nothing in between. It was all very time-consuming and sometimes completely impossible. It was vital to dress them properly because of the cold, which made many of them permanently blue.

When I had first heard about the state of the Romanian orphans who had been relegated to the 'madhouses' my naïve dream had been to get them outside into the fresh air; to have them up and stimulated on day one; to give them some fun in life. That was still my ultimate aim but before I could think about that I had to work out how to get the children out of the cots and walking about, and before I could do that I had to think of ways of getting them to stand. But it was hard to make them feel enthusiastic about doing anything as long as they were cold and hungry, so the first priority had to be to make them more comfortable. Then they might be willing to start expanding their sadly limited horizons. My dream of taking a few children out to see the sky for the first time in their lives was beginning to look more distant every minute that I spent struggling alongside Jenny just to clean them up a little and dress them.

I remember thinking that if we could just sort the laundry system out, things would go more smoothly. As it was, the children were constantly being dressed up in things that were far too big or far too small for them. Often the washing came back from downstairs still damp so they would be changing from one set of wet clothes to another. Many of the children appeared to be rheumatic in their joints and I began to think their constantly damp state might be a major contributing factor.

Once I had done everything she asked me to, Jenny suggested I just started to get to work on walking and talking with whichever child I thought fit. She didn't give me any specific ideas about what to do, just left it up to me. The best place to begin, I reasoned, was to try to get them out of their cots onto my lap. That way I would be able to give them a cuddle and a tickle to get them used to being touched and try and stimulate a response. I sang game songs like, 'Walking round the garden, like a teddy bear,' or 'This little piggy', whilst doing all the appropriate actions. I thought I might try putting the more placid ones on the floor, push a toy or something to them in the hope that they might then push it back. A few allowed me to lift them out of the cots without complaint but did not look at me or change their deadpan expressions. They just lay still and stared into space. It is hard to know what to do with someone who shows no reactions or responses at all, not even anger or frustration. They allowed me to do what I wanted to them, remaining completely passive throughout.

Those who did react to my efforts screamed horribly when I tried to pick them up from their cots and at first I was terrified of hurting them and was tempted to leave them where they were, rocking aimlessly to and fro in their own little prisons. What was the key which would unlock the doors to these children's minds? I wanted to release them from their mental and physical shackles, to show them what life could be like – but where did I start? I realised that I would need to go more slowly with the screamers and work with them inside the cots for a while before trying to get them out. One little girl, Corrina, hid underneath her cot every time I came near her that first day, sitting hunched over in a sort of squatting position. She had no trousers on and constantly rubbed her hands from the front of her bottom round to the crease, ritualistically smelling and licking her fingers like a chimp. Whatever the particular form of ritual behaviour, whatever the reason behind it, the children were using it to retreat even further into themselves and to shut the rest of the world out. Corrina's was only one of many strange and inexplicable rituals I saw every day.

As we went about our chores, Jenny told me as much as she knew of the children's histories, which wasn't much since none of them had any medical records to speak of. There were fifteen children in Salon One, aged from three to fourteen. None of them had ever been out of their cots until a few months before and some of them still hadn't allowed themselves to be lifted out.

Until the revolution a few months before, and the sudden exposure of the orphanages to the world's media, the children had had their hands tied behind their heads and their legs tied up against their chests to make them easier for the women workers to manage. Lucia later told me that at one time one woman had been in charge of forty children. If they were tied it was quicker and easier to wipe their bottoms. If the children were tied to the cots they wouldn't get out and cause trouble. She didn't explain what she meant by trouble. Many of them were still in the same foetal shapes, simply lying all day in the same positions in which they had been tied. Their bonds might have been cut but their muscles had atrophied and their joints had completely locked. There were still not enough people in Ungerini with the physio-therapy skills to help them gain the use of their wasted limbs so there they lay, waiting to be fed.

The only food they received in most of the upstairs rooms was a milky, semolina-like substance dispensed from the huge beer bottles with teats which I had seen stacked on the kitchen floor the day before.

Because the workers were still using the passive feeding method, which did not require the children to exercise any sucking or swallowing muscles, they were unable to take food from spoons or to use their tongues. Perhaps it was due to the lack of properly developed face and tongue muscles that they were unable to talk beyond making low guttural moanings.

Some months before there had been a terrible fire in the room, Jenny told me. All the children had still been tied up to the bars of their cots. Corrina, and a boy called Maricel who had been horribly burned, were the only two to survive out of twenty-two children. As a result of the fire our room had been re-painted more recently than the others and had quite clean, white-washed walls.

A week after my arrival Jenny returned to England, leaving me in charge of the room, which was a very daunting prospect indeed. I was much more comfortable doing what I was told, rather than sticking my neck out and taking decisions, but I was starting to get a few ideas about what I would like to do – what I instinctively thought would help the children. I wanted to move towards my dream of walking the children out of their terrible prison into the light. I felt excited at the prospect of putting my ideas into practice and yet fearful that I wouldn't be able to cope.

There was a staff of 142 women carers in Ungerini, working in shifts. In Salon One, we had Lucia and two Marias. One was known as 'Grande' Maria due to her size and the other as Maria 'Frumos' (beautiful). Maria the Beautiful was much younger than the other carers and very shy of me. At first she seemed surly and unco-operative, seeing every innovation as more potential work for her. The women were charged with keeping the children alive and the rooms tidy, and that was the limit of their responsibilities. They would be fined should any of the children die, and I soon realised that they lived in fear of Madam Augustina who would happily beat them if they didn't keep things up to her standards.

One or two of the children under our care seemed so weak and close to death that the only thing I could think of doing for them was dropping milk onto their tongues from some little syringes I had brought with me, hydrating them just enough to be able to sustain life in the hope that we would be able to do more for them later. I was working on instinct, wishing all the time that I knew more about childcare.

Where do you start when there is so much that needs to be done? One of the first things I had done, with Jenny's permission, was to find out each child's name and write it up above their cot, making each one a little sketch of some sort of animal in brightly coloured felt-tips, even though I couldn't draw for toffee. It helped me to learn their names as well as giving them a little bit of individuality. I asked the helpers to try to put the children back in the same cots each time. This would also be a great help for those children receiving medication – ensuring that each got the correct treatment.

Once Jenny had gone back to England, I decided that the next priority was to get some light into the room, so I took down the filthy nets which hung at the windows and set about washing the grime off the glass to allow a little daylight through. The job was made harder because there was only cold water and no soap, but I kept going until I was satisfied. I noticed Lucia watching me work so I motioned to her that perhaps we could do a window each. Reluctantly, sighing deeply at the appalling way in which I was squandering both our energies, she joined me. None of the children gave any sign of noticing our endeavours.

I was determined to get a supply of hot water into the room so that I could soothe some of the tenser children and wash them more thoroughly at the same time. I went down to the kitchens to ask if I could heat a pot on their range each morning. To begin with the women working there shook their heads, jabbering at me to go away. They seemed frightened that they would get into trouble because I was in the kitchens at all. When I realised that was the problem I went to Madam Augustina and asked her permission, which she gave happily. Once the kitchen staff realised they weren't going to get into trouble from her they became more friendly, chatting away to me when I returned for the vast cauldron of hot water. I would then get one of the big girls to help me stagger upstairs with it, each holding one handle, so that I could use it in the baby bath. After watching me labouring away for a few days the kitchen workers started to wave me away when I tried to lift the giant pot and took it off themselves, carrying it upstairs for me single-handedly, with no apparent effort. I never ceased to be amazed at the strength of these women. Later, in a bout of high spirits, a woman who must have weighed considerably less than me lifted me up, tucked me under one arm and ran the length of the corridor before setting me down again, apparently not the least bit out of breath.

The carers kept the large ceramic kiln in the corner of Salon One stoked with coal, just as they did in their homes. Some ladies from a village in England had sent out some curtains, which I put up. They were perfect, even though they were never drawn, because they were bright, pretty colours. It didn't seem to impress the locals but it raised my spirits and I felt sure that anything which improved the atmosphere in the room must produce some long-term benefits.

The posters which the producers of *Blue Peter* had asked me to bring to Romania were supposed to have been collected by someone from another orphanage in Bacau, but the contact never materialised. I thought my children were just as deserving as any others and since I had lugged the four huge parcels all the way to Ungerini with me, I didn't want to see them go to waste. I stuck some of the brightest and most glittery pictures around the walls in another attempt to brighten the place up and give the children something to look at. I then passed the rest of the posters to other workers for their rooms. Just these few simple things changed the feel of the room completely and made workers visiting from other rooms exclaim with surprise and smile. Sadly, the children living there still showed no sign of noticing any of the activities going on around them. I attached the old net curtains to the ceiling, hanging little toys and other brightly coloured objects in them so that those still flat on their backs had something to look at too, but their eyes remained blank and unfocused at first.

Every morning I would rush into the room, saying, 'Come on, you lazy brats, rise and shine, upsy, upsy,' and go round kissing them all, calling each one by their name and trying to liven them up. Each day was a new start and I wanted to help them enjoy life. To begin with, Lucia and the Marias used to look at me as if I was insane and very possibly dangerous. After a couple of weeks they began to lose their reserve and rush at me with massive bear hugs, kisses on both cheeks and shrieked greetings. One day, after I had been there for about a month, one of the translators told me that the women said they really liked working in Salon One with me as I treated them nicely and injected some life and fun into the place.

One girl in my room was up and walking. Monika was twelve, but no bigger than my three-year-old niece in England. An educationalist, paid for by the Star of David Organisation in Sweden, came and took her out each afternoon for some exercise. It made me feel hopeful that if Monika could do it others might follow. I was determined to get as many of the children up to her standard as I possibly could before I had to return to England, but many of the more backward ones still wouldn't even let me lift them out of their cots.

There was a little boy called Lazlo, whom I nicknamed 'Lazy Lazlo', who did allow me to lift him out onto the floor, but he would immediately become very bad tempered, demanding to go back into the cot. The very fact that he had a temper made me think that there must be a spark of life in his brain that we might be able to fan into something more. So, I would push toys up his jumper, to annoy him, making him pull them out and throw them back at me, often with surprising accuracy. After a while he started to enjoy this game and then gradually he began to play with the toys he was given instead of throwing them and then actively to seek them out for himself.

With Corrina, who had spent the first day hiding underneath the cot, I started by getting her to sit on my lap while I stroked and massaged her in order to win her confidence gradually.

I did a lot of gentle touching and stroking of their faces and limbs with the less responsive children. I would start by doing it in their cots to get them used to me, in the hope that they would eventually trust me to lift them onto my lap and then eventually to put them down on the floor. I would try to spend five minutes with each child, getting round to each of them twice in the course of a morning. With the very nervous ones I would start off by just stroking their faces, although even this would make many of them freeze with blank-eyed fear.

I found a chair downstairs in the basement where the rubbish was thrown and asked Madam Augustina if I could have it. She said yes and then screamed for a worker to come and carry it upstairs for me. When a child had grown sufficiently relaxed about me stroking them in the cot I would put the chair next to the bars and lift him or her out onto my lap. To make them feel more secure I wrapped them tightly in blankets, like newborn babies. I reasoned that if they were warm and comfortable they would think that being out was a good thing and might even start wanting it. I then stroked them some more and sang and talked to them as if they understood every word I said, while they stared straight ahead of them, not moving a muscle. Often they would empty their bowels and bladders onto me but Jenny had left me her plastic apron so that only parts of my clothes became soiled.

I believe I was fortunate to go out as part of the second team of volunteers because we had more time to plan what we wanted to do. The existing team had established a routine of one British person to each room, getting both the carers and the children used to their presence. It must have been even harder for them to know where to start when there was no structure at all, and their valuable ground work allowed us to develop what we did in each room.

I asked Madam Augustina if I could have the manic piped music turned off, to give us a little peace and tranquillity. She agreed and it was an enormous relief when it stopped, as if a tremendous pressure had been lifted off my brain. I reckoned that if the quiet made me feel calmer it must have an even greater effect on the children. Although I thought that listening to music was very good for them in principle, there should also be quiet times. Eventually it was turned off in all the other rooms as well. Other volunteers had paid visits to Salon One with their children, to get them used to being out and about and to indulge themselves in a bit of adult gossip. They could see how much easier it was to talk to the children and soothe them without the music blaring out and forcing everyone to shout in order to be heard.

Adina had spent nine years living in total darkness under her dirty old blanket and became hysterical at the thought of coming out. I tried to put myself in her position and imagine how frightening the world must seem without the blanket around her. I needed to find a way of keeping her feeling safe while allowing her to see what was going on around her and to grow used to it. I contacted John in England and asked him to send a cellulose blanket that she could stay under while looking through the holes and gaining enough self-confidence to be willing to enter the outside world herself. The whole process took months.

For the first time out of their cot, I would hold a difficult child for no more than a minute before putting them back and moving on to the next one. I gradually increased the time that I kept them on my lap while at the same time increasing the distance between

Ungerini Irrecuperable Orphanage

Kitchen ranges – serving buckets and feeding bottles

Bathing
facilities

Diane, Matthew, Roger, Jacqui and 'Nelly', Bucharest

Typical cottage, Moldavia, March '91

Bacau – coming to market

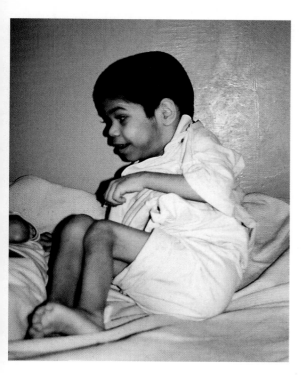

Lazy Lazlo

Marian

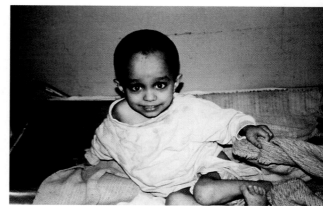

Szulita

(Some of the first photographs taken at Ungerini in 1990 by Mrs Barbara Herne.)

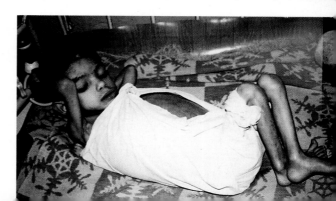

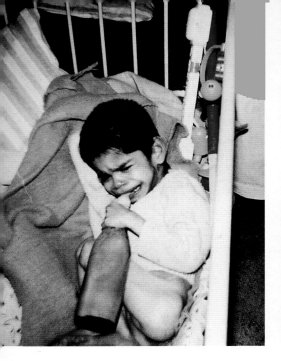

'Maria-my-room' with feeding bottle, Salon One

Bev and Maria and new decorations

Lucia and Monika

Adina – having abandoned her safety blanket

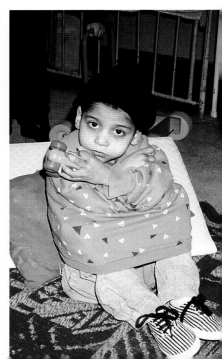

Mobiles, toys and curtains
– May '91

One of our first trips out
– with Mark

Outdoor disco, Ungerini – showing belt shortage!

Bev with some of the bigger children at Ungerini

Ciprien being visited by his parents

Illeana and Jill just after Gabriel was taken to Gisteni

Maria Grande and her children at home

Bev with Maria Frumos
and her mother

Sister Fabiana, Sister Camilla, Sister Jane and Sister Ida – Bacau

Mother Teresa's home, Bacau

Andrei and Alena – both six – on arrival at MT's

the chair and the cot and gradually unwrapping them from the swaddling blankets, until eventually we were sitting over amongst the more adventurous children. Even the most reluctant would finally allow me to put them down on the mat – although it took three months to lift one little girl from her cot – it felt truly marvellous each and every time this happened.

The Norwegian arm of the Red Cross represented them in Romania and in the mornings their trainee nurses worked with the downstairs children and in some of the upstairs rooms, although sadly not mine. Dr Kari, the woman who had smiled at me across the dining room on my first night, and her team were visiting and assessing all the institutes in the country, both adults' and children's. They would come back to the hotel in the evenings, their faces grey with fatigue.

'Do you know, Bevey,' Dr Kari told me one night, 'We think we have seen the worst, then another one we visit is more terrible than the last, what to do?'

After building up an overall picture, their task was then to decide where to direct the Red Cross aid, and establish what exactly was needed in each place. They found the decisions hard. 'We have to act like God himself,' another of the doctors confided in me, 'deciding who shall have and who shall not. We can only pray that we have got it right.'

It was still far too cold for me to contemplate taking the little ones outside, but I began to feel more optimistic that by the time Spring arrived I might have managed to get them sufficiently confident for a trip out to at least be possible. The next step after getting them to sit on the floor was to persuade them to come out through the door of Salon One into the corridor, which was as traumatic for many of them as getting out of the cots had originally been. If I tried carrying them out the door they would scream and cling painfully to me like demented little cats, trying to clamber over my shoulders to get back into the familiar safety of Salon One.

I had to go through the same gradual process as before, sitting each child on my lap on the chair and each day moving the chair closer to the door, allowing them to see outside the room and watch whoever might be passing by outside. Eventually, with the braver ones, I would move my chair out into the corridor when there wasn't anyone around. There was always a danger that one of the inmates from the 'bad boys' room' might come out and run at us screaming, which would terrify the child on my lap and set us back weeks.

I discovered later that one of the side-effects of malnourishment is that you don't want to be touched; you just want to be left alone. Everyone becomes bad tempered when they are hungry and if hunger was a continuous state we would all start to withdraw into ourselves as these children had done.

I spread out the one floor mat we had for the more able children and tried to get them to sit on that. This terrified Lucia who was afraid they would pee on it and get her into trouble with Madam Augustina, so I went in search of some more potties. When I arrived there had been two pots in the room which Jenny had persuaded a couple of the brighter children to use.

'What do you do with the full pots?' I asked her on the first day.

'Oh, one merely puts the wallahs outside the door for the women and they just magically disappear,' she told me.

The system did indeed seem to work, and although I can't say that they came back exactly clean at least they were empty!

I suggested to Lucia that we try to put all the children on pots first thing each day before placing them on the mat. I soon realised the impracticality of this since it took twenty minutes to get each child up, leaving us no time to do anything with them once they were on the floor. Perhaps it would be better to get them all out of their cots at once, if they were willing to come. If they did pee everywhere we would just have to clear it up, and we would try to train them to use potties as we went along. Potty-training was a priority for me, for selfish reasons as much as anything else. I found the job of wiping them up in their cots without water, paper or rubber gloves fairly gross. Not having had to deal with nappies for children of my own I had never been able to face changing and wiping the bottoms of other people's, even my own family's. The one time I had to do it for one of my nieces I could be heard gagging and retching from outside the public loo that we were operating in. It was only when I got the child back to her mother that I was told she had been wiping herself for two years! The incident remained a family joke from that day on – even more so when the news got out that I would be working with incontinent children in Romania.

If simply left alone on the mat with toys the more advanced children wouldn't play with them – they would just sit, staring and rocking as they had been doing in their cots. So I got them out in groups of six or so, whizzing from one to another like a spinning plate act in a circus, tickling them and trying to stimulate them in any way I could to get them to take an interest in something outside themselves. I got them sitting on my lap on the floor as much as possible because it occurred to me that no one in the room had ever touched anyone else. They might not even have looked at each other, and I wanted to break down some of the barriers. They were like fifteen little separate units, despite the fact they had spent most of their lives hugger-mugger with others. Towards the end of each session on the floor, I would line them all up next to one another and then roll them over my legs into one another like parents do with normal children in games of rough and tumble, to try to get them used to being with one another and part of a social group.

I asked Diane, the Irish physiotherapist who had come out with us as part of our team, to teach me some simple physiotherapy. Because of the way the work had been allocated she was in another room, doing the same menial jobs as me, which was a shame because she could have done so much more if she had been able to concentrate on physio. She was an excellent teacher and could have made a much greater difference to the children's lives if she had been allowed to concentrate on training the volunteers and women carers in some elementary techniques.

At midday the women carers would disappear for half an hour into another room where they would chatter away to one another, ladling the milky substance the children lived on into the beer bottles from a dirty-looking old bucket. The children would begin to become agitated, knowing that feeding time was approaching. The women would then return as we went for our lunch and would give the bottles to the children. The children's tiny, frail hands were barely able to support the weight of the heavy glass bottles as the slushy mixture poured directly down their throats, creating the curious side-effect that none of them ever had wind. Those who were unable to hold onto the bottles at all went without.

Sometimes I would return from my lunch-break to find that a few children hadn't been given anything – normally it was the gypsy children, like Maria and Szulita, who were considered to be the lowest of the low by all the Romanians.

'But, Bevey,' Lucia would protest when I wanted to know what was happening, 'they are gypsies; they have AIDS.'

'They don't have AIDS,' I would explain patiently, through whichever translator I could find. 'They just look like that because they are so hungry and malnourished.'

Despite all our efforts there were some traditions at Ungerini it seemed were never likely to change – like shaving the children's heads every few weeks with cut-throat razors, which always left them scarred and bleeding and looking even more hideous than before. The children were so used to this sort of treatment that they seldom made a sound during the ritual, even when they were cut painfully. Sometimes Valentina would come round brandishing a pair of scissors and cut the smaller ones' hair, which I thought was very unsafe. I have never seen anyone who kicked as hard and viciously as she did when she was angry, and trusting her with a sharp implement so close to the eyes of other children seemed very unwise to me.

I felt it was very important to get on well with Lucia and the other women. Without their co-operation anything we achieved with the children would be useless because they would simply revert to the old routines once we had left. When we arrived all they cared about was keeping the children alive and the rooms tidy. They did not want to do anything for the children beyond giving them their bottles and wiping up their excreta. If the rooms were not cleaned to her satisfaction, Madam Augustina would beat them with a stick. They did not talk to the children, get them out of their cots or seek to stimulate or comfort them in any way.

When I introduced some of the toys which I'd brought with me from England into the room Lucia had been horrified because she said they made the floor untidy. Everything possible was done to minimise the amount of work which these women had to do and they were very afraid that our methods would create more work for them. Why waste your energies doing things for children who didn't appear to appreciate it? It was all very well, they reasoned, to stimulate the children and get them up, but who was going to have to control them once we went home? I had to admit they had a point but I was sure that overall we could make their jobs easier by making the children more able to look after themselves.

I thought we would also encourage the children to be more

co-operative by making them more comfortable and happy. If they had exercise, for instance, they would stay healthier and sleep better, which would make the women's lives easier. If we could potty-train them there would be less mess to clear up. I put a lot of effort into explaining all this to Lucia and the two Marias but they were very sceptical. I could tell that they often thought I was stupid and they were just humouring me. They were completely mystified as to why we were there at all.

'Why do you want to come to a place like this from England?' they wanted to know. 'Who pays you to do this work?' When we told them we were not paid they would shake their heads in disbelief. They were very curious about me, John and Russell, and surprised that any husband would let his wife come out to work in another country for several months. A married Romanian woman would not even attend a social function alone because it would be a direct insult to her partner and construed as being 'up to no good', they told me.

I simply had to get the Romanians carers' co-operation if I was going to make any long-term difference to these children's lives. They had to see that they would also benefit from the changes, if there was to be any chance they would carry on the work after we had gone. One of the first things I needed to do was learn some basic words in Romanian, just so that I could communicate with them and show that I was trying my best to integrate, even if my attempts at conversation didn't get much further than 'Hallo', 'How are you?' and 'Hasn't the weather improved?' Once I could greet them I moved on to asking about their families and their lives at home.

Lucia, being a little older than the other helpers in Salon One, had quite a lot of influence, so she was my first target to convert to any new practice which I wanted them to start following. Like all the women, she was very resistant to any new ideas or changes. When I started to do a little physiotherapy with the children she was sure I was wasting my time. 'Oh, Bevey, Bevey,' she would say, shaking her head and clicking her tongue. 'These children will never walk.'

'Probably not, Lucia,' I would agree, 'but please could you try and help me. I know I'm a crazy Englishwoman but let's try because it might just help some of them a little.' Then she would humour me and do a little work with them but I knew that she only ever did it while I was watching and she and the other women would tell each other in wonder how ridiculous I was. I felt that it was better to have her laughing at me than resenting me. She was quite a jolly personality but very strong and determined about what she would and wouldn't do. I found that when I got Dana, the interpreter, to come in and help me to talk to her, asking her advice and help, offering to be her assistant in the room, making suggestions rather than telling her what to do, she began to respond much better to me. I could then start to suggest to her things I would like to do, such as cutting down the amount of faeces the children did around the place.

As I got to know her better I found that she had quite a good sense of humour, particularly when it came to sexual and lavatorial matters! She and the other women were always joking about the size of their men's private parts and mocking their amorous Saturday night performances, wanting to know if men's willies were different in Britain. There was one boy in Ungerini who had a very long one: 'Like a horse, Bevey,' they joked in Romanian, 'like a horse,' and one of them galloped around the room while another one put her arm between her legs to make a giant erection as they laughed, showing mouths full of rotten and missing teeth. If Dana or one of the other managers came in they would sober up immediately, like naughty schoolchildren caught playing up a student teacher. I felt pleased that they were willing to relax enough to share their jokes with me.

A boy called Nichusorui, from downstairs, did an enormous 'blow' one day. Grande Maria, shaking with giggles, asked me what it was called in English. Putting on my poshest voice and exaggerated face movements I told her, 'Fart'. From then on every time someone came in I would have to point to Maria and say, 'Sponi, Maria' and she would reply, in a voice so upper class it sounded almost bored, 'Fart'. We would then all become weak with hysterics, like naughty schoolgirls. I sometimes wondered if we were all going mad. We certainly used to crack up at the silliest things but it was probably just a way of coping with stress.

I had to try to do something about the children's diets, too, because I was sure that they would never thrive or progress as long as they were living solely on the bottled gloop. I tried to think through the feeding process for normal children in England and I realised that we actually needed to wean them onto solid foods, just like the babies they resembled. The first step seemed to be to try to give them something a little thicker in the bottles.

Jenny had explained to me that the children were frightened of eating from spoons because they associated them with having medicines like paracetamol rammed down their throats – one helper pinching their noses and another holding their mouths open with both hands. (The other way they dispensed medicine was up the children's backsides, forcing their legs right over their heads, which must have been equally, if not more, painful.) Not knowing how to use spoons, the children would throw their heads right back, as they did with their bottles, and I realised it was because they had never learnt how to pass food from the front of their tongues to the back of their throats.

After checking with the nurse who was in charge of the British team that it would be all right, I started by putting a teaspoon of powdered milk from the team room into each bottle, not wanting to overdo it in case the sudden shock to their digestive systems was too much. They seemed to be all right, despite the dire predictions that Lucia doled out when she found out what I was doing.

Initially all my efforts in Salon One were met with looks of blank puzzlement and open hostility both from the children and the Romanian helpers, but I kept going and I found that my confidence started to grow.

When Jenny got back to England she wrote me a very sweet letter telling me how brave she thought I was for coming to a place like Ungerini without any medical training or experience. She was sure she had seen a difference in the children I had been helping, even in the first week. I felt very pleased because no one else had given me any encouragement or advice at that stage and I had no idea if I was doing the right things. Many of the other volunteers who had excellent professional credentials and experience in dealing with children like these seemed to be as sceptical about my methods as Lucia, but they didn't offer me any alternatives so I kept going. It was important to keep trying and for these children any attention was better than being ignored. Independence was the greatest gift I could give them – to be able to wash and dress themselves, or to go to the toilet, were simple but vital steps in a normal child's progress, but how do you teach them to fourteen-year-olds? I could clearly see the women's argument that it was much quicker to do everything for the children yourself and, indeed, the children were so used to this and so very tired all the time that they were happy for it to continue. I knew, though, that they would never get out of their own personal prisons if we didn't battle on.

I believed that there must be places with better facilities than Ungerini, and if the children could walk and be independent perhaps we could talk to Madam Augustina about transferring some of them. I imagined there must be places where they could receive some practical training or useful occupation which would keep them out of the local adult institute which the Norwegians had told us was similar to Ungerini, only more terrible. If we could get the younger ones up and running maybe they could go to school, or perhaps their families might have them back.

Everything I did seemed so basic and obvious and natural. I was becoming very fond of the children and even proud of them when they achieved even the slightest improvement. My goals were little things but for the children each was the equivalent of climbing Mount Everest.

The grumpier Lucia and the women were to me the nicer I was back to them. Some of the other British workers were treating the women like servants, ordering them around and being very unpleasant, rather as I imagine the British behaved in Victorian times when they went out to the colonies, convinced that the natives were inferior to them in virtually every respect. I couldn't see how that attitude could be anything but destructive. Surely, I reasoned, we were there to assist them not to rule them. Most of the women carers were kind and warm people, just a bit lazy and badly guided.

Maria Grande came from a very large family. She herself was in her thirties and had older brothers and sisters in their forties as well as brothers and sisters who were younger than her own children. This was a fairly common situation since Romanian women marry young and continue having children right into their fifties. She told me that her family would have been even bigger if some hadn't died of things like flu and measles. Although health care was meant to be totally free, I was informed that it was always necessary to bring gifts to the doctors if you wished to receive their full attention. (Even when the doctors prescribed suitable drugs they were rarely available and small infections often progressed quickly and ended in amputations or death.)

At Ungerini there were no wheelchairs. Any child who could not walk had to shuffle on his or her bottom or not move at all.

I suppose it did not occur to the authorities that anyone would wish to take the handicapped out. We never saw any wheelchairs in the streets so perhaps there were none in the country.

As part of my attempts to befriend them, I taught the women at Ungerini how to belly dance – a sight worth seeing! It had been a hobby of mine in England which had always surprised people who thought I was too demure, and certainly the wrong shape, for such things. ('Does it make you hot?' some men at work had teased me when they found out about my hobby – and in my innocence I had assumed they meant did I work up a sweat!) Some of the other workers in the orphanage asked for a demonstration and the Romanian women were watching, laughing and clapping their hands, begging me to show them how to do it. Before long they were all sashaying around after me, undulating their ample curves. Some of the children started to copy as well. Grande Maria was like an ironing board when she danced but how we all laughed. From then on, whenever I passed the women in the corridors they would laugh and dance. A translator called Ionel told me that the women could not believe that an English-woman could move like this as they thought us all to be rather 'rigid', or was it 'frigid'?

Ionel was a young man of about twenty who had arrived at the hotel one evening with a box of apples for the children. He had just been discharged from the army and didn't have a job to go to. He spoke very good English and asked if he could come up to Ungerini to help. Some of the established British team said no, but I pleaded his case. I thought that he would be a brilliant addition to the troops for a number of reasons. Firstly we needed all the help we could get, but we specifically needed more men to help with the boys because there were very few male role models for them. Secondly, I thought it was great that a Romanian was coming forward and volunteering and I thought it was possible he might bring some of his friends along as well in due course. The fact that he spoke English made him doubly valuable. Even if all he did was to speak to the children in Romanian, this was surely to be encouraged – they met few enough adults who wanted to befriend them.

I felt surprised at my boldness. I must have been becoming more assertive by then because I was amazed to find that the others gave in and agreed to try him out.

Ionel helped me a great deal in Salon One – while making sure he put in time in other rooms as well so that no one would feel I was monopolising him – and proved to be a real ally.

Day after day I worked away at coaxing the children out of their cots and stimulating them; massaging them, singing and dancing with them, playing with and tickling them, getting them used to being touched and showing them that although becoming upright might be frightening to start with, it would be better in many different ways once they had mastered it, getting them to focus and concentrate on things, to try new experiences like blowing and bursting bubbles. I managed to find a rusting old table and chairs in the basement which I carted up to the room for them to sit at, just to get them off the floor and closer to normality.

Once I had persuaded Madam Augustina to turn off the ghastly piped music we were able to use individual cassette recorders in each of the rooms so that we could control when we wanted music and when we wanted quiet times. I played nursery rhymes and other more gentle music. Strauss waltzes were a firm favourite with children and carers. I would put the music on and get everyone sitting around the table. I would clap my hands and then I would clap their hands. I would give Lazy Lazlo something that he could bang the table with, which he enjoyed. He and a couple of the others always hated sitting at the table and would constantly get down and crawl back to the mat, but I figured that at least they were getting some exercise and it showed they were beginning to demonstrate some initiative. It was always a challenge to find things that would catch the children's interest.

I shook rattles, and bells on shapes, and the other simple musical instruments that I had brought out with me from England, in front of their fixed, staring eyes. Eventually some of the children started wanting to have a go themselves, but they were never that interested in doing things unless I coaxed them. I sometimes felt a pang of conscience and asked myself whether I was being fair in forcing them to do these things if they didn't want to. But any doubts were outweighed by the conviction that if I could make them more active they stood a chance of being transferred to a better place at a later date.

As the first step in my grand plan of getting every child onto its feet, I tried to encourage them to stand in their cots, holding their hands to begin with and then showing them how to support themselves by gripping the sides. I would hold my hands under their bottoms to support them, encouraging them all the time, 'Good girl, isn't this good, look how much you can see now.' I wanted them to feel secure up in the air and to experience how much more interesting life would be for them if they were upright. I had some wind-up toys which I would set going to give them something to watch and to provide a reason for them to persevere, otherwise they would give up and sit down as soon as I let go of their bottoms. I was watching the weather warm up and the snows begin to melt and I wanted to be ready to get at least some of them outside by the time the air was warm and the ground was dry.

I was very careful to explain every one of my plans to Madam Augustina, because I didn't want her to think I was doing anything without consulting her and I wanted to give her time to get used to the ideas so that she wouldn't dismiss them. She was a woman who didn't like to have her powers threatened and I made sure that she never thought I was trying to push her into doing anything she didn't approve of. She was very amenable about the idea of taking the children out, although she did ask me not to do it while there was still a lot of mud around because the children would bring it all back indoors and create extra work for the staff, a point I was willing to accept. She still used to come up with strange little rules, though, even once we started to venture out. One day she announced that no one was to go outside without a baby bonnet on. So Roger wore a rather fetching pink bonnet with a bobble on the top all afternoon. Even Madam Augustina smiled. 'Oh, Roger, pardon,' she laughed, 'I didn't mean you.'

To keep Lucia and the other women in the room keen, I drew up a series of diagrams of ways to handle the children and asked Ionel to write explanations in Romanian as to why it was good to do things like talk to the children, get them up and help them to help themselves. I also illustrated them as it occurred to me that not all of the carers might be able readers. I wanted to be able to leave something in the room after I had gone to guide the next people who came out to replace us. I've never forgotten how completely lost I had felt on my first day.

Once the children were standing in their cots I would then start to lift them out and keep them upright on the floor by playing games with them, just like babies, dancing around to the music or holding onto their hands and getting them to sway backwards and forwards, telling them to, 'Go away ... Come here ... Go away ... Come here,' making them smile and turning their exercise routines into fun. Lazy Lazlo was the first immobile child we actually got walking and it made a huge difference to the morale of Lucia and the Marias – it was the first time they really appreciated what was possible. It had taken eight weeks or more of constant encouragement. Suddenly they had a rush of enthusiasm and wanted to get more of the children walking. They even started taking initiatives, sometimes getting the children up and onto the potties before I arrived in the morning, looking mighty proud of themselves and the children. They began to show off to other women in the orphanage.

'Isn't that Lazy Lazlo walking?' I heard a women from another room asking Lucia.

'Yes,' Lucia replied proudly. 'I have been giving him gymnastica, and now we are working on the others.'

The job of helping these children seemed so enormous and awe-inspiring I didn't stop to think about it. I just did what my instincts told me day by day and, to my amazement, I found that it worked. We were beginning to get a very happy atmosphere in the room and achieving some stunning results. Some of the children were beginning to react and smile when I came in, making little noises and coming towards me. I noticed that if I was working with a child in one corner of the room, perhaps reading to them, as if they understood, or just talking to them, I would find the others would also start to move across the room towards me. It felt marvellous; they were beginning to show an interest, not only in me, but in life! Some of the other volunteers laughed at me for talking to the children in English most of the time, but it seemed to me that all the children needed to hear was the sound of a human voice, and since they didn't speak Romanian either it didn't much matter what language I used.

Children who had been written off as never likely to do anything began to get up and walk. Other workers and carers would come to Salon One to visit us during the day, and word spread. The Norwegian Red Cross, seeing me in the corridor outside with a child that they had tried to work with and had given up on, asked if they could come into Salon One and do some filming, which gave Lucia a chance to flash her gold teeth and ostentatiously cuddle the children for the cameras, and why shouldn't she?

The Red Cross workers were very constructive and encouraging to me and pointed out that my main problem now that I had encouraged the children to come out of themselves was in making sure the stronger characters didn't monopolise my time. They explained that I would have to learn how to show the more demanding ones that they would have to share me, teaching them that they would get their allotted time with me just like the others, but when it was someone else's turn they couldn't have my attention. I hated having to reject any child when I had spent so much time encouraging them to communicate but I could see that the Red Cross people were right and I simply didn't have enough time to do everything. If I didn't control the situation the stronger children would push the weaker ones aside. Corrina, who had spent the whole of the first day hiding from me, became one of the most demanding, so I now had to spend a lot of my time peeling her off and saying, 'No', which was horrible.

Lucia and the Marias could tell that some of the jobs, like cleaning up excrement, made me retch, and once I had won their confidence they would laugh and take over from me when the most disgusting jobs had to be done. 'Bon lav – are you ill – Bevey?' they would enquire and I would reply, 'No, it's just the kaka.' I had no hesitation in letting them see my fallibilities. I wanted to show them that I didn't have any special skills, that anything I was doing they could do too. I needed to know that the children would continue to be cared for after I had gone.

The cough I'd arrived with grew gradually worse with the pollution and bad living conditions and many of the women would bring me in herbal teas and other remedies to try to help, like goose fat to rub on my chest. Illeana Grande, one of the kitchen workers, used to brew me up some real throat-grabbing concoctions. It amused the other staff no end to see me holding my nose as I swallowed things, trying to stifle a retch afterwards. I think they were amazed and amused to see that we were just like them.

I would respond to their concern and kindness by finding them paracetamol tablets when they had bad period pains, or antibiotics for the abscesses which caused their whole faces to swell up. Other volunteers said that I shouldn't waste the supplies which were meant for the children on the women, but I believed that we should be helping the whole community and that if we made the carers' lives more comfortable they would be kinder to the children in the long run.

I was constantly surprised by the level of superstition amongst all the Romanians working at Ungerini, management and carers alike. They believed, for instance, that cold air would make the children ill. When I tried to get some fresh air into the room by opening the windows and the door they all became hysterical, crying, 'Current!' (draught!), certain that I was going to kill their charges off with pneumonia. They had been happy to leave them malnourished and sitting in their own excrement for days on end but were terrified of them catching a chill from an open window.

I had seen a British health visitor bringing some water into a room for the children to play with which looked like a good idea, letting them get their hands wet and learning about different textures. I had brought lots of bubble bath with me from England because I had seen from my own experience of entertaining nieces and nephews that all children love to play with bubbles. So I found an old baby bath down in the team room and filled it up to do some water play with them. Madam Augustina happened to come into the room that morning and was horrified, certain that the children would catch their deaths of cold.

'No, no,' I assured her earnestly. 'It is a scientific thing that we do in Britain; it encourages the measuring capacity of the brain.' Baffled but impressed she withdrew her objections and insisted every room upstairs was to have water play from then on.

I found that once I had won Madam Augustina's confidence she was quite open to my suggestions and as helpful as she could be, given the pressures of being permanently afraid of the 'authorities'. The whole system in Romania seemed based on fear. The children were afraid of the women workers, the women workers of the management and the managers of the government authorities. No doubt the officials that terrorised institutions like Ungerini had others above them wielding even bigger sticks. Ultimately everyone was responsible to the Minister of Sanitation, a title which, more than anything, demonstrated to me the national attitude to people with mental and physical handicaps.

Just as the children were beginning to respond to me I discovered that one woman was beating and scratching the children at night when I was not there. The carers worked on a three-shifts per day rota, and I saw two women a day – not always

Lucia, Maria 'Grande' or Maria 'Frumos'. At first I didn't know where the cuts and bruises on the children were coming from. I was certain that they weren't doing it to themselves because they rarely came out of their cots unless I was there, and I also noticed that some had started to withdraw back into themselves again, cringing away when I went to get them up.

Lucia and the Marias took me to one side and begged me not to believe that it was them hurting the children, telling me that it was one other woman. They seemed as upset as me that all our good work was being spoiled. It nearly broke my heart to think that just as the children were learning to trust people someone was doing this to them. I went to Madam Augustina and explained that we were trying to boost the children's confidence and this ill-treatment undermined all our efforts.

'No one at Ungerini is hurting the children,' she insisted and by now I knew better than to argue. She had taken in what I was saying and would act on it in her own good time, leaving a long enough gap between my complaint and her response so that she didn't lose any face. A couple of weeks later the woman concerned was moved to a room with much more active children. Knowing, however, that it would take some time before anything was done, and being unwilling to allow the children to be subjected to another minute of abuse if it was within my powers to stop it, I confronted the woman myself.

She swore that she had done nothing and that she knew nothing about it, but it was obvious that her conscience was heavy. She kept crossing herself at the very suggestion that she would be such a monster, but I was not in a mood to pull any punches.

'Oh, no,' I shouted at her. 'It's no good starting all that. You are not going to heaven. You will go to hell for this!'

When she realised that she was not going to convince me of her innocence she started to tell me about the horrors of her own life, how her man beat her about and how she had a child but no husband and how she was pregnant again now. I felt myself softening a little. 'That is very sad,' I agreed, 'but it is no reason to hurt the children here.'

'But, Bevey,' she protested, 'they are just the handicapped.'

'Then you must be kinder to them, not unkinder.'

I'm fairly certain she did not lay hands on them again in the next two weeks and once she had been transferred out of the room we got back onto quite good terms. I could understand exactly why she might feel so much frustration about her own situation and why she would see no reason not to take it out on children who seemed not to know what was going on and who could prove to be so frustrating themselves, but it didn't mean that I could allow it to happen.

One of the older girls living at Ungerini was called Illeana. She was a pleasant and attractive girl whose only reason for living there seemed to be that she had very severe squints in both eyes, which made her alarming to look at. She was close friends with a boy called Gabriel who had tight, dark curls and velvety brown eyes which didn't work very well. He pushed his face disconcertingly close to yours when he spoke to you.

One day I came into the dining room to find the normally gentle Illeana giving Gabriel a terrible pasting and throwing chairs at him as he crashed and bumped into the tables. She was being cheered on by the kitchen staff.

'What is happening?' I wanted to know.

'She caught him kissing Valentina,' one of the women told me. 'Valentina has run away, but Gabriel is not so quick.'

A few days later I noticed a large white van parked at the front of the building and heard Gabriel's fearful wailings long before he appeared. He was dragged out by two large men and flung into the van. Several of us ran down to find out what was happening.

'He's being taken to the Adult Institute,' we were told, 'before he makes one of our girls pregnant.'

As we stood helplessly by, watching this distressing scene, Illeana rushed out of the building, hysterical with despair. Neither of them had been told what was to happen; Gabriel had just been grabbed and hauled out, given no opportunity to say goodbye to Illeana or to have a last few words. As the van drew away we could see his face at the window, tears streaming down it as he tried, unsuccessfully, to get a last glimpse of his friend. Illeana fell to the ground, screaming in uncontrollable grief and I felt the tears coming to my eyes at such a pitiful sight. She mourned for many weeks after that, a grief so real and deep that you could almost see her heart breaking. When you have nothing – no possessions, no clothes of your own, no space, no cupboard, no bag, then friendship must seem very precious indeed. Used to being treated with disdain and harshness by all, Illeana had actually found someone who thought she was worthy of their love; someone who wanted her despite the fact that she was a gypsy with terrible squints. To have that person torn away from her without warning must have seemed like the end of the world. In the days following Gabriel's departure, she developed a stoop, her head down and shoulders rounded as she walked. Dark rings formed under her eyes. She stopped eating and shuffled about like a haunted zombie.

Eventually Illeana collapsed onto my lap one day, sobbing her heart out, and Ionel translated for me. She told us that several of the British workers whom she had thought to be kind had promised to take her to see Gabriel but they never had. She said they had also promised to get her an apartment in Bacau so that she and Gabriel could be re-united, but of course nothing had been done about it.

'I hate you British!' she spat. 'You promise to find my family, but you don't. I hate you. Go away and leave us alone!' She sobbed and wailed, her emaciated body shaking in my arms, her tears drenching both of us. 'And they promised me a piece of soap and a pair of knickers so I could be clean – nothing, nothing, nothing!'

Illeana had been told she had no family and was an orphan. I queried this as she had told me a lot about her family and that she had come to Ungerini as an older child. I was told many of the children imagined things like this, and everything possible had been done to trace her family. Taking this to be the truth was to be a decision I very much regretted later on.

I worried so much about what would happen to her once I too left. Illeana was an attractive girl and was bound to attract the attention of the men, if she hadn't already. Illeana spent much of her time sitting in the corner of Salon One, to the annoyance of Lucia and the Marias, who didn't like any breaks in their routine. Others of the bigger children used to help me, especially at meal times. They did tend to take six spoonfuls themselves for every one that went into the little ones' mouths, but I thought on balance that it was good for the little ones to see how the more capable children handled spoons and bowls – they might learn to copy them.

Giving up hope that any of us would ever help her, Illeana eventually escaped to the local village where she was found trying to catch a bus to see Gabriel by a kindly worker. Fortunately Illeana's conversational skills weren't up to explaining what she wanted to do. She didn't have any money and the bus was going in the wrong direction anyway.

She then tried to send Gabriel a note, asking one of the workers to write it for her, hoping that a member of staff at the Adult Institute would read it to him. She wrapped it round a sweet and asked one of our team to give it to him when they next visited the Institute. She later found the note discarded inside Ungerini's gates. This was the final straw. She withdrew to her bed and looked as if she would never speak to us again. I began to wonder if, for all our good intentions, we might actually be making some things worse for some of the children by bringing hopes that we could never manage to bring to fruition.

At about this time I noticed that there was a door opposite Salon One that was always kept padlocked. On one occasion someone forgot to lock it and I decided to do some investigating. I pushed my way in and found myself in an Aladdin's Cave of blankets, sheets, clothes, soap, soap powder, cream and shampoo. I couldn't believe my eyes and immediately shot downstairs to have a word with Madam Augustina.

'Would it be possible to use some of these supplies and improve the laundry system?' I asked politely.

To begin with she came up with a list of excuses about how the things would be spoiled, soiled and stolen, but eventually she relented and let me have some more blankets. I also tackled her on the subject of giving the children some zips and buttons to protect their modesty. It was very hard, I pointed out, to teach a child to walk when you were trying to hold both their hands and then hitch their trousers up at the same time.

'But the children cut them out and steal them!' she protested.

'How do the children cut them out?' I demanded. 'Do they have knives? If they are stealing them where are they hiding them? They have nowhere to hide them. It can't be the children, it must be the women in the laundry rooms.

'When the girls menstruate you do not even give them anything to pad themselves with – the blood is just dripping down their legs. Would you allow children of your own to walk around like this?' I asked. She shook her head and I pressed my advantage. 'Then why should we expect them to?' I had a horrible feeling I had gone too far but she seemed to be agreeing with me. I even suggested that we get some Velcro sent out from England as that might be a less desirable commodity to steal than buttons and zips. She promised to look into it but I could tell there wasn't much she could do about it in the short term.

I also used to ask the carers, especially the women in charge of the bigger children downstairs, 'Would you let your son go around with his dick hanging out or your daughter with her fanny showing?' This usually brought hoots of laughter as they were shocked that I knew and would use such words. Their reply was invariably the same old, 'But, Bev, they are handicapped.'

'All the more reason for you to protect them since they cannot protect themselves,' I answered. 'Pull them up! Let's get some string around them!'

In a phone call home to John, I explained the problem and he duly sent out an enormous ball of string so that I could create some makeshift belts to keep us going. Each morning I would tie everyone's trousers up, but by the next day all the pieces of string had disappeared because the women had taken them home. I took the ball back to the hotel with me every night in case the team room was broken into and that was stolen as well.

'Bevey,' Madam Augustina said, in the course of one such talk, 'You know you need only call me Augustina, that is my first name.' I felt rather foolish, having always assumed that I had been addressing her correctly by her surname. From then on I tried to address her just as Augustina, but I never quite managed to think of her as anything other than Madam Augustina.

I would spend my mornings in Salon One and in the afternoons I worked downstairs with the bigger children, which gave me a chance to start fulfilling my ambition of getting some of the children outside into the fresh air. I must admit it wasn't just for their sakes. I was as keen as anyone to escape from the horrible, damp, dark rooms into the beautiful countryside surrounding the orphanage.

I wanted the children to feel the breeze on their faces and hear the birds singing for the first time in their lives; to see the blue sky, to watch clouds go racing by, to smell their first flowers. On our first ventures outside I felt like Julie Andrews running around in the mountains singing. I used to get Mark or Ionel to come with me because they were better sprinters than me and if one of the children ran off they could go after them. Not that any of the children had enough stamina to be able to go very far or very fast, but many of them had a turn of speed I did not.

To begin with they were terrified of everything they saw.

Patrika, a big, fat, unset jelly of a boy whom I had often had to stop from dominating other weaker children, was particularly upset when we came to a lane where a horse or ox cart had left a trail of clods of earth. There was one lump, about the size of a small melon, which he refused to go past. Never having seen anything like it before he just stood staring at it and jibbering with fear. I spent ages coaxing him to put his foot on it to show that it was harmless and that he wouldn't fall off the edge of the world if it crumbled beneath him. When we got him to the top of a hill, which was a battle in itself, Patrika had a panic attack about coming back down. He was practically an adult but had never walked on anything but flat concrete floors. It took two of us, one on each side, to gradually bring him back down, step by step as he hung onto us, quivering and moaning, 'Bevey, Bevey.'

Trips out meant we always had to ensure that there were enough adults to control our charges – there were potential dangers everywhere we went. On our way to see the orphanage pigs one day we came across four enormous open pits where the workers used to dump sewage. Because everywhere at Ungerini smelt bad, we hadn't realised that all the human waste was being dumped in unfenced holes so close to the building. Nothing had been done to ensure that the children couldn't fall into these cess pits.

There was also a chance that they might fall down the wells which we stopped at in order to draw drinking water. Some of the villagers we came across during our walks were kind to the children, although they were always puzzled as to who we might be. Others became angry and seemed frightened that our charges would bring diseases to the area, polluting their drinking water with their madness, and would chase us off. I soon realised that this attitude towards the handicapped is widespread in Romania and is one of the main barriers to progress in this area of health care. I suggested that rather than leaving the local carers in the rooms when we went out we should take them with us. That way we could take more children along and communicate more easily with curious locals and perhaps allay some of their fears. I thought it might be nice for the women to get some fresh air as well and to talk to the children in Romanian, encouraging them to learn their own language.

On one outing we found a little stream which we dammed and

I showed the children how to float twigs in the current. One of the Florins was with us (it's a common name), a gentle smiling lad with dimples, who held my hand, blushing profusely, and liked to hear stories about my cats and dogs in Britain. He loved the water and rushed about screaming as his twig boat began to float downstream. Doina, a ten-year-old who was known as 'Doina the face slapper' because of her habit of dealing unsuspecting volunteers stinging, welt-inducing blows to the face, was with us too that day and for the first time I saw her give a small, exploratory smile, as if practising a new-found skill.

Later we discovered a pond which had thousands of frogs in it, so we got everyone out to look at that, whole roomfuls of them. Other British helpers worked desperately to keep their children clean when outside, laying out blankets for them to sit on, but I wanted them to touch and feel everything, to dig their fingers into the earth if they wanted to, or pull up handfuls of grass. The saddest thing was having to take the kids back inside once they had got used to going out. On one occasion a beautiful blond-haired boy called Mihai wept and begged to be allowed to stay outside. We had to drag him back and I felt so sorry for him that I cried too, knowing that he might not be able to get out again for a whole week.

I longed for the day when I would be able to take some of the little ones from Salon One out for the first time. I imagined the awe on their faces when they saw the brightness of the sky and felt the breeze on their skin. When the weather was finally dry and warm enough, we started to ferry them downstairs in small groups. Instead of the wonder and awe which I had imagined, they were all terrified, clinging to our legs and skirts. I would take them downstairs a few at a time, leaving them hanging onto Lucia or one of the Marias while I went back up for more, wondering if I was doing the right thing or if I was simply indulging my own fantasy. But gradually, day by day, they became less scared and would sit calmly on the grass with us in the sunshine, tolerating the fresh air and awesome space all around them, but they still didn't have the initiative to play independently, and they didn't show any interest in their surroundings. One day it rained and this caused all the children to panic for they had not seen or felt anything like it before. The sound of birds or even the wind in the trees was a disconcerting experience for all the children at first, too.

I was shocked by how rarely I ever saw a family come to visit their child in the home, for they weren't all orphans despite Ungerini's title. One day, however, while the children were eating, two workers rushed in and grabbed a very handicapped but gentle boy called Ciprien. He had skin covered in sores, and bite marks on his ears and nose, almost certainly inflicted by some of the bigger boys in his room who were known to pick on him. Thick snot always ran down his upper lip and he was usually dribbling as well. The workers quickly washed him and put him into the best clothes available. When I came out into the corridor a little later I saw two elderly, proud-looking peasants sitting with Ciprien on their laps as a never-ending parade of screaming people passed by, pushing and shoving and staring at them aggressively. They were feeding him little bits and pieces of food which they had brought with them. The father was sitting bolt upright with a Cossack hat on his head, and when he took it off and gently put it on Ciprien, the boy gave an excited shout. Ciprien's mother was weeping silently and as I watched I saw two big tears run down the old man's cheeks. I felt a bit of a wobbler coming on myself at this and went outside, not wanting to intrude on their privacy. I remembered that when we had taken Ciprien out one day he had run over to a peasant's cottage and we'd had to pull him away as he fought to get in the gate. I wondered if it had been because it reminded him of his home.

The old couple were going to have to get back to Bacau to the big Auto Gara bus station that evening and Mark asked if any of us minded him squeezing them into the van for our trip back to the hotel. Ionel was also with us so we were able to talk to them during the journey.

'We have only just been able to get here,' they explained, 'because we had to wait for the snows to melt on the Carpathians before we could get across.' They told us Ciprien was sixteen. 'The authorities took him from us when he was nine, so that he could be rehabilitated in a better place. We can only come twice a year because of the distance and the cost.'

When the time came to part, Mark and I pressed whatever lei we had into the old lady's hand. She looked at the money and kissed my fingers. I felt very humble.

'How much would the return trip cost them?' I asked Ionel once they had gone.

'About thirty pence in your money,' Ionel answered. It seemed so little and yet for them was probably more than they had to spare.

My admiration for the Norwegian Red Cross people grew with every day as I watched them at work. They seemed so professional and they never allowed their own egos or personal problems to get in the way of doing their best for the children. Even though I had no experience at all they often asked my opinion and listened to what I had to say, which I found very surprising but flattering all the same – perhaps I was doing all right after all? They were extremely happy that the children were progressing under my care and I felt I had been given a vote of confidence that I was very grateful for. I so desperately wanted to do something tangible for the children and give them skills that would help them after I had gone home. The Norwegians' encouragement was a boost to my belief that there is no such thing as a hopeless case, that everyone deserves a chance – even if the chance comes to nothing. They never tried to put me down just because I was untrained, saying that they were intrigued by the good results I was getting and were pleased to see the children in Salon One coming out of their prisons.

Dr Kari was in her seventies and Norway's foremost expert in mental illness and welfare, a world leader in her field. She was petite with slightly wavy grey hair, twinkling blue mischievous eyes and a lovely smile. I watched her fix many a violent child with those eyes, smilingly saying, 'No, now vee don't vant to do zat, do vee?' and they were always instantly calmed.

One of the things the Red Cross asked my advice on was the way in which the older children were fed in the dining room. They said they would like to have my help at mealtimes because I was 'non-confrontational' with the children. Having seen the mess left after lunch that first day I was shown round Ungerini, I knew that it was a problem which needed fixing. All the big children, about ninety of them, were herded into the dining room to be fed at the same time. The food was dished out into big bowls, though there were nowhere near enough bowls to go round. When the kids were released into the room there was a mad, screaming free-for-all, with food ending up on the floor while desperate children scrabbled around on all fours trying to scrape it up, fighting each other and tearing at the few loaves left out for them. They even forced food out of the mouths of smaller, weaker children. They ripped at each other's ears, scratched at mouths, grabbing bread out of hamster-like cheeks and quickly stuffing it into their own. The noise was deafening; women shrieking, children frenzied and hysterical because they were so hungry, terrified that the others would get to a scrap before they did. It was a sight so bestial and savage that I will never forget it. The best of the meagre meals went to the strongest, fastest and most ruthless children, who would become screaming, fighting, greed machines. I saw Patrika take hold of a smaller child and force his hand into his mouth, grabbing the bread and anything else he could scoop out and immediately transferring it into his own mouth before going on to his next victim. It wasn't so much the act of a bully as that of a boy desperate for food. Within a few minutes of arriving the carers were chivvying the children along, hurrying them to finish and get out so that they could clear up. The children would then go back to their rooms, covered in food debris.

Having watched this chaotic spectacle a second time, 'Why the hurry?' I wanted to know. 'They're not going anywhere except back to their rooms.'

'The shifts are about to change and the staff want to be ready to leave,' the Red Cross people explained.

'Why don't we bring the mealtime forward a bit to give them more time?' I suggested.

It took us a while to persuade the helpers in the rooms not to let all the children out to lunch at once, but to divide them up into groups of ten to fifteen at a time, washing their hands and faces first.

One day, when they had failed to do this and nearly a hundred children were thundering down the corridor together, I found Roger fairly hysterical and as beautifully if crudely articulate as ever, screaming at the women: 'If I threw one brain amongst you all,' he yelled, 'it would be f...... lonely! Oh, only ninety-six children in for lunch at once? Oh, definitely not nearly enough! Quick! Take the keys, drive to the villages, round up the children and drag them here by the hundred! Then we can have a real f...... luncheon party!'

I led him quietly outside, put a cup of coffee in one hand, lit him a cigarette for the other and went back an hour later to find him a bit more like his usual self!

Once there were groups of more manageable numbers we were

also able to find sufficient old tables and chairs and individual bowls and spoons. We then set about showing the children, despite much protesting, that if they sat down and used the spoons they would actually get more to eat. To begin with they leapt onto the tables and on top of us, screaming because they thought they weren't going to get anything to eat this way but we persisted.

I was trying to think how we train children at home when they first want to feed themselves with solid food. The big difference here was that these were starving teenagers who most definitely did not want to wait long enough for satisfaction to feed themselves with spoons. Where on earth should we begin?

Each of the volunteers would take one table and would stand behind the children, guiding the spoons up to their mouths in their hands until it became an automatic reaction which they did for themselves. I took the table with the maddest boys because I seemed to have a soothing influence on them. Some of the other workers tended to get into confrontations and then the children would start hurling things at them. Everyone got pretty good at ducking bowls of steaming food as they whizzed by. One time I did not duck quickly enough and a whole bowl of very hot beans landed on my head, dripping down my hair and into my ears. There was a stunned silence. It was such a shock I thought I was going to cry. Everyone was staring. I was so embarrassed all I could think of saying was, 'Do I take it the beans were not to your liking, sir?' Whereupon the English team all relaxed into helpless laughter. The Romanians hesitated momentarily and then they laughed too as they helped de-bean my hair.

Some staff wanted to separate the most violent children off from the others but the rest of us talked them out of it – we felt they all had to learn to live and hence eat with one another on a daily basis. The food was always far too hot to begin with, scalding the children's mouths and making them wild with frustration. I asked Madam Augustina if the kitchen staff could turn the heat off earlier, so that the children could eat it straight away. It was also suggested that it would be better if the bones were removed from any meat dish before the food came to the children because they tended to throw them at one another and some of them received quite bad head cuts as a result. In the past the women had always served the soup from the top, where it was thinnest, so that all the goodness and the vegetables which had sunk to the bottom were thrown to the pigs with the dregs. We taught them to scoop from the bottom so that the children received more nutrition per bowlful.

Adding to the general air of mayhem, the Romanian helpers always seemed to be shouting and screaming at one another. This agitated the children and made them nervous, so I tried to encourage them to be calm, quiet and a bit more gentle. It seemed to work. I also suggested the kitchen staff should slice the bread in advance so that the loaves weren't torn to pieces in a feeding frenzy. 'Oh, no,' they told me. 'We don't have time.'

'Okay,' I smiled sweetly. 'I'll come in early and do it.'

It took me about half an hour each morning and I would then leave the bread covered in paper to protect it from the flies. I only had to do that a few times before they saw that I wasn't asking them to do anything too difficult and they relented. 'Don't worry, Bevey,' one of the cooks told me, tapping her fingers above her ample chest, 'I will do that for you.' She was much faster at the job, being more experienced with knives and much less cack-handed than me. To begin with the children would grab as many slices as they could, cramming them inside their clothes, their eyes darting protectively from side to side, then, when they realised they could have as much as they wanted, they became calmer and were willing to accept one slice at a time. They still tended to shove it into their mouths, leaving only the smallest gap to suck the soup through, and there were one or two who would always dive head first into the pig bucket, sucking up the slops, if you didn't hold onto them.

After a while the children began to eat fairly well, quite calmly, and they actually started to look better. Their skins were clearer and they had a little more weight on their bones. They even seemed to enjoy mealtimes. We used to stay with them and talk and began to put cups of water alongside the food. The children were always thirsty because the women generally tried to dissuade them from drinking from the buckets in the rooms in order to cut down the amount of pee they had to clear up. I noticed that Roger had started to sit down at the children's level so as not to loom over them, and I began to do the same. Even after we had got them sitting down at a table to eat there were still a lot of loud troughing noises. Most of the kids were still liable to scoop everything up from their bowls and stuff it into their faces with their fingers rather than using the spoons and when finished would immediately turn their attention to whatever their neighbours had in their bowls. The contents of their noses were usually streaming into the food but they still kept on shovelling it into their mouths. Sometimes, in their haste to get everything in before it was stolen from them, they would gag and throw up into the bowls and then quickly wolf everything back down again before it could be taken away from them. It was quite hard to hold your own food down with all this going on around you.

There were more than a few things the cooks produced in the kitchens which were quite edible: the soup, which had been boiled for so long you could be fairly confident it was safe, and mashed potatoes with cheese added. They really did their best with the limited resources available, and it is only fair to note that the children were often eating better than the kitchen staff and their families did at home.

For some of the children the highlight of mealtimes was having their hands and faces washed again – although the floor cloth would be used for the job if you didn't watch out – while others put up the most awful struggle. As time went on the women began to see that if things were done in an orderly fashion there was less work for them because they didn't have to clean food off the walls, ceiling and floor, and the children's clothes weren't quite as plastered in food either. After only four weeks we were really beginning to make some visible progress.

And I was happy to see improvement, not only because the children's eating habits were now more socially acceptable, but it showed they were enjoying their food and mealtimes. Already the children were adapting to new routines and their general health was benefiting.

CHAPTER FIVE

Making Friends

*

When I first arrived at Ungerini everything seemed very black and white. I could only see the terrible plight of the children and couldn't understand how the adults could allow it to continue. Gradually, as I came to know more about the home lives of ordinary Romanians, I began to see things very differently.

As volunteers, our main contact with the Romanian people was through the staff at Ungerini, those who befriended us and those who came to us for help. Many of the women carers were distracted from their work by concern for their own children. If the child of a poor family fell sick there were not many people who would be willing or able to help. When they saw what I was doing for the children in Salon One, some of the local carers started to ask me to tend to their sick relatives. I had little or no idea what to do medically, but I decided that even if I did no more than just visit it might make them feel better because at least it would demonstrate that someone cared. Once John started to get parcels through to me I used to be able to take a few bits and pieces to the local village children and give some to the carers for their families.

The first to ask for my help was Maria the Beautiful. She used to wrap up carefully whatever I gave her and after a while I discovered that she always took it home to her mother. One day she very coyly asked if I would visit her mother. She wanted me to bring a medical kit along, although I couldn't work out quite what was wrong from Maria's descriptions. Mark, the young man I had seen working in one of the rooms on our first tour of the home and who had become a good friend, drove Maria and me out to her simple cottage during our lunch hour. This was the first time I had actually been inside one of the villagers' homes. All the houses had dogs outside and I already knew not to go near unless they were chained up. Dogs were only used for hunting or to guard properties, never kept as pets. They were accustomed to being stoned and kicked if they came too close to humans. (There were a number of dogs that we used to see skulking around outside the buildings at Ungerini, searching for scraps or hidden carcasses. At one time they had been allowed to roam around inside the rooms, savaging the children in the process. A French team who slept inside Ungerini told us that on nights when the children became very agitated, for instance if there were thunderstorms outside, the carers brought dogs in to frighten and subdue them into silence. It was later confirmed that many of the scars on the children came from dog bites.)

Mark stayed outside Maria's house for a smoke. As my eyes became accustomed to the gloom inside, I saw the bar of soap I had given Maria proudly displayed on the only shelf alongside a tiny bottle of shampoo – neither had been touched. The house was bitterly cold, its floors just hardened mud, and Maria's mother had only a few old rags on the bed to cover her.

In the dark kitchen two wooden beds were pushed close to a little stove. There was a terrible, sickly smell of putrid flesh in the air. In the next room I could see another bed, a wooden chair and table. On the walls there were faded hand-woven rugs in the traditional Moldavian patterns that had obviously once been very beautiful. News of my arrival spread rapidly through the village and within a few minutes there were at least twenty relatives and neighbours crowded into the two tiny rooms. Even with my extremely limited medical knowledge I could see that Maria's mother was suffering from advanced breast cancer. She had no dressings and her clothes were stuck to her open wounds and to bed sores so big I could have fitted my hand inside them. She had nothing to alleviate the pain of her condition.

Nausea stirred in my stomach but I forced myself not to think about it. All these people were expecting me to do something special. Pots of water were put on to boil and a few of the people asked to leave so that we could give the old woman a bed bath. Luckily I had brought some fresh clothes with me, kindly donated by Jacqui and Diane since mine would have been much too big, which we were able to put Maria's mother in after I had gently dressed the cancers and sores, applying soothing antiseptic creams and gauze. The pain from even my most gentle touch must have been excruciating, but she gritted her teeth and did not cry out. A few tears fell from her eyes as she squeezed my hand, whispering 'Multumesc,' – thank you. I could feel her pain as I worked and I was told she had been ill for five years, steadily going downhill until finally she was bedridden. She apologised that she could not get up to make me a 'chai' – tea.

The next time I visited we took the old scarf off her head and washed her hair. The poor woman was so grateful she kept wanting to kiss my hands to say thank you. I gave her the ring with the wooden cross on it that I had been given by Janet Stevens at Abbey National in England. I felt very humbled because I had done so little and I wished I could have done more. Later I managed to get hold of some paracetamol that Maria could crush up in camomile tea, giving her mother a little respite from pain.

Maria's mother was terrified that she would die without candles. In the Romanian Orthodox Church it is believed that the dying must have a candle at each of the four corners of their beds to light their way to heaven. John was able to send some out from England and they brought her immense relief. I went back to see her every couple of days after that and she finally died just before I was to due to leave Romania. The family insisted that I come in to see her, which worried me a little as I had never seen a dead body. They pushed all the poor, ancient relatives out of the way so that I could sit right by her head. I was surprised she looked so much better, very peaceful; her skin was wrinkle-free and had a sort of glow to it. There appeared to be a slight smile on her lips. I joined in with their prayers and Maria indicated that she wanted me to kiss her mother on the lips. I was frightened to do this but realised that it meant a lot to Maria. On contact she seemed cold to the touch but most definitely at peace.

I was able discreetly to give Maria enough money for the funeral – a few pounds in our money but from her response you would have thought I had made her a millionairess; it meant so much to her that she could bury her mother with dignity. I discovered that the poor old woman I thought I had been helping to die peacefully was actually five years younger than me.

Another of the women carers, Maricica, brought her sick, seven-year-old son all the way to the hotel in Bacau. It was a very brave action for someone like that to walk into a hotel, and she received a very poor reception from the staff there who tried to shoo her away. But Maricica was determined and just kept asking for me until they were forced to call up to my room. The boy was feverish and I couldn't immediately tell what was wrong with him, so I asked one of the Norwegian Red Cross doctors to come down and take a look at him but he didn't have many ideas either. I asked Maricica to wait while I went back up to my room and packed up a food parcel of chocolate, biscuits and a Fanta for their return journey; it was all I had but the best I could do. I also gave her the bus fare back and some vitamin pills as it looked to me as though the boy was badly malnourished. I made sure she understood that 'more was not better', and just to give him one at a time. The hotel staff wouldn't let me give her the parcel in reception so we had to go outside. I felt very frustrated and helpless because there was nothing else I could do and she had come with such great hope. Maricica was relieved when her son did eventually get over his fever, but we never found out what had caused it. I couldn't help but imagine how John and I would have felt had Russell fallen ill without good health-care services to rely on to make him well.

One of the interpreters, a lovely woman called Betty who was good with the older children and very interested in us, really caring and worrying about us as if we were family, took us one Sunday to visit her mother-in-law's home. It was a beautiful wooden house with a carved verandah, vines and fruit bushes outside and hand-painted wallpaper inside. The interior was very dark with net curtains at the small windows. The wooden floors and walls were covered with rugs and carpets in gaudy reds, blues and purples. There was always a lot of red around in Romanian homes because they consider it lucky. They tie red bows into the manes of their horses for luck. The old lady of the house had to draw all her water from a sixty-foot well a short walk away.

Betty's mother-in-law prepared a feast of eggs, lamb and garlic for us. It was a beautiful day and we played football in the garden. The old lady then took us on a long walk to a reservoir set in spectacular scenery. We were practically mountaineering but she was as agile as a goat in her thick stockings, leggings, woven skirt, jumper, headscarf, sheepskin waistcoat and boots. At one point she took my arm to help me up a particularly steep hill. She said she liked me because I smiled a lot. She insisted on sitting next to me during the meal, continually touching my face, holding my hand and thanking me for coming to Romania to look after the children. She asked Betty to ask me what my husband thought about me doing this sort of work. Like many of those I told of John's unselfish attitude, I don't think she believed me when I said he supported me. I remember thinking how nice it would be if we could bring the children to an idyllic place like this. I had suggested at one point that we take them on outings to Bacau, but was told that this would not be allowed as the children might 'try to escape'. Since none of them had much energy, a full set of clothes or a pair of matching shoes with laces, and the majority could barely walk or speak, I thought the risk of escapes was minimal but the authorities were adamant.

We saw another side of local life altogether when we visited Dana, the interpreter we had met on the first day, at her flat in town. Each week she would generously prepare a meal for us all, a vegetarian feast. Finding all the ingredients for such a big meal must have been a major job for her. As well as being a vegetarian, she was also into alternative pastimes like yoga and mysticism. I have never seen such a good selection of English language versions of the classics as she had in her flat. She was one of the most well read people I have ever met and had a great awareness of world affairs. She was in her twenties, married with a small child, and had a local girl living in to look after the boy while she was at work. The girl used to sleep on the sofa in the lounge and had filled Dana's sitting room with Catholic paraphernalia, which Dana wasn't too happy about. Whenever we were visiting she would play loud music because she was worried about the neighbours listening in to our conversations and reporting her to the authorities. I couldn't tell if her fears were well founded or whether that sort of thing had gone with the Ceauçescus. They were wonderful evenings when we all let our hair down and forgot the problems we had been dealing with all day. Dana made great efforts to show us the more positive side of her country, and many of her friends were eager to invite us to their homes to make sure we were eating enough and to tell us about their history and culture. I used to go to the concert hall every Thursday with Dr Irina Tiron, a paediatric consultant from Bacau Hospital. The Bacau Orchestra was splendid, good enough to tour the major concert halls of Europe.

It was such a strange contrast to my daytime activities, to be part of an audience of educated Romanians. What would our children have made of it I wonder? It was so far removed from

Andrei (6), Patreascu (4) and Ionuts (4), April '91

Sister Jane feeding Catalin (8) –
from a spoon!

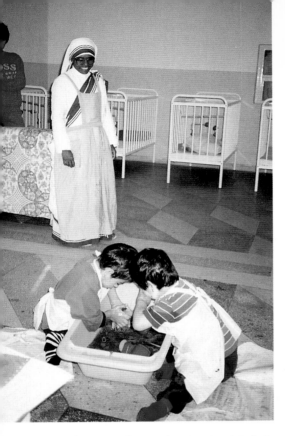

Water play – Sr Ida watches Lucien Maftei and Patreascu

Dom Patreascu with Tractor Lucien and Mariana (ex-Salon One)

Ring-a-ring-a-roses with Sr Ida and Ramona Patreascu

Lunchtime at MT's – eating from bowls now

Maria-my-room, Gillian and
Crenguitsa painting at MT's

Helen and Valentina, Christmas '91

Saying goodbye to Maria – Jacqui
and Bev in 'those' nighties

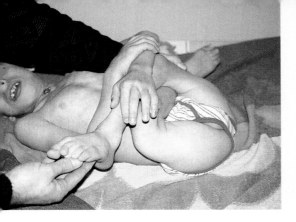

Lucien lying as he was tied

Aged 14 and permanently cross-legged

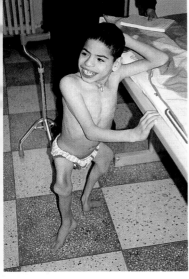

Dr Nigel examining Patreascu at MT's

Standing to show deformity

Patreascu with leg pinned

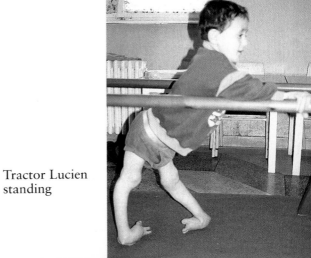

Tractor Lucien standing

Patreascu arriving at
Stansted

Szuzannah de-planing!

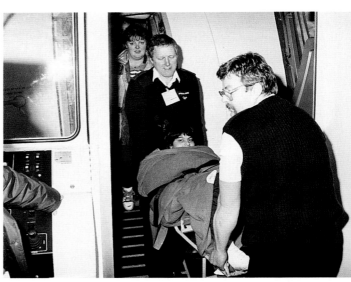

Daniel surrounded by
six 'adopted' cousins
and sister Karen

Diane and Jacqui with
Szuzannah and
Ungerini hairdo,
March '91

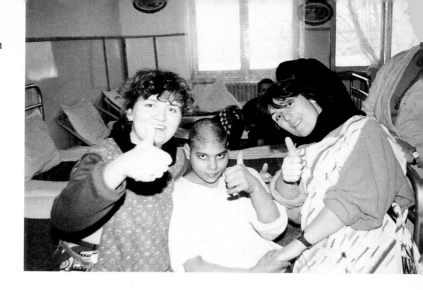

Misty and Russell
supervising Szuzannah's
calipers

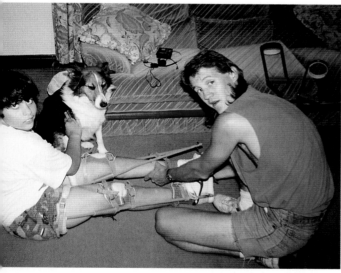

Szuzannah upright!
with Dr Nigel and Dr
Bobby, December '92

Florin, Illeana and Simona,
Ungerini, March '91

John and Illeana in Milton Keynes,
pre-op...

Illeana's 17th birthday and leaving party

their experience yet took place almost on their doorstep.

Life was hard for the Romanian middle classes as well as the peasants, albeit on a very different level. There were shortages in the shops to deal with and water was constantly being cut off during the day without warning. Wise householders would always keep the bath full and a bucket beside the toilet for the many hours when the pipes were silent and dry. We learnt to use water very sparingly. If we could get enough for a bath we would wash ourselves and then climb out and put soap powder in for our clothes. Roger used to roll up his trouser legs and climb in on top of his washing, treading it like grapes.

Although I grew to understand why the women carers behaved as they did towards the children, given the hardships they had to endure, I still became angry with them on occasions. I had taken musical instruments out with me – things like chime bars, triangles and drums (no wind instruments because of the dangers of exchanging mouth fluids) – and one day they all disappeared. I had only been out of the room for five minutes. The women swore blind that they hadn't taken them.

'All right,' I challenged them, Ionel interpreting my every word, 'all of you jump on the spot.' As they reluctantly began to jog up and down there was a series of clanks, clatters and clangs as my precious instruments cascaded out of their hiding places. I was so upset. 'You bloody bitches,' I screamed. 'I've sincerely tried to help you, to be nice, coming to visit your families and helping to nurse your sick, and this is how you repay me!' I ranted on for ages until their eyes were watering up with shame and they were crossing themselves and begging forgiveness to try to calm me down.

'Oh dear,' I said to Ionel once they had gone, 'I'm afraid I went rather over the top.'

'Not at all, Bev,' he assured me. 'Before they loved you, now they will respect you as well.'

When I stopped to reflect I could quite see why toys were routinely stolen, and why everything else that wasn't locked up or nailed down disappeared. Having seen the conditions the locals were living in I can't honestly say that I wouldn't have behaved in the same way. If I had a child with no toys and saw things being given to children who appeared not to appreciate them and very often smashed them to bits, I would be more than tempted to take those things to my own child, who I could be sure would enjoy them. When I first arrived at Ungerini I had thought the carers were monsters, but I gradually realised that their lives, too, were unimaginably hard and that more often than not it was ignorance not unkindness that made them behave the way they did. But just because I understood the reasons for their behaviour, I didn't believe it was justified.

As the weeks passed, several of the children too showed themselves to be true friends to me. Szuzannah was a gypsy of about fourteen, with horribly crippled legs. She had lovely, flashing black eyes and used to look up at me from the floor like a sad, faithful old dog. She was always desperate for attention, love and approval. When some of the more articulate children shouted abuse at me, like, 'Old cow,' Szuzannah would spring to my defence saying, 'No, Bevey beautiful.'

One afternoon in early March I was working with some of the larger lads when Szuzannah crawled in to see what we were doing. A particularly unpredictable boy, Bordisan, suddenly became very agitated, started howling like a wolf and then charged across the room intent on hitting me. I froze, unable to move as he approached. Szuzannah grabbed hold of the end of the bed and pulled herself up onto her twisted legs, putting her frail body between Bordisan and me, taking the full impact of his fist which knocked her backwards. Through her tears she told him to 'leave my Bevey alone'. For a second I felt relieved at having been spared the blow and then guilt that she had been hurt while saving me.

Two other girls, teenagers called Simona and Loridana, also used to come to my rescue, telling the more energetic children, 'Be gentle with Bevey; you will all get turns.' They both made tremendous efforts to keep themselves clean, despite having no warm water, soap or shampoo, and both obviously had severe problems with their legs, walking with strange gaits. They loved nothing better than having one of the helpers bring in some nail varnish and paint their nails for them. Although Simona sounded gruff and bossy, she had a very well established sense of right and wrong. She loved to touch my hair, making a strange, cat-like moaning sound as she stroked it. When I gave her my shoulder bag with black cats on it she wept for joy. I came to look on many of these older children as close friends.

CHAPTER SIX

Slow Progress

*

*T*here were a great many heart-breaking set-backs at Ungerini, like the day when Lazy Lazlo seemed even more miserable-looking than usual when I came in singing my usual 'rise and shine' message. He just lay there, looking very yellow, particularly the whites of his eyes. My first thought was that he had contracted hepatitis, or jaundice as it used to be known. He felt hot to the touch and seemed too disinterested in life even to be grumpy with me. Adelina, the 'Chief Nurse', came as soon as I asked. Luckily we had some antibiotics in our team room and she started to give him these, even though they weren't prescribed for his condition. For two weeks he was too weak even to whimper. I couldn't help thinking of all the drugs available in Britain and other Western countries and which couldn't be got out to the children who needed them most in the world and it saddened me to my very core. It was weeks before Lazy Lazlo was well enough for us to resume our efforts to get him to stand up.

Incidents like this made some of the other members of the team think we were getting nowhere, but I found that we were progressing a tiny bit day by day, giving the children more and more to live for, slowly making their lives more comfortable. To any newcomer the situation would still have seemed almost unbearably bleak, but working closely with the children it was possible to see little breakthroughs every day; a child smiling for the first time or looking you in the eye, moving outside Salon One without screaming for the first time or starting to show interest in a toy unprompted.

I was beginning to see the children as individuals with very distinct personalities, rather than as categories or degrees of infirmity. There were a few volunteers who were willing, like me, to spend their afternoons with the big children downstairs. Many of the others found that even half a day at Ungerini was as much as they could stand and they would return to the hotel after lunch. Since I was there I thought I might as well do whatever I could to help. There was never anything much to go back to the hotel for.

The difficulty with the big children was always finding things for them to do that they would enjoy but which wouldn't get out of hand. Their, expressionless faces were like those white masks they use in Japanese Kabuki theatre, registering no emotion other than blank disinterest or stark fear. If the children looked at you at all it was with haunted, frightened eyes. I felt a great sense of achievement the day I persuaded twelve-year-old Monika to smile at me with her mouth and her eyes both at the same time.

I tried them with things like the colouring books I had brought out from England with me, but they weren't really up to the required level of manual skill. How do you get someone to colour in a picture of a beach ball if they have never seen one? They liked to blow bubbles, but you can't do that every day and we had to be careful they didn't snatch at the liquid and spill it, so we would hold the bottles and wands and they would puff away. I believed the blowing motion would help them to develop their muscles and put some life into their blank faces, but I don't know if there was any truth in this. With some of the more aware ones I would try to encourage them to do facial exercises like sticking their tongues out, simply to get their muscles working.

In most cases just the fact that we were there at all cheered them up. I used to play a game where they would pretend to be asleep and I would have to wake them up. They would then sit bolt upright and open their eyes very wide, like dolls do. It was the same little charade every time and always made them scream with laughter. Sitting the children on my lap like giant ventriloquists' dummies, I tickled their faces with paint brushes, feathers and silk and put hot and cold things against their skins so that they could feel the different sensations – anything to make them less introverted and more interested in whatever was going on around them.

Jill, an older lady who had been a nurse and was part of the first team to go out to Ungerini, was very kind and helpful to me at the beginning. We got to know her the first weekend we were in Bacau. The rest of her team had decided they needed a break as soon as we arrived and had gone to Bucharest for a few days. On the Friday evening, when we got back to the hotel, it was bitterly cold. The British Army had sent out loads of rations which were stored in the team room and Jacqui and Diane decided to cook us all a delicious chicken curry and rice. My job was to lay the coffee table. I found some old champagne bottles into which I put some even older candles, while Roger went off and bought some rough old wine and champagne. I put on a tape of Strauss waltzes and the mood was set.

Suddenly we heard a little voice say, 'Oh, it's you!' and we saw Jill's head disappear out of the room and off down the corridor. I raced after her and invited her to join us. She was a little reluctant at first and explained that she guessed she hadn't been invited on the Bucharest trip because she was so much older than the other team members.

We found an extra plate and each donated a portion of our meal. Roger poured her a glass of champagne and we all squeezed up. We had a hilarious evening, swaying in time to the music just like they must have done in the beer halls of Vienna, and getting quite squiffy since some of us were not used to drinking such strong stuff. Jill was amazed that none of us could waltz and was persuaded to try to teach Diane. Diane, tall, slim and with cascades of beautiful, curly, honey-blonde hair and sparkling green eyes, waltzed around the candle lit room with her shorter, very pretty, but slightly plumper partner. The next day Jill quietly told me that it was the first time she had been included in anything since she had arrived two months before.

I enjoyed working with Jill. We all came to respect her dedication to the children, and we knew she would be a loss to the team when the time came for her to leave. Jill and Mark used to have a sparring kind of fondness for one another. If he was driving the van she had a habit of shrieking 'Stop!', forcing him to screech to a skidding halt and enquire as to what it was that Jill had seen. 'There's a peasant in the road!' she would offer.

On her last morning Mark, Jacqui, Roger and I went to the station to see her off and as the train pulled out Mark shouted, 'Stop!' Jill screamed back, 'What is it?' Mark mischievously held up a passport, calling back, 'Passport!'

Jill looked flustered for a couple of seconds, then brought out her own passport, waved it gaily and hooted with laughter.

She was very helpful to me from the start, popping into Salon One to see how I was doing, bringing along two or three of the children from her own room. She would clap her hands with obvious enjoyment when she saw a difference in one of my charges. 'You know, Bev,' she told me one day, 'it's not so long ago that "madhouses" in Britain and other European countries were like this.' She's right and we shouldn't be too quick to judge others without remembering this.

There was only one key to the team room and we all used to waste a lot of precious time going from room to room trying to find out who had it. Jill, being highly organised and hard-working, found this particularly irritating. One day I bumped into her on the stairs and she shrieked, 'Who's got the key?'

'Please don't shout at me, Jill,' I replied. 'I haven't got it.'

'I have only got one voice,' she shrieked again. 'This one and a louder one for when I'm annoyed. It is nothing personal, dear.'

At the next meeting I suggested we put a nail in a convenient wall and keep the key on that. Most people remembered to comply.

Jill used to like to take her children for walks around the orphanage, to give them a change of scenery. Sometimes we had access to a plastic slide and she would bring the children from her room up to Salon One for a bit of recreation. I enjoyed her visits because it gave me someone I could talk to without recourse to an interpreter. Jacqui used to come in from Salon Two next door as well, often bringing a pale, lifeless little scrap of a girl called Cristina. It took Jacqui a month to coax Cristina out of Salon Two and still she clung to Jacqui with a look of terror. I used to run my fingers across her cheeks gently, a little bit more each day, until eventually she would actually put her arms out to come to me.

Jill was an extremely skilful artist, specialising in water colours, and always bursting with energy. Every morning she would go out and get bread for our picnic lunches, organising everything we needed to take with us and unpacking and washing up when we returned. She had an immense talent for calming the children, even the most difficult, able to stop the most formidable of the bigger boys despite being in her sixties and not powerfully built. She was never rough or unkind; she would just fix them with her grey eyes, place her hands very gently on their shoulders and say firmly, 'Not beautiful! Stop!'

She used to go into the big girls' room and play games like ring-a-ring-a-roses with them. I thought that looked like a very good idea and I asked if she would mind me copying her ideas for the boys' rooms and whether she had any other brainwaves. It was very successful and I realised that this was the answer. They wanted and needed physical exercise and these simple games provided it. I started to try out all sorts of things like elementary aerobics, doing the hokey-cokey, the Birdie Song and 'Simon Says'. I wasn't sure if this was the sort of thing I was supposed to be doing but no one came forward with any information or advice or encouragement so I just kept going. I would put on Strauss tapes and waltz with them if they were willing or sit them on my lap and cuddle them if that was what they needed. Some of the bigger boys used to want to dance with me when they had the most enormous erections. I found this impossible to tolerate so I would suggest we jived. Jiving meant they didn't get so close and had to concentrate so hard on not falling over that their sexual urges faded.

We did lots of clapping songs and games. I thought that if they got the idea of copying my actions, they might also copy me speaking. I started with simple words like 'water, hungry, toilet,' reasoning that the basis of most simple communication is necessity, so we should start with the words for their basic needs.

The problem with the big children was that the moment you walked into the room they would all bundle on top of you and if you weren't careful you lost your balance and ended up under a pile of bodies. No harm was intended, but sometimes you got hurt by mistake and the kids that couldn't get to you would start savagely biting themselves in frustration or snapping at one another like hyenas around a carcass. To prevent this I made them take turns with me, just like the little children upstairs. Szuzannah was a particular problem because she often used to be around our feet and none of the volunteers or workers liked her very much. Because she was a floor child she had developed an immensely strong upper body. She used to latch onto my legs and refuse to let go. I always felt very guilty about shaking her off because she was so desperate to be loved and because she had been so noble in taking Bordisan's punch on my behalf.

There was another badly crippled boy called Mihai – aged seventeen – who had a horrible, ugly looking old plastic doll which he munched ferociously, making manic noises as he did so, whenever he became anxious. The doll had lost all its clothes and most of its face, but its eyes still stared fixedly out at us. Mihai did wonderful imitations of us all, just like a parrot. The children all thought it was hysterical that I made them say 'please' and 'thank you' for things because they aren't words Romanians use very often and Mihai used to squawk them back at me, his imitation impeccable.

I could see from their faces that some of the other volunteers thought I looked ridiculous waltzing or disco dancing around with these children who spent a lot of their time falling over, or cuddling and rocking boys who were as tall as me, but they didn't seem to have any better ideas. They would sometimes ask me, 'Do you really think that's beneficial?' their faces telling me exactly what they thought. When directly challenged like that I would flounder for answers because I didn't know for sure. But I kept doing it. As long as the children were happy and laughing I must be getting something right. It seemed vital to gain their trust and make them feel comfortable with me, getting them to lose their fear and relax sufficiently so that we could begin a more specific programme of rehabilitation.

The women carers seemed to be becoming kinder with exposure to good examples ... The cooks would sometimes come round the rooms in the afternoons bringing special treats like slices of apple. Many of the children didn't know what to do with such luxuries, either throwing them at one another or chewing them up and spitting them out, but many were grateful for these little gifts.

Mark, the blond chap I had watched at work the first time I came to Ungerini, started to bring his ghetto blaster into the rooms when he helped me in the afternoons and the children loved it. He and Jacqui were both very keen to help and sometimes we would put two lots of children together. Although every room looked virtually identical, moving from one to another made the children feel that they were going on some sort of outing and they would become very excited.

The only problem with this physical activity was that the rooms became very hot as the weather warmed up and the bigger children would develop the most terrible body odour as they pranced and leapt about. By the end of the afternoon the pong would be almost enough to knock you out. Mark and I had the idea of moving the whole thing outside into the sunshine and organising discos for all twice a week. There was an almost secure courtyard out back and we decided to ask Madam Augustina if we could use it. I was getting more and more confident about asking for things now and although she was doubtful about it at first I wasn't going to be discouraged. Madam Augustina was worried that the authorities might make a surprise visit and want to know why all the children weren't sitting in neat lines on the beds as usual. I told her that it would make the children sleep better and fight less if they were given some exercise during the afternoon. This gave her the excuse she needed should her superiors challenge her and she agreed to let us try.

Mark and I had to give Madam and the other staff the impression that we knew what we were doing, which or course we didn't. At our first disco we let all ninety children out at once and the stronger ones thundered dangerously over the weaker ones in their eagerness, so the next time we asked the women to bring the kids out one room at a time. We were learning as we went along and thankfully no one suffered too badly as a result of our ignorance.

Mark was a heavy-metal fan and had brought some Status Quo tapes from England with him which the children loved – head-banging suited the repetitive, rhythmical movements so many of them made all the time. 'Whatever you want, thump thump, whatever you need, thump thump', or, 'You're in the army now, thump thump,' was perfect for them!

Mark put the cassette player up on a shed roof out of reach because it would have been all too easy for someone to smash it in a moment of madness. To begin with they grew excited at their newfound freedom and did things like throw stones at one another, but we threatened to send them back to their rooms if they didn't stop and none of them wanted that; they all wanted to stay outside where the music was. It was physio that was fun, a relief to all. One boy used to dance with me very sweetly and then excuse himself and dance for a while with an imaginary friend, before returning.

At first the local helpers just stood on the sidelines and watched us making fools of ourselves, but one by one I managed to coax them to join us and they began to let their inhibitions go, folk dancing with the fastest footwork imaginable. It was astonishing to see these huge, muscular peasant women, who normally moved at the speed of snails, flying around the dance floor. Madam

Augustina declared the disco a great success and even allowed some of the smaller but more mobile children from upstairs to join in as well.

What Mark and I really needed if we were going to supervise the crowd safely was more manpower and I finally managed to persuade some of our more reluctant team members to come and assist. There were some surprising grumbles along the lines of: 'The children can't just have music all the time,' and they agreed to help only on the condition that we played some local Romanian music rather than just imposing British rock on them. I could see some sense in their argument and Mark duly put on a Romanian folk tape. All ninety children immediately stopped dancing, the music more than likely re-awakening their memories of the dreadful piped racket that they had been forced to listen to inside their rooms for all those years, and they began to spit.

'What shall I do, Bev?' Mark asked.

'Put Quo back on, Mark, quickly!'

Some of the big boys were very good at spitting. I had seen one of them hit Madam Augustina on the back with a spitball from a distance of about twenty yards. She didn't even know it had happened – real skill. The same boy got me once when I came round a corner unexpectedly. I chased him all over the orphanage, pretending to be crosser than I was. He stopped eventually and gave a low, theatrical bow. 'Pardon Bevey,' he said. 'I thought you were another person. I was dismayed to find it was you!'

It was a great relief to be outside and it was wonderful to see the children having such a good time. The carers were, quite rightly, rather nervous of having so many of the children in one place and one of them forced all her children to sit in line, with the help of her 'boss' child, in exactly the same formation as in the room, but even they gradually became more confident and relaxed. Several of the rooms had 'boss' children, the most able, who would be put in charge if the women had to leave the rooms for any reason. They would be left with the sticks and lumps of wood to help them keep order. It was not something which any of us liked. Madam Augustina used to be furious if she found any of the women out of their rooms as they were supposed to stay there throughout their shifts. It was because all the carers had been in one room, smoking, drinking and gossiping, that so many children had died on the night of the fire in Salon One. I could quite understand why they did it. I was always pleased to get a visit from another of the volunteers when I was alone in Salon One.

These privileged children were always easy to recognise because they were better dressed than the others and could often be seen holding hands with the carers. They were also generally fatter and healthier because they were better fed. Patrika had grown fat because he was strong and had managed to get the lion's share of any food on offer. Because he was also a favourite of the staff assigned to his room they would ensure he got what he wanted. Because they believed big people needed more food than thin people they became very worried when I started to lose weight and were always trying to feed me up with pancakes and gogoshi – a sort of doughnut that they made in the kitchens. Patrika was very aggressive about getting his way, screaming and shouting for everything. And the disco was no exception. He started to slap and push people and I stopped him immediately, certain that if he was allowed to continue he would gradually exert more and more force until someone was seriously hurt. I asked him, in my simple Romanian, 'Do you wish to return to bed or stay on?' – subdued he stayed!

Several of us had noticed that both Patrika and a girl called Vassila had recently become much more aggressive. Some of the helpers suggested that it was because the two of them had been made to sleep together. This bore out stories we had heard from a French team who had come to install a proper plumbing system and slept inside the orphanage. A few of the women thought it was good sport to get the children into bed with one another, but those who disapproved were becoming braver about speaking up and telling us what was going on. There were also terrible stories of savage beatings and screams in the night. I went to Madam Augustina and told her our suspicions.

'No one here would do anything like that,' she assured me, and I knew that if I left the matter with her it would be dealt with without any individual loss of face. Sure enough, we heard nothing more about the children being exploited in this way.

The French plumbing team spent many months at Ungerini, moving tanks around and trying to improve the water supplies throughout the building, but without much success. There were endless disagreements between the Ungerini Orphanage Trust (a British charity that had grown out of the Romanian Orphanage

Trust) and the French over exactly whose fault it was, but in the end they left with things only very marginally improved. Some new toilets were installed but they were porcelain and stainless-steel fitments would have been better suited to withstand the likely level of wear and tear. It remained a mystery to me that something so fundamental to the health and well-being of everyone living and working at Ungerini couldn't be rapidly sorted out, and it illustrated how complicated solving simple problems could become and how hard it was to make any lasting improvements. I was surprised to find that people become amazingly parochial when undertaking charitable works and it seemed to me in my innocence a very silly, negative and wasteful way to behave.

Each volunteer reacted to the pressures of life at Ungerini in different ways, and sometimes we behaved like naughty school children in an effort to release the tensions. On 1 April, Mark challenged Jacqui to a potato-throwing competition in the hotel corridor – first one to drop one had to cook supper. The battle commenced and Mark started baiting Jacqui by shouting out 'Wee spuddy' in a mocking Irish accent. Suddenly he let out a blood-curdling yell. Jacqui had substituted an egg and it had exploded all over him when he caught it. He chased her, screaming, all over the hotel until a large and aggressive man came to his door and shouted abuse at Jacqui. Pulling herself up to her full five feet, Jacqui showed him the spare egg she was carrying and indicated that she would gladly break it over the top of his head. He rapidly retreated back into his room.

For a change, we would sometimes take a group of children on an outing in one of the vans. One particular day Roger, Diane, Jacqui and I had crammed a van far too full with children – all of them looking even more barmy than usual because Madam Augustina had insisted on them wearing baby bonnets to keep out the cold – and we broke down in a little village that didn't look as if it had changed since the Middle Ages. The only one of us who spoke more than a few words of Romanian was a schizophrenic boy, called Nichusorui, who was sporting a rather fetching pink bonnet with a bobble on top and a fine-looking embroidered coat sent from France. He immediately took control, strutting around the van sounding off at the few bemused villagers who came to see if we needed help. The two Romanian words I used almost constantly with the children seemed to be 'Injet' which meant 'slowly, gently' and 'Gata' which meant 'stop'. When it came to explaining why I was parked in the middle of nowhere with a van full of nutters I was a bit stumped.

Eventually we managed to get the van started again and set off, only to find one of the children, a seventeen-year-old called Radu, starting to projectile-vomit within minutes of our departure. He reminded me of one of those wooden dolls on a stall at the fair, their mouths permanently open in fixed grins, ready for us to throw a ball in. He turned, mouth wide open, and a cascade of evil smelling vomit gushed out. He did it four times in all and managed to hit Roger every time. Wherever Roger moved to, the vomit seemed to follow, with Radu smiling benignly between bouts. For Roger it was the final straw, his patience had been tested to the full and found wanting.

'I don't f...... believe it!' he exploded. 'I come all the way out from England to help these people and all they do is vomit over me!' At which point he was hit with another full frontal stream. Jacqui, Diane and I couldn't look at each other – slowly, like a volcano getting up steam to erupt, we began to lose control and laugh. It started with sniggers, but soon we were shrieking and howling, shoving each other and falling off our seats, carefully avoiding the sick, clutching each other helplessly as we fell out of the van. I had to walk cross-legged in an effort not to wet myself. Every time one of us stopped the other would look – and then it would start all over again. Our sides ached and our tears flowed until we were exhausted.

Poor Roger, he could not understand why we were laughing and I couldn't either really, for it was unkind and by now his normally dry and acidic wit had disappeared altogether. The more serious he became the more our mirth was fuelled.

The more we laughed the angrier Roger became. 'And then,' he stormed, 'apart from orphans puking over me at every f...... opportunity, bird-brained bimbos find it f...... amusing – go on, laugh! What shall I do for an encore? Dive head first into a f...... pile of horse-shit? No? Not funny enough? Shall I sever an artery, would that suit?'

'I'm so sorry,' I started, but I couldn't finish the sentence because I was hysterical again.

I learnt so much from Roger. He was highly intelligent and academic and our rather mundane daily routines must have seemed very tedious, but he was gentle and kind with the children, always treating them with respect. However, he did not suffer fools on the team gladly. There was a sort of local bar in the village and one afternoon he decided to take some of the more mobile lads for a pint! I was just coming back from a walk when I saw them sitting round a table in their bedraggled, torn and ill-fitting clothes and unmatched shoes, with Roger dispensing the little glasses of beer. He was always encouraging the children to enjoy themselves and to learn to live fuller lives and would become infuriated with any pettiness or unnecessary rule-making. Taking the lads on such an unorthodox trip was just his style! He refused to waste any time on 'in-team' fighting, when there was such enjoyable work to be done.

There were many wonderful volunteers working out in Romania at that time. As well as the Norwegian Red Cross workers I had come across in the home, I was particularly impressed by the VSO (Voluntary Service Overseas) workers. There did, however, seem to be some volunteers who had come for reasons I couldn't fathom. Perhaps it was some sort of ego trip, or just something to do, but rather than inspiring the local workers in the orphanages, by showing them what was possible and helping them to find new ways of doing things, they were as uncaring as the local women had been, and tried to get away with as little work as possible.

I always admired people who realised quickly that they couldn't cope and went back home, making room for someone else to come out and try. I completely understood that actually coping with the children on a day to day basis was not everyone's cup of tea. One man told me he felt very ashamed that he couldn't bring himself to touch some of the children because they looked so grotesque. I told him he mustn't feel bad about that, that we all had different things we could and couldn't do. Those people who admitted they had made a mistake were more honest than those who simply stayed on, trying to get out of doing anything unpleasant by taking days off or arranging day-long meetings with local politicians. I guess I was there with my own needs just like everyone else and I know that the work was often very stressful, but I was happy. I learned to overcome my fears and to help others to do the same. It didn't happen overnight but after several weeks I realised that although I was still aware of the dangers I wasn't quaking in my boots any more. I had chosen the path which was right for me but I certainly didn't expect it to be right for everyone.

One evening Mark told me he really enjoyed my company.

'Oh, do you, Mark?' I replied, somewhat sceptically. 'That's nice.'

'I've been invited by one of the carers to lunch on Sunday,' he continued casually. 'Would you like to come?'

'I've got quite a lot to do,' I said vaguely. I had been hoping to catch up on both my letter writing and my sleep that weekend.

'Oh, please come. I don't fancy the drive on my own. It'll be fun and the family really want to meet you,' he went on.

There was a desperate edge to his voice, almost as if his life depended on my accompanying him, so eventually I gave in and we set off. The carer, who was an extremely attractive young lady, looked as if she had sucked on a lemon when she saw me arriving in the van. She had prepared a delicious Sunday lunch – for two! I could have thrashed Mark – it was obvious that the girl concerned was not at all happy to have this middle-aged old bat cramping her style. The day seemed to last for ever and there was nowhere for me to disappear tactfully. When it was finally time to leave we drove away with her gazing lovingly at Mark and sending invisible daggers into my back.

It wasn't the last time that he conned me into playing gooseberry when some rampant female was after him. Several times he arrived breathlessly at the door of my hotel room, inviting me up to listen to some music. After the first few times he gave up pretending it was because he enjoyed my scintillating company.

Towards the end of April I was passing one of the rooms downstairs when Marius, the boy who had punched me on my first day and I had since befriended, called me in. There were no other workers around and I hesitated for a second at going, but decided it was time to show him some trust. I sat down on a bed and he climbed up onto my knee. Paladin, another large and rather mad boy who I did not know as well, climbed onto my other knee. Paladin used to chatter away to us all day, asking so many questions that we had thought he must be one of the normal children. It was only when Ionel joined us that we discovered he spoke complete rubbish and we realised that he wasn't quite with it.

For a while the boys enjoyed cuddling and being cuddled then, without looking at each other or appearing to exchange any sign, both of them grabbed my hair from each side in an apparently synchronised movement and threw me savagely back onto the bed, pulling great tufts of hair out. I was terrified and managed to fight my way free of them, furious with Marius for his betrayal of my friendship. Paladin was really beyond understanding that he had done wrong, but I punished Marius by refusing to take him outside for a walk I had promised him later. He was very apologetic and didn't know why he had acted as he did. Incidents like this reminded me that these children could be physically dangerous, particularly the ones who were virtually full grown, and that I should never allow myself to become over-confident.

Some of the other volunteers used to become quite annoyed with me for always being so cheerful. I suppose that's what caused them to think I must be stupid. 'Bev is to intellectualism what Saddam Hussein is to peace,' the leader of the project once quipped. In Romania we had a Team Leader, Operations Director and Operations Field Director – all British and provided by the Ungerini Orphanage Trust. I was never sure what claims to exceptional intelligence he had given such a tasteless remark, but was hurt none the less to think that I gave the impression of being so dim. They behaved as if they thought they were showing their respect for the plight of these people by always moaning on about how terrible everything was. At one stage I innocently announced that I was planning to keep a diary during my time in Romania. I suddenly received a lot of very earnest visits from people anxious to find out what I actually planned to record. As it was I couldn't find the time to write and have relied on my memory.

When we first arrived I had been very worried by the difficulties which the different teams of volunteers had in gelling. The existing team had obviously been through a lot together and some of them seemed to feel that we, the newcomers, were there to usurp them. So, instead of giving us guidance on how to set about helping the children, they tended to ignore us as much as possible. I felt rather at a loss as to how to deal with this and badly needed to do what I would always do if such a situation arose in England – talk to John. I had not counted on just how hard it would be to get through to the UK. It took a week to book my first telephone call home and I was very relieved to hear his voice on the other end and to be able to pour out my woes down the line.

'Just carry on being yourself,' he advised wisely. 'Don't take any of it personally and get on with the job you are there to do, working with the children. If your presence there worries anyone it's their problem, not yours.'

I did, and it worked. However, I determined that I would welcome any new team members and give them as much help as they wanted. It was vital that there should be a person who was interested enough to listen and help if needed.

CHAPTER SEVEN

The Arrival of the Sisters

*

*J*ust before I arrived at Ungerini, Mother Teresa of Calcutta had visited Romania and was so appalled by the state of the orphanages that she immediately set about opening four of her homes in the area – two in Bucharest, one in Bacau and one in Transylvania. In February 1991 two Sisters came to visit Ungerini, surrounded by the senior workers from our British team who escorted them from room to room and didn't let us volunteers near them. They stayed for quite a while in Salon One observing me at work with the children and since no one introduced us I just kept going as if they weren't there. I watched the way they talked to the children and I was impressed by how gentle and unassuming these fragile-looking women were. The children were unafraid of them as they stood there, quietly smiling in their beautiful white saris with the thin blue lines around the edges, their eyes sparkling behind their spectacles. There were several of these visits. We were then told that the Sisters were opening a home in Bacau and would be taking three children from each room. I was asked to select three children from Salon One.

'This is very good news for the children,' one of the Norwegian Red Cross workers told me. 'The Sisters run wonderful homes; the children will be much better cared for and will also receive a good education.'

I felt very happy at the announcement but worried about who I should put forward for transfer. At my level of experience there was no scientific or fair way of selecting which of the children should receive this opportunity for a better life. I worked on emotional grounds. I chose the children I thought had the most to gain and the potential to achieve it and which most desperately needed help. It was heartbreaking to deny any child the chance on any grounds, and once I had made my three choices I found I couldn't bear the thought that despite my careful deliberations little Maria, who was so horribly deformed and crippled, was not going.

The children I eventually settled on were Szulita, Monika and Ionuts, two girls and a boy, all aged six. Szulita weighed only a few pounds, no more than four bags of sugar, and each day she seemed to become more frail. Feeding her regularly throughout the morning with syringes of milk was having no effect on the sad and very visible decline of her emaciated body. One of our nurses declared her days, if not hours, from death. I believed Szulita's only hope was to go to the Sisters; perhaps they would be able to save her ... If not, at least she would die surrounded by love and warmth.

Monika was a very gentle and sweet child and I thought her disability was to have one leg shorter than the other (it turned out to be hip dysplasia when properly diagnosed). Monika desperately wanted to get up and walk and was almost there, as was Ionuts. I was certain that once with the Sisters they would soon be walking, talking and independent.

Maria was an extremely malnourished, waif-like child of twelve, so small I used to hold her in the crook of my arm like a small baby. Her knees were permanently pulled up to her chest and her arm was so curved that her hand was cupped round her ear the whole time. She had black eyes and hair, and skin so thin I could see the blood coursing through her veins. It was terrifying to lift her out of her cot because she would usually scream and I could never be sure if it was from pain or fear.

Of course my choice of Maria was totally illogical. We were told that she would never walk, talk or be independent, and she was probably much too old to be able to change now. She was so fragile, terrified, vulnerable – I couldn't honestly say whether she would progress much beyond her current capabilities, but I was sure she would be happier with the Sisters – could I deny her that just because she was older than the others?

After several nights of tossing and turning I plucked up the courage to ask Sister Jane, a beautiful Indian woman, Sister Superior in Bacau, if Maria might be included as a special case. When I was told that they would take her too I felt an overwhelming sensation of joy. I wrapped her up in her filthy, smelly rags and ran out into the corridor to take her to Diane's room so that I could share the good news. I had tears pouring down my cheeks and I was talking away to her as we went in a mixture of English and Romanian.

'You are going somewhere beautiful, to live with a proper family. The Sisters are going to be your Aunties. I'll miss you. I love you.' To my horror I realised that I had walked into a couple of the Norwegian Red Cross team, who were wandering around with a video camera, filming. If the corridor hadn't been so dark they would have seen how brightly I blushed at being caught making such an exhibition of myself.

'That was beautiful, Bev,' they smiled understandingly. 'Could you do it again for the camera?'

'Oh, no,' I protested, 'I couldn't.' I didn't think I could re-enact something so emotional, despite my earlier ambitions to be an actress. I did think to myself, 'I'm British; I can't do this in front of people,' but the sheer joy I felt for Maria and her new life overcame any inhibitions I had. I suspect that if I ever saw the footage it would be one of the most embarrassing experiences possible but at that moment I was so happy I didn't care what I did. I just began to tell Maria where she was going and tears of joy cascaded naturally down my cheeks.

A few days later I bumped into the Sisters unaccompanied by their usual entourage of charity workers and plucked up the courage to ask some questions about the home, eager to know what sort of place my children would be going to.

'You must come and visit,' they said sweetly.

'Oh, could I?' I blurted. I was very surprised by how warm and friendly and open they were. 'When would be the best time?'

'Come any time you like,' they assured me. 'We would be delighted to see you.'

I was very excited at the prospect and made the mistake of telling the rest of the team about the invitation. The senior workers seemed to stiffen at the news that I had actually spoken to the Sisters myself. 'We would rather you didn't do that Bev,' they said. 'We will arrange for everyone to go together at a later date.'

I didn't dare to ask them why this was and just accepted the decision, assuming that they knew best. For a week I waited for this arrangement to be made but, when no one mentioned it again, Diane and I decided to take our courage in both hands and go round one evening on our own.

'I would like to give them some notes on the children from Salon One,' I said. In my vanity I thought I was now the only one who properly understood the children in my room. Over the previous few weeks I had got to know these children very well and I was anxious to pass on everything I knew to the Sisters so that they could settle them as quickly as possible. I wanted to tell them about each child's likes and dislikes and the different ways they preferred to be comforted when they cried. When Maria was on the floor, for instance, she would look for things to pull round her for protection. It was always best to sit her with her back to a cot so the other children could only approach her from the front, because they made her nervous. She liked to sit on my lap and have her face stroked while I sang, 'What are we going to do about Maria?' but became agitated if you touched her legs for any reason. Each child had toys and music that they especially liked and I wanted the Sisters to know all this. I was also very curious to find out more about the Sisters themselves. I'd once read a book about Mother Teresa and her order, written by Malcolm Muggeridge, and what it said had seemed almost too good to be true.

Without telling anyone else what we were doing, Diane and I set off on our own into the back streets of Bacau late one evening. The home was in a gypsy ghetto, which was by far the poorest part of town that I had seen. There were four Sisters setting up home in a very simple house. The walls were painted in pale, pastel colours; the cots were white and there were Z-beds waiting for the bigger children. There were few toys or other luxuries around, but what we noticed immediately was the wonderfully warm atmosphere which enveloped us the moment we walked in. The Sisters had made sure that they had the basics, hot and cold running water etc, they needed to keep the children and home clean and to operate a system of modern lavatories, before they opened their doors to the children.

Sister Jane told us this had all been brought out to Bacau by a co-worker of Mother Teresa, George Bushell, and a team of workers from Britain. They had been helped by local workmen who had been glad of employment and to learn new techniques.

We explained that we had come to give them the children's notes but they seemed overjoyed that we had come to see them at all. They proudly showed us their home and asked us about ourselves and what we had done before coming out to Romania. Sister Jane took the notes from me and sat down to read them. Afterwards I learned she had been very moved and had said to her sisters, 'How come this woman, who is just a secretary, can write such sensitive and beautiful notes about these children in her care?' I almost cried with pride on hearing this, but also felt rather puzzled as I hadn't imagined I was doing anything out of the ordinary. It was an obvious thing to do in the circumstances.

'Tell me, Bevey,' Sister Jane said after we had been talking for a while, 'Why is it that so few of the British volunteers at Ungerini are actually working with the children?'

I didn't know the answer and said something about there being a lot of administration and liaison to be done by the senior workers, but I could see that the Sisters were genuinely puzzled.

Many weeks passed and I was still very worried about Illeana who did not seem to be recovering her spirits after losing Gabriel and being let down so badly by the British volunteers. I thought that she would benefit from the more intimate atmosphere – more like a large family home – that the Sisters were trying to create and wondered if they could be persuaded to take her in. I decided to chance my luck once more. One evening, at about nine o'clock, I went back to the Sisters in Bacau. I could hear excited chatter and laughter coming from inside. I hesitated to knock, frightened to intrude. Sister Jane came to the door and invited me into their little parlour. She listened patiently as I recounted Illeana's story. I told her how helpful she was to me and that perhaps they could take her on as a junior worker.

'She must be saved, Sister,' I ended my special pleading.

'We are really planning to take younger and more handicapped children,' she told me, 'but if we did take Illeana it would have to be as a child not as a worker. We would want to educate her for a better life. Education is a very high priority for our children and those we help. I will think about it.'

The next day I caught sight of the now familiar white sari from my window in Salon One. Sister Jane had found Illeana and was talking to her. Had I not been an atheist I could have dropped on my knees and prayed at that moment. Later I was told that Sister Jane had been to see Madam Augustina and the Romanians were reluctant for the older children to go to Mother Teresa's, frightened they would be used as slaves. Sister Jane told Illeana not to give up hope, that they would try to help her, but I had a horrible feeling that once again her hopes were going to be raised, only to be ultimately disappointed. I only hoped it wouldn't be the final straw for her.

By the time I returned to England at the end of May, I had been able to persuade the Sisters to take five more children from Salon One. That meant nine in all from my room and fifty-two in all from Ungerini. The Norwegian Red Cross also asked them to take some very needy children from Gemesh, a smaller institute in the Transylvanian part of Romania. Although I was happy for those nine children, I hated having to be judge and jury, writing down the names of those who would be given a chance of a new life, deciding to omit other names and thereby damning them to a life of almost certain misery. Not a day passed when I didn't agonise over whether I had made the right or wrong choices. I will never know and it is something which will be on my conscience for the rest of my life.

On the day the Sisters came to collect the first children I was asked to travel with them, as a familiar presence that would help calm their fears. It was the first time the four children from Salon One had been outside the building – they were the most handicapped – and they were all terrified. Maria sat on my lap, her twisted little body uncomfortable no matter what I did, and screamed deafeningly all the way down the mountain. We sang throughout the twenty-mile journey to try to distract the children from their terrors, but it was impossible to drown out the noise. Although they were on their way to somewhere far nicer than anything they had ever experienced, we had no way of letting them know it. They only knew that something strange and frightening was happening to them and they were all very unsettled by the time we got to Bacau.

Sister Jane asked me to stay for a while and try to calm some of the older ones, particularly a boy called Lucien, who was going berserk. There were piles of new clean clothes already laid out and waiting and I thought I would give him a bath to settle him down. All eight of the big children then decided they wanted to have baths too, their first ever experience of hot water, shampoo and soft, white, scented baby powder. Bathtime at Ungerini had always been an ordeal, entailing being flung into a bath of ice-cold water (two baths to cater for 186 children, with the water unchanged between bathers until our arrival). There had been no washing and no soap, just a sluice down with cold water and then sitting or lying on the cold concrete to drip dry.

Once safely in the bathroom with me, the children became ecstatic with joy at these simple, physical pleasures. Getting Lucien, who was then fifteen years old but only three feet tall, into the bath was hard because his legs always went all over the place, his feet pointing forwards, backwards or sideways. I was frightened of hurting him and didn't quite know where to hold him because his chest and arms were deformed too. As I gently lowered him into the tub, the bubbles rising up over his grotesque little body, he put his thumb up: 'Foarte bine, Bevey!' ('Very good'.) All the children had learned to put their thumbs up to signify something good; what a legacy I have left them! Once he was in, Lucien made me wash his shaved scalp with shampoo over and over again. Each time I had to smell his head and say, 'Oh, Lucien, foarte frumos' ('very beautiful') with great exaggeration and he would crow with happiness.

By the time the American Sister, called Sister Shanti, popped her head round the door she could barely make us out in the clouds of powder and steam. 'Do you think the children might be ready for bed now, Bev?' she enquired.

'Certainly,' I replied. 'What's the time?'

'Eleven-thirty!'

I couldn't believe it; we had been in there for hours.

One of the rituals which all the children enjoyed was the 'Indian' or 'Mother Teresa' bath. They would stand in the bath and have jugs of warm water poured over their bodies. They would then be soaped up by hand and rubbed all over, then more warm water was poured over them, the Sister using her hands to rinse them. They just loved the caresses and undivided attention.

One of the smallest children to come to the Sisters was called Ionel. I had not come across him often because he had been in Salon Eight at Ungerini, and he had spent most of the time in his cot. He was very tiny and needed nursing night and day by Sister Ida. He was not expected to live long because of chronic bronchial problems and general ill health. The Sisters were determined that his last few days would be as loving and happy as possible, and that he should die with dignity. My initial impressions of this poor little scrap were very negative. He showed no signs of life apart from permanently whinging. Very few people seemed to like Ionel but Sister Ida was dedicated to him, staying with him all the time. Despite expectations, his health appeared to improve a little in the first few weeks, although he was still a long way from joining in with anything that went on around him.

Ionel had been born in hospital. His mother, who was not married to his father, had not been able to keep him and he was sent straight to a state orphanage. At some time he had contracted polio, although we didn't discover that until some time after his arrival at the Sisters'. When it came to the three-year test he failed and was sent to Ungerini. Many of the physically handicapped children there became mentally handicapped simply because they were starved of affection, exercise, stimulation and nutritious food. By the time we got to them, however, it was hard to tell which children were genuinely mentally handicapped and which had become so through deprivation. Ionel was one of these unknown quantities but it was generally agreed that due to his perilous health he was probably a hopeless case.

Like the others, he had been tied up in his cot all day with his emaciated arms behind his head and his knees in his chest, lying on lino, cold, filthy and uncared-for. There were cigarette burns on his chest and on his body were bite marks from the stray dogs which used to roam the orphanage freely before the revolution. On the way to Mother Teresa's he hadn't had the strength to scream – he had just lain in Sister Ida's arms and stared blankly into space, struggling to breathe.

Within a few weeks it became obvious that Ionel was not going to die after all, and he started to eat at a tremendous rate. Because he couldn't move about this led to him putting on weight and he began to look like a fat little old man. The Sisters were fond of giving their children nicknames. There was one little girl called Lachrymora who had the most beautiful blonde hair and blue eyes, just like Sister Shanti, so she was renamed Shanti. As he put on weight, Ionel began to bear a strong resemblance to Dom Patreascu, the elderly night watchman, a burly man who was almost as wide as he was tall. So the Sisters started to call Ionel 'Patreascu Mic' ('small Patreascu'), and the name stuck.

Once she was more confident he wouldn't die, Sister Ida started to be firm with her charge, as well as encouraging. She was frequently heard to shriek, 'Immediarte Patreascu!'

('immediately!'), which seemed to work. As a result he absolutely adored her and was soon able to eat by himself, very cleanly and nicely, and he loved to try to say his prayers before meals and at Mass, although he still had no speech. He had achieved far more than I had ever thought possible when we first took the tiny little wretch into the home but he was still the most irritating whinger and everyone but Sister Ida found it hard to warm to him. I went off him even more when I was sitting on the scruffy old sofa which they had in the hallway one day, trying to avoid the pee stains, with a pile of children climbing around me, and he decided to gnaw his way up my leg as if it were corn on the cob.

Despite not liking him very much, I did notice, as the weeks passed, that Patreascu Mic showed a fairly adventurous spirit. As soon as he was strong enough to come out of his cot he used to find ways of escaping even when we didn't want him to. He learnt how to lift the edge of the mattress and wriggle out between the bars and, when he grew too portly for that, he would trampoline up and down on his slightly better leg until he was going high enough to land with his stomach across the top of the bars. He would then vault out surprisingly athletically. Because he didn't have the muscles to support his back he had to sit propped up in a baby seat, but whenever he was set free he would try to crawl through to a room with bigger children in it. I also noticed that when a tape finished in the tape recorder he was able to work out how to turn it round and start the other side. Daniel, who was very intelligent but confined to a wheelchair, would stand guard over the machine and if Patreascu came anywhere near he would smack him on the hand with a ruler. Patreascu would go off screaming but would soon be back to try again. I began to suspect that there was more to this little chap than we had initially thought, but still didn't feel myself warming to him.

The Sisters were always keen to get the children eating from spoons so that they could vary their diet more effectively. The problem was that the children's experience of spoons was confined to the medicine spoons rammed down their throats by uncaring helpers and they were consequently terrified of them and the pain they had brought. It took a lot of work to coax them into trying again. Patreascu was quite naughty about throwing his food around and Sister Ida used to smack his hand with a wooden spoon. Sister Ida's rule was that the hand which threw the food was the hand which received the smack from the wooden spoon.

It worked. After a while he began to take the spoon off her and smack himself!

Quite soon after the Sisters had started to take children from Ungerini we had some new children brought into Salon One from another orphanage where they had failed the three-year tests. They arrived in the most beautiful travelling clothes, which were immediately ripped off them and never seen again. One of the children was a little boy called Costel who had cerebral palsy and was horribly bent and crippled. He was also blind and had the sorest, reddest bottom I have ever seen. He looked like a little baboon. The medical staff came and gave him an injection, stabbing the needle into his bottom in the customary brutal manner. Although they must have received some medical training after school, these workers had never been taught how to give injections gently. Often two staff members would hold a child down and the third would jab the needle in without any preparation of the site. It must have been extra painful when they were so thin and scrawny. Poor Costel was in no position to put up a struggle.

Adelina, the Chief Nurse at Ungerini, was a very attractive, green-eyed woman in her late thirties. She was kind and always tried to be helpful. If she was approached in a professional way she would listen to new ideas, and would pass them on to her staff. Perhaps my view of her was rather biased by the fact that after I had been there a couple of weeks she allowed me the glorious privilege of using the only flushing European loo in the whole orphanage! By then I was coughing so badly and frequently that I needed to spend pennies fairly regularly. When John heard my cough down the phone line he said I sounded like a Charing Cross tramp after a rough night.

By the time Costel arrived in early April, I had persuaded the kitchen staff to boil water for me and I started work on him by giving him a warm bath to try to relax his muscles, ease his pain and soothe his poor, raw bottom. I then put on Sudocrem, something we used an awful lot of and had to keep locked away in the team room to prevent it disappearing, and the rough, odourless talcum powder which we were supplied with. To try to get him to relax his hands I would massage his palms until Diane told me that this would have the opposite effect and that I should massage the back of the hands to make the muscles flex and the hand come open. The children with cerebral palsy were often locked into position so that when the helpers tried to straighten them out in their rough and ready way they would simply snap their little limbs. If the children didn't straighten out, the women didn't think to wash in the creases between their stomachs and their legs and they developed the most horrible, foul-smelling sores.

I told the Sisters about Costel and what a pitiful little thing he was and they said they had to have him. When Sister Jane went to see Madam Augustina she was told that it would take several months to prepare the right paperwork for the transfer.

'Oh dear,' Sister Jane said. 'What a shame. Tell me, Madame Augustina, that powdered milk you asked for, when were you hoping to get it?'

'As soon as possible, please, Sister.'

'Oh dear,' Sister Jane averted her eyes, 'I'm afraid it might take me a few months to arrange that.'

Madam Augustina thought for a few moments. 'If I was to get the paperwork for Costel this afternoon, would that be helpful?' The Sisters were learning fast...

Within a couple of days it was arranged that Costel would be transferred to Bacau along with Marian, a boy with club feet and hydrocephalus, a condition whereby enormous amounts of fluid make the head swell and compress the brain. Marian was being transferred because his head was so heavy everyone was frightened that his neck might snap if he was knocked over by one of the bigger boys in his room.

It was a beautiful sunny day; a little snow was still clinging to the trees and the mountain flowers were coming into bloom. I felt so happy that Costel was escaping from Ungerini I couldn't stop weeping. Months later Sister Jane told me that my pitiful snivelling had struck her as so comical she had told Sister Ida to travel in the van with me and she would follow in the car because she was afraid she would laugh.

When we arrived at the Sisters' home they treated Costel like visiting royalty, taking him off for a warm bath and to change into a whole new set of clothes. They put Marian into a cot with Lucien, because they had been in the same room together at Ungerini. Marian had no speech and Lucien only used foul language but the two of them just kept touching each other, smiling and hugging. It was such a touching reunion that even the Sisters ended up with tears in their eyes.

Poor Costel continued to suffer the most terrible pain and

would cry at night when the other children were asleep. The old night watchman, Dom Patreascu, was supposed to patrol the building but, very sensibly, seldom went outside, spending most of the night comfortably settled on the old settee in the hallway. When he heard Costel crying he used to get him up, wrap him in his coat and cuddle him on the sofa until both of them finally dropped off. He was a kind, gentle man.

One night I went into Sister Ida's room to kiss all the children goodnight before the Sisters went round to deliver their nightly blessings and the mobile children started trampolining out of their cots. There was total chaos. As soon as I got one back in their cot another child got out. What could I do? I know, call for Dom Patreascu. He surveyed the scene and laughed, clapped his hands and spoke a few gentle words and they all went back to their beds without a murmur. I bowed to a superior talent.

I used to work at Ungerini during the day and then go to help the Sisters in the evenings. The van taking us back to the hotel would drop me, and whoever else was coming, at a nearby crossroads so we could walk down to the home. Mark often used to come to see the children who had been transferred from his room, but most of the others were too tired after a day at Ungerini. Jill was very worried that I would wear myself out, but I preferred being with the children and the Sisters to sitting around the hotel listening to people complain. To begin with I used to talk a lot about what the Sisters were doing, wanting to share with the others the joy of seeing the children change so much – sometimes from one day to the next. But I soon realised that the others thought that by praising the Sisters I was somehow criticising their own efforts, so I shut up. There were some people who thought that the Sisters were just creating an 'oasis' for a few children which did little to help the overall situation. I never thought that accusation fair as the Sisters did a considerable amount of medical work in the surrounding areas, helping the poor, the elderly, the handicapped and anyone else who needed them. Sister Jane held a dispensary every Friday and the poor used to queue in freezing temperatures, sometimes from two in the morning, in order to attend. They also helped at the hospital, which had no bandages or medicines, and dispensed soup and bread each day to people who would get no other meal.

But even if this accusation had been true I still couldn't understand why people should think it a bad thing. Sometimes a task seems so huge that people are intimidated into doing nothing about it. But if you only help one child amongst tens of thousands it must still be better than doing nothing. And if enough people create enough small oases eventually they will add up to something greater. Each small improvement in conditions showed the way forward and gave the ordinary Romanian people hope.

At about nine o'clock most nights the Sisters would make me a little supper and I would sit eating with Dom Patreascu and then either he or their English volunteer, Ashley, would drive me the short distance back to the hotel so that I didn't have to walk on my own at night.

I had explained to the Sisters that I was an atheist, in case they didn't want me around, but they just laughed and said that I could be a Buddhist, Moslem or Jew for all they cared, I would still be warmly welcomed. They never made any attempts to convert anyone to Catholicism, believing, I think, that they would be more likely to bring people to God by their example than by preaching. They were far too busy anyway with their work. They used to disappear off to Mass and to their Adorations and I used to think what a bore it must be, to have to spend so much time praying. I was very happy to be left out, although I did hear some wonderful singing sometimes. Mark brought his ghetto blaster down some evenings, so the children could have the music they had loved at Ungerini. After a while I realised that we were playing it at full blast while the Sisters were trying to do their Adorations. I apologised to Sister Jane. 'Don't worry, Bevey,' she smiled sweetly. 'Only those who want to be distracted will be.'

Back in England, John and my friends at the Abbey National had been working hard to fill a lorry with toys, medical supplies and everything else that I thought was desperately needed for the orphanage and the Royal Mail had offered to bring it out for them. When I brought this to the attention of the Team Leader the people at the Ungerini Orphanage Trust told me that they did not need anything to be sent to Ungerini because they had their own sources of aid. This surprised me as on the ground there still seemed to be a shortage of virtually everything, but the Sisters had no such reservations so I asked John to direct the Royal Mail to the home in Bacau.

I was on a walk in the mountains around Ungerini with some

of the bigger children when Mark came searching for me and shouted across the hills, 'Bev, the Royal Mail's in Bacau!' He drove me down to help with the unloading. John had told me how hard all the people in the post room at Abbey National had worked, and the security staff and porters who helped with the loading. They all came in at the weekends to get the job done and I could see why. There was a mountain of stuff and the Sisters could hardly believe their luck. A little of it they kept for the children in the home, but most was distributed to proud but destitute local families. I have to confess to being disappointed that they did not keep more for the children, but decided it was given freely to them by me and therefore it was their decision what to do with it. They probably knew best anyway.

During the first few weeks with the Sisters I could see an enormous transformation in the children under their care. They began to smile, to take notice, to be happy and to grow. Some of the ones who we had been told would never walk, slowly struggled to their feet and took their first faltering steps. Their behaviour was still wild and unpredictable at times, but they were certainly looking healthier. I was desperate to try and work out what the Sisters' secrets were so that I could go back to Ungerini and apply them to the children who were left behind. It wasn't that we were doing badly at Ungerini – some tremendous steps forward had been achieved; it was just that they were doing much better. There didn't seem to be any mystery or miracles involved; the Sisters simply appeared to do it with love, fun, happiness and hard work. The children would hear them laugh and hear them row and shout as well, just like in a real family. They even had a cat and a dog. I was very pleasantly surprised to discover that nuns didn't walk around with their heads bowed, praying all day long – they were human beings like the rest of us, and such wonderful human beings, too. There were only four Sisters and four Romanian staff, including Dom Patreascu, and I don't know how they managed the workload. They cooked on a single gas ring and had very little in the way of bowls or even food. What they did have was an abundance of enthusiasm and jubilation. In this atmosphere of love and security, the children visibly thrived.

I worried when I heard that Mother Teresa's were thinking of taking on Valentina, because I knew her as very wild and unpredictable. She had been known to steal at the workers' request. The first time I gave her a colouring book she ran off with it and I didn't see her for two days. After that I gave her one sheet at a time. I reluctantly expressed my fears to Sister Jane. 'Oh, Bevey,' she ticked me off. 'You must try to find it in your heart not to judge people. Can you honestly say you would be any different had you lived as she lived, had you endured and seen what she did? You'll see . . . with love, warmth and security she will come to change.' I felt very small at this reprimand and when Valentina arrived she immediately became a vital part of the community.

Valentina did have parents, and had always dreamed that they would one day come to fetch her. She so desperately wanted contact with them that the Sisters decided to trace them for her. Sadly, her family wanted nothing to do with her, which was dreadful for Valentina, but freed her of the fantasy that she would one day go home and she was able to concentrate on becoming a real part of the Sisters' family in Bacau.

'I can't understand how you do this work, Bev,' Sister Shanti, the American, said to me one day.

'But you do it,' I said, surprised by her words.

'But I was always brought up a Catholic. It is my religion and it is in my blood. You have no religion.'

'You don't have to have religion,' I said, 'to want to help people.' I did, however, see that having a strong sense of belief and faith could help in some situations.

'Do you know what, Bev?' Jill had said to me one day when I was quietly singing the praises of the Sisters to her, 'I think you'll end up joining those nuns.'

'Good Lord, no, Jill.' I was shocked that she even suggested it. 'To begin with I love it when family and friends call me and would need to have the telephone surgically removed from my hand if I became a nun – I'd look like a marquee in a white sari, I'm married, I couldn't get up that early in the morning (4.30), and anyway I'm an atheist and I would never be good enough to do their wonderful work or have their unselfish commitment.' She just smiled enigmatically and went on with her work.

CHAPTER EIGHT

Coming Home

*

As I approached the end of my three-month stint in Romania I asked if I might be allowed to stay for another month. In my arrogance I was beginning to believe that the children really needed not just anyone, but me, and I thought that in another month I would be able to make real headway.

I was enjoying the work enormously now, sharing in the children's joy at their new-found freedoms. Many of them were beginning to show little glimmers of independence, wanting to get up, wanting to join in things, putting their arms up to try and help when getting dressed. Small things, but they were huge steps forward for these kids. They were dragging themselves out of their mental and physical prisons, breaking free of their chains, awakening from their dark, isolated lives and seeing the light. One day Lazy Lazlo had a fight with a boy called Iulian over a toy and I was just about to stop them when I thought, 'What am I doing? This is what I have been working for all these months – normal childlike behaviour!' It was wonderful that they were both sufficiently interested in a toy to want to fight over it. But there was so much more to be done and I wanted to stay on and continue what I had started. I felt I was abandoning them when they needed me most. I was worried about them regressing just as their lives were beginning to have meaning. I felt so much part of a team alongside Lucia and the Marias that I didn't want to be parted from them either.

Not only that, I was very worried about coming home to England. I had been happy before I came out, but I now believed that my life in Milton Keynes had been purposeless. I had discovered I was good at something and it had opened up the world

119

to me. I have to admit that by that time I felt I was on something of a mission. It was a lovely feeling to discover such a talent so late in life. I didn't believe I was the only one who could do the work, but I had come to realise that I did have a gift for it. Dr Darmady had been right to accept my application after all.

My interest in news from England had begun to diminish over the weeks. Whereas I had been desperate to get letters from home in the beginning, I now just glanced at them, never bothering to re-read them as I had done at first. The idea of being free of family ties and able to continue concentrating on helping other people seemed very tempting. How could I go back to my old, humdrum life after all I had experienced? How could I listen patiently to the petty problems and moans of my colleagues and family as I used to after witnessing so much real suffering? Would I ever be able to get back into the mundane routine of office and housework again? Would it ever seem worthwhile? How could I bring myself to leave the children whom I had grown so fond of?

All these questions kept spinning through my head. I wasn't even sure that I could face going back to John, much as I loved him. I had experienced so much on my own that I couldn't imagine how I would ever be able to make him understand my feelings, share my experiences. He had been wonderful, keeping things going in England without complaining, and ringing regularly to see how I was getting on. The funny thing was I had begun to feel irritated by his calls, not able to think what to say to him or how to bridge the gulf which had opened up between our lives.

In the beginning it had felt wonderful to hear his familiar, friendly voice down the line. It was a terrible problem for me to get calls through to Britain and as John often got through very easily, I think he began to doubt if I was trying hard enough. Perhaps he sensed my not really wanting to speak to him. I tried hard to be pleased when he rang, to sound interested, but it was becoming more and more of an effort. I ran out of questions to ask as I began to forget about home and to only think of what was happening in Bacau and Ungerini. Often the calls I booked would come through in the early hours of the morning, jerking us both out of deep sleep and leaving us stranded on the line trying to think of things to say that the other would find interesting. John actually complained once or twice that I didn't seem to be interested in what was happening at home any more, which shocked me because I had thought I was covering up my indifference very well. I denied it but I doubt if I sounded the least bit convincing.

I seriously considered leaving him and coming back to Romania to work, a thought that filled me with guilt as John had always been so supportive of me and had given me absolutely no reason to hurt him. I felt very confused as the date for my return drew closer, wondering how I could break the news to him that although he was a lovely man and I had loved being married to him, I had now found something bigger and more important which I wanted to do with my life. I knew he would not understand, how could he? These children, so dreadfully handicapped, the workers, all of them were at that moment more important to me than him. No words could explain it.

I confided some of my fears to Sister Jane one evening in the parlour outside the chapel. She very wisely cautioned me not to make any decisions yet, but to see how things worked out. She was very understanding and supportive, but firm, and told me I *must* return, that my marriage was important and it would be unfair to let John down. Things would seem different, she assured me, after a little settling-in time. At that moment I couldn't believe that I would ever readjust. I just kept meditating and asking anyone who was listening to give me an indication of what I should do.

The thought of saying goodbye to all the children that I had come to love so much made me terribly sad, as did the knowledge that I was leaving so much work unfinished. We had barely scratched the surface for these children and I had to leave them. I couldn't imagine a day going by when I wouldn't lift them from their cots, hug them. The thought that I might never see them again was abhorrent to me. With so much still to be done, where was the point in going home?

Two weeks before we were due to return in late May, we were told at a meeting that a team of eight people were coming out to build an outside playground at Ungerini. The whole thing had been organised, and the funds raised, by an energetic lady called Jenny Marsh. The people in charge of our team disapproved of the project, believing it to be a complete waste of time and money.

'This Jenny Marsh is bringing a very grand group with her,'

our Operations Director told us, 'all ex-public schoolboys from places like Eton and Harrow. You mustn't feel intimidated by them or their conversation.'

'Sure,' Jacqui's dark eyes flashed, 'just so long as they take their turn at making the f...... tea and washing up they'll get along fine with me.'

When they arrived, we discovered they were a wonderful group, full of fun and energy and willing to work from early morning to late evening with a joy and enthusiasm which was an inspiration to see. They got on famously with the children, involving them as much as possible in the work. In the evenings they liked to relax and party and they made our last week much less painful. I felt enriched to have met them, particularly Will and Tommy Leigh-Pemberton, sons of the then Governor of the Bank of England. Tommy had ridden his motorbike out from Britain and Will had driven the huge lorry. I was saddened to read about Tommy's death some time later in Africa and I count myself lucky to have met such a free-spirited and generous soul.

The playground was ready two days before we were due to leave. The skies were sunny, the wind was warm and the ground was now firm and dry. It was glorious to watch the children, still shaven-headed and dressed in rags, getting used to the sensations of swings and slides, behaving almost like normal kids. Nichu-sorui used to delight in getting his swing as high as possible, ecstatic with the additional range this gave his spitting!

The night before our departure we had a big party at the hotel with lots of Romanian guests. I was making an effort to be sociable but felt real dread at the thought of boarding the train next morning. Ionel had brought some local brandy which he insisted I try. It tasted like medicine and burnt like firewater, but a wonderful red glow came over me, taking away some of the pain.

As the evening wore on Ionel came and sat very close to me, taking my hand. 'Bevey,' he murmured, gazing into my eyes, 'I am so happy to have got to know you. You have helped me in so many ways. The tireless work you have done with the children is remarkable. If I could think of the best possible woman in the whole world; if I could go to every country in search of the greatest; if I could choose who I wanted from the whole world ...' I could see Jacqui looking across the room at us with an alarmed expression as the tears fell down Ionel's face. Clinging to my hand he went on, '... to be my mother, it would be you.' I was both honoured and relieved!

From that moment on I sort of flowed along until I was lying happily under the table. Various gallant, and suitably strong, team members offered to winch me up but I was very happy to stay there for a while.

We arrived at the station the next morning after two hours' sleep and with only minutes to spare. The others were ecstatic to be returning home, but Jacqui and I just wanted to be away from their happy chatter to sort out our thoughts. I think some people thought me very off-hand but it was nothing personal and I suspect I did such a good job of covering up with a sickly grin and a 'hey I'm cool' attitude that most of them hadn't realised the inner turmoil I was in.

I couldn't imagine a time would ever come when I wouldn't be thinking about the children whom I now loved so dearly. At the same time, how could I consider abandoning John and Russell and our families for a bunch of children I had only known for four months? How could I contemplate hurting John so much after eighteen years together?

I clambered onto the train for Bucharest dressed in Bacau's finest nightwear, a brushed cotton nightdress the size and shape of a bell tent. It was covered in divine pink roses and was a parting gift from Jacqui, intended to liven up John's and my first night back together. I wasn't sure it was up to the task, given my state of mind.

Despite my confusion the major concern at that moment was physically getting on the train since there was no platform. Roger had quietly reassured me that no task was too big and that he would put his shoulder down, Mark would haul me up, he would push Benny Hill-style and between the three of us I would make it onto the train. However, my fears were unfounded and pulling my considerable weight up onto the four-foot high train step, huffing and puffing and climbing over chickens, children and the luggage of the peasants, I heard someone shouting that I had a visitor. I pushed my way back down to the door and found Sister Jane holding the hand of Maria, whom the doctors had said would never walk. She was standing beside Sister Jane on her tiny crippled legs and even managed a shy, gentle little wave.

I saw Sister Jane looking at my nightie as I climbed down. 'I've joined this bizarre religious cult,' I explained.

'Oh,' she said, with a glint in her eye, 'a bit like us, then.'

We stood looking at each other and I felt the tears which I had been suppressing for so long well up. I had kept myself busy counselling everyone else in the last few weeks but finally it was here, the real thing. I was going home.

Sister Jane knew the torment I was in. She took both my hands and looked deeply into my eyes. Standing very close she squeezed my hands hard and said, 'We will pray for you. God will be your guide; he will not forget you and you will not be alone.' She pressed a little black prayer book into my hands. 'Read this. Learn to pray from it. Many answers are there.'

I suddenly pulled my hands away and, not knowing if it was allowed or not, hugged her and kissed her on both cheeks. 'Don't forget our children,' she whispered. 'Poor Bevey...'

I choked back the tears as best I could, said goodbye and got back onto the train, struggling my way through to my compartment, pushing past the people to get to a window for one last glimpse of Maria.

As the train drew out Jacqui and I pulled out the footrests and pretended to doze so that we could avoid conversation. I was now feeling sick, as well as miserable, wondering how I would break the news to John that I wanted to abandon him. The plane journey was no better and I still felt horribly ill. People were talking to me and it was as if it was all a dream. I was answering but not really aware of what I was saying. I felt so guilty because I knew that John was looking forward to my return and had missed me lots. His sister, Joy, and some friends from Abbey National were all taking the day off work to meet me at the airport.

When we landed at Heathrow I had an idea: maybe I could resurrect some humour to mask my true feelings. I decided to give John a real shock. He had warned me not to return home with a baby or a toddler, so I asked the others to take my luggage for me after going through customs, knowing that John would be waiting to collect me on the other side. Taking Tough Ted, my faithful teddy bear, I wrapped him up in Jacqui's brushed cotton nightie, which looked a lot like a cot sheet, and cradled him in my arms like a baby – as I came through the gate John wasn't there. I couldn't believe it. He had never been late for anything in his life. In fact, I had on several occasions in the past rather unkindly told him it was like being married to an alarm clock. Yet he was late to meet me after we had been apart for the longest time ever. Despite all my doubts about returning I felt let down by this anticlimax.

He turned up three quarters of an hour later, having been given the wrong time for the arrival of the plane by the airline. As I went towards him with the bundle cradled in my arms, his face was a picture of horror. He turned to Joy, white-faced, 'Oh, my God,' he said, 'What has the silly bitch done now?' Relief fairly flooded into his face when he realised the little bundle was Tough Ted and we all laughed together. It was a relief to have something to laugh about, to break the awkward silence I had dreaded.

I said a sad goodbye to Roger. 'I'll miss your witty and intellectually stimulating conversation,' he teased.

'I'll send you a tape,' I promised in return.

And then came a very extended goodbye to Jacqui, neither of us wanting to be the first to go. I could tell that John and my welcoming group were getting impatient. Finally we vowed to stay in touch and she left.

Our friends had wanted to organise a 'welcome home' party, but John had vetoed it. They had all been very disappointed and told me later they thought John was wrong. 'We know how jolly you are, ' they told me, 'and how you enjoy a bit of fun.' True, but not if I was to be the centre of attention, and John knew it.

They were all round me, asking questions, tugging at me, insisting I went for a meal and disappointed that all I really fancied was a banana, a yoghurt and a cup of tea. Everyone was chattering and laughing and I felt like I was drowning. We sat down in the restaurant at Heathrow, the questions still flying around me. I felt as if I was sinking, being dragged under the water. My head and eyes hurt from tiredness and, more than likely, the after-effects of Ionel's brandy. It all seemed so bright, so colourful, so noisy and so final. I was back.

I thought the journey to Milton Keynes and the questions would never end. I began to feel travel-sick. The house had been festooned with balloons and banners. It looked grand but I felt like I was being nailed into a coffin. Moss and Misty came rushing out to greet me, leaping up, licking me, knocking me over, barking, whining and slobbering. I was waiting to feel happy to be home, but it wasn't happening. The phone was ringing and everyone wanted to talk to me at once – there seemed no escape. I was exhausted and wanted none of it.

John had prepared a huge meal. I managed to eat some of it but I could see that my lack of appetite hurt his feelings. He had imagined I would be starving.

'I'll take the dogs out,' I said, trying to make my escape.

'Oh, no, Mum,' Russ said kindly, 'I'll do that for you.'

I sat down on the couch while John went to get a coffee. I pulled my boots off and curled my legs up into a foetal position, pretending to be asleep.

'Oh,' John said as he came in, 'I thought we could go over and see your Dad. He and Margaret are so looking forward to seeing you. My dad is waiting to see you too, oh and Rob and Margaret want to come this evening...'

After a few minutes I genuinely fell asleep. John put a quilt over me and I slept through the night, there on the couch.

The next morning was Saturday. I dragged myself upstairs for a shower. I felt a deep excitement; hot running water, on tap! I wandered around the bedroom, poking into things. It seemed so strange to see a drawer full of socks when I had been so used to them being a rarity. I opened my wardrobe and was amazed to see how many clothes I had, remembering my friends in rags in Romania. The kitchen was the same, stocked full of food. When I went to take the dogs out I found I had five coats. Did all my friends have that many? I wondered. Perhaps I'd be able to persuade them to part with one or two so we could send them to the Sisters for distribution...

The house seemed stiflingly hot, or was it that I felt so tired? I could hardly breathe. John went shopping and I continued to look around the house. I felt irritated and trapped. I went out into our lovely garden and felt annoyed to find John hadn't done the weeding.

When John returned he was smiling. 'Oh, not unpacked yet, then?' he said innocently. I felt infuriated but didn't know why. I had returned with just one small bag, having given all my clothes to various Romanian friends and workers at Ungerini.

It was a dull day and we had some lights on. Everything seemed so bright after the low wattage bulbs in Ungerini and Bacau. The phone went on ringing and people were being so kind. I kept up a pretence but underneath I was panicking. How long could I keep this up? John knew something was wrong. Everything he tried to do was wrong, every thoughtful gesture, every hug he tried to give me was brushed off. I just wanted to have some space, to have time to settle back in. I asked him to tell people who rang that I was out.

'That's not fair,' he protested. 'They're ringing because they care; you can't be so rude as not to talk to them.'

'Oh, cut out the moralising and lecturing – who are you, my headmistress?' I thought, but I held my peace.

Jacqui rang. She was having similar problems and we talked for hours. John kept hovering around and saying things like, 'Haven't you finished yet?' I knew I should finish but we felt so comfortable talking to one another. Poor John and Russell, what a homecoming. At nights I found that the very things I had missed so desperately about John when I was all alone in the hotel room now annoyed me. The warmth of his body and his arm around me seemed suffocating. His snoring and even the way he turned over infuriated me. I couldn't sleep. I just dozed lightly and the slightest thing would instantly wake me.

John was very tolerant. He wanted to hear about Romania, to find out what I had been doing and why it was so important. He wanted to understand what was going on, but I didn't want to talk about it. I had turned into a tired-out, irritable old hag. Nothing I could do seemed to resurrect my normal high spirits. I really tried to appear enthusiastic and to most people I probably seemed like the same old Bev, but John knew. If only I had had the courage to talk to him about it, but I kept it all bottled up and suppressed. This was my fault, my doing; no one, I believed, could possibly understand the torture I was going through. I felt split in two – one minute I planned to return to Romania within days, the next minute this seemed like an act of extreme folly. What to do? Where to go? There wasn't a minute in the day when I didn't think of the children, of Lucia and the Marias, of the Sisters.

I went back to work at the Abbey National two days after my return, which was much too soon, and the adjustment to normal working life was just as hard as I had feared. At lunchtime on my first day back, on my way to the canteen I was directed to the executive dining room and found thirty Abbey National friends waiting for me, having arranged a special luncheon. They all clapped and I had to really force a smile onto my face and look as if I was about to enjoy myself. The catering department had made a beautiful welcome-home cake in the shape of a belly dancer and it was all so lovely and special that I couldn't understand why I wasn't enjoying any of it. I felt I was being very ungrateful but I am a very low-key person, much happier beavering away behind the scenes than being up on stage in the glare of the spotlight. I made a supreme effort to put on a show of having a good time. It was the least I could do after all their kind efforts.

I was desperate to keep up my contact with the friends I had made in Romania, like Jacqui and Diane, and I spent hours on the phone to them and to Sister Jane, endlessly talking about the children. It must have driven John mad. I approached Dr Darmady who had set up the Ungerini Orphanage Trust and asked if I could help with fundraising or the organising of relief lorries for Ungerini, but she said no thank you because she had plenty of professionals to do that sort of thing. I was a little hurt because I felt that I really wanted to continue helping the children and had proved my worth to them over the past months. The others who had come back with me all received similar rejections. I guess we had done our time and were now surplus to requirements; it was someone else's turn. The Trust had a committee of friends and colleagues who were handling the British end of the operation, and they were already winding down the number of people they wanted at Ungerini. They no longer had the funds to pay for things like the volunteers' airfares.

I frequently rang Felicity MacPherson, who was no longer connected to the Trust, and she listened to me very sweetly as I poured out my woes. Later, when I had recovered from the culture shock of my return home, I rang her to apologise for having been such a nuisance, but she very kindly told me she had been flattered that I had felt I could talk things out with her.

I was surprised by how many people knew I had been out to Romania. Dave Metcalf and Peter Lazard, who I worked for, were very tolerant about the constant stream of people who came to my desk, asking questions. I could see that many people were disappointed that I had no horror stories to tell them, but I simply didn't want to talk about an experience which I was still trying to come to terms with and get into perspective. I did, however, give an interview to the company magazine in which I was able to thank everyone who helped with the sending out of the supplies.

For weeks I kept thinking of Salon One, glancing at the clock, hoping someone would be getting the children up or feeding them, depending on the time of day. The Abbey National had moved to its new building and it was like starting a new job that I didn't really want. I couldn't remember any of my computer codes or people's phone numbers and sometimes I couldn't even remember their names. Everything seemed so tiresome and futile and I just wanted to go straight back to Romania and get on with some real work. Gloria, the temp who had been covering for me, was wonderfully supportive and I could not have survived without her.

Having had my offer of help turned away by the Ungerini Orphanage Trust, I was determined not to let the whole thing just fizzle away and I set about helping the Sisters instead, organising lorries of clothes, food and medical supplies. I asked everyone I knew to give me spare coats, shoes and clothes. I spoke to the catering department at work who promised to ask their suppliers about making donations. As the parcels began to arrive, Denise Harris in the post room persuaded her boss, Don O'Connell, to let her store them until I found somewhere more suitable. My next problem was getting the stuff out to Romania. I contacted Relief Fund for Romania and spoke to Jessica Hellings, a volunteer, who sent me a list of the people planning to take lorries out, all of whom had to approach the Fund for validation letters. I started phoning these groups and persuaded them to take hundreds of boxes. I had no money to offer, so I was completely reliant on their goodwill. The Abbey National porters and security men were a terrific help too, because by now the parcels were coming in by the hundred.

About five minutes from the office I found a village hall that we could use as a distribution base. Various friends and colleagues started coming to the hall and helped me sort, bag up, box up and label, and soon we had an impressive pile of goods. I was desperate to get it out to Bacau. I knew all this activity was only a stop-gap for me, but at least it was a beginning.

One lunch hour a forty-foot lorry arrived at reception. I had already assembled a team of ten fit young men and we all hurried out. We formed a chain, passing the heavy boxes along like rugby balls. The Abbey National were very tolerant of my moonlighting and encouraging others!

By now I was also writing to other companies, asking them for throw-outs, seconds, wrongly labelled goods or anything else they could spare. I received soap, shampoo, candles, biscuits, sewing machines, wool – the list was endless. People seemed so happy to give; to know exactly where things were going; to think that they were making a difference.

Mother Teresa will never allow people to raise funds or get publicity using her name or the names of her children, believing that people should be willing to give of their own volition – that their work should speak for itself – but I was able to campaign for Romania in general and direct whatever was donated or sacrificed towards the Sisters. They would then distribute the goods to the needy in the locality, taking the minimum required for their own children's needs.

John was patient with me and was an enormous help. Though I returned from work one day to find he had put a large painted sign on our garage, which was bulging as usual with clothes and other goods, saying, 'Forward Transit Camp for Mother Teresa's, Romania'. The only time I saw him get really cross was when we came home one day and found we couldn't get into the house because someone had piled so much stuff onto the front doorstep.

A number of people came to me saying that they would like to do the same as I had and would I put them in touch with the Ungerini Orphanage Trust? One by one they were all turned away and so I put them in touch with Sister Jane who was always happy to welcome them to Bacau. Janet Stevens, the management trainer who had given me the wooden cross ring all those months ago, was one of the first. People were quick to point out that she had no experience or training in working with physically and mentally handicapped children. 'Well, I have trained the Directors and Senior Managers at Abbey National for many years; there can't be that much difference, can there?' she said. When she was rejected by Ungerini she was initially reluctant to go to the Sisters because she felt the children there were better off and not so much in need of help. I assured her, as I had to assure all the others, that just because they were slightly better off didn't mean that they didn't still have enormous needs. I also felt that if we could help the Sisters they, in turn, would be helping the children at Ungerini whenever they could. I typed a helpful little package of everything you needed to know about voluntary work in Romania – how to get there, inoculation, money, etc.

In October 1991, while walking the dogs in the woods, I met a man who told me that his daughters had just finished college and were thinking of doing something like VSO. When he found out where I had been he asked if they could come and talk to me. One of them, Gillian, who had been at art school, came round the same evening and ended up travelling out with Janet.

After an exhausting journey, weighed down with urgently needed supplies, they eventually arrived at Mother Teresa's. Sister Jane gave them one of her most glittering smiles, saying, 'Oh, so happy to have your help – you have arrived just in time for tea!'

Oh, great, thought Janet, feeling parched and in definite need of a pick-me-up. Sister Jane thrust bowls and spoons into their hands and gave them a child each to feed. Some time later Janet, plastered in food from Andrei who still liked to blow raspberries even with his mouth full, began to wonder what she had done to upset me enough for me to send her to this place.

When I heard from Sister Jane how well Gillian and Janet were doing and how much the children loved them I felt a distinct pang of jealousy and had to speak to myself very firmly. I was afraid that the children would forget me and would love others more. Then I thought how beautiful that would be, that they could love and trust other people, not be dependent on me alone. I felt shame at my original jealousy and realised how silly it was. Perhaps now I was finally coming to terms with being back home.

Initially Sister Jane was horrified by the mess which the children got into when doing art with Gillian but she soon realised that they were concentrating, becoming totally absorbed. Above all, the children were occupied! Both Janet and Gillian wrote to me telling me all the news and Gill complained about 'an awful little boy called Patreascu who is always whinging'. She said that he did the most horrible dark paintings of black tunnels but, in his favour, he was always the keenest to help her tidy up the room and wash the brushes afterwards. 'The Sisters asked me to make some decorations by cutting up coloured tissue paper and sticking it onto card,' she said, 'and he was the only one who was actually able to help me with it.'

*　　　*　　　*

About four weeks after I returned to England I received a phone call from Romania. It was Sister Jane. 'Bevey,' she said, 'I have someone who wishes to talk to you.' Who's that I wondered? Perhaps Sister Ida?

'Bevey,' another voice came on the line, 'It is Illeana. I live with the Sisters now!' My heart stood still. It took a few seconds for the news to sink in. Sister Jane came back on to help translate for us. 'I have my own bed,' Illeana babbled happily, 'some clothes and knickers. I have a toothbrush and handkerchief and I am allowed to have a bath and wash my hair with shampoo. Nobody hits us! Oh, and we have food at a clean table, and Sister Jane says I will go to school, and learn to read and write!'

She chattered on as I tried to take in everything she said, listening to her voice, happy and animated in a way it hadn't been since Gabriel had gone to Gsteni. She was soon to discover that she was wrong about the 'no smacking' rule. Sister Jane told me a few weeks later that one day when she had visitors, Illeana stripped off and deliberately walked completely naked past the little parlour in an effort to attract attention to herself. This happened twice more and on the third occasion Sister Jane gave her a good whack across the buttocks with a wooden spoon. Illeana did not do it again.

Edward Parry and Jessica Hellings of the Relief Fund for Romania set up a mobile medical unit to establish health programmes at the village level. It was a wonderful idea, welcomed by the Romanian medical authorities and, of course, the people, and they asked the Sisters for somewhere secure to store their caravan and drugs. It was the start of a very fruitful co-operation. A British GP and nurse and a Romanian translator, worked closely with Romanian doctors. This is definitely the way forward.

Helen was the daughter of a health visitor who had been out at Ungerini as a volunteer. She had come for a week to visit her mother and had helped instead of holidaying. Helen wanted to go back to Ungerini as a volunteer herself but the Trust wouldn't accept her because she had no qualifications – it was a shame since she had already proved she was great with the children. I persuaded her to write and ask Sister Jane if they needed help. They did. Helen had cascades of gloriously wild hair, wore Doc Martens, lime-green leopardskin leggings and was quite a sight for the unworldly townspeople of Bacau. Sisters, workers and children all adored her. One Sunday afternoon, as she prepared to go out, one of the Sisters asked her where she was going.

'To the footie,' she replied, 'to see Bacau United.'

The Sisters were alarmed as the football stadium was a hotbed for drinking, fighting and bottle-smashing and they thought she might attract unwanted attention with her eccentric appearance. They tried to dissuade her.

'Now look here, girls,' she purred. 'You have your religion, and it is God – I have mine and it is football, okay?' And off she went. Needless to say, she came to no harm.

Before long I had helped around thirty people to go out to Bacau as volunteers. I became quite experienced at picking those people who wanted to go for the right reasons – people who would be able to make positive contributions to the work of the Sisters. Sometimes they settled in immediately and loved the work, the children and the Sisters. Other times it took them longer to adjust, but the Sisters were always patient and understanding and most volunteers came to enjoy themselves. When Janet first went out she told everyone out there that she worked for 'the Abbey', not realising that our employer's fame had not spread quite that far; she found herself being treated with extreme reverence. They must have thought she was a nun travelling in plain clothes.

My stepson Russell went to Bacau several times. I told the Sisters that they mustn't give him any preferential treatment, and that if he upset them they were not to complain to me but must deal with him direct. During one of his many visits I was talking to Sister Jane on the phone and she told me that Russell had turned up two hours late for an appointment. 'I was chasing prodigal son all through orphanage with largest wooden spoon,' she said in her heavy Indian accent, 'Through every crook and nanny, beating buttocks wherever I could catch him. With all the children running after me screaming and laughing and saying, "Go on, Sister, catch him".' Needless to say, Russell was on time thereafter. The Sisters also noticed that whenever Russell arrived all the levels of the local girls' skirts appeared to rise a couple of inches and they seemed to find a lot of excuses to walk past the orphanage whenever he was outside painting.

Not all the volunteers were happy with the way the Sisters ran their home, feeling that perhaps they were too regimented and set in their ways. There were so few staff and so much work for everyone to do that it was necessary to have strict systems. Had these people seen the chaos and misery that resulted from a lack of any sort of order, or short- or long-term planning, at Ungerini they might have felt differently. At Ungerini there were 186 children and 142 staff, plus the British and other volunteers. In Bacau there were four Sisters, six staff and fifty-two children, plus the dispensary to run, the elderly and handicapped to be visited, and the distribution of goods to the villages to be organised. The Sisters also found time to visit the prison regularly, the adult institute and Ungerini. It would be impossible to achieve all that without rotas and strict routines. There simply isn't any other way to do it and the very regularity of it all makes the children feel more secure. I used to think that if they didn't stop for prayers so often they could fit a bit more in, or take a well-earned break, but I came to realise that it was prayer which gave them the strength to carry on, re-charging their batteries.

A couple of the volunteers commented on the firmness with which Sister Jane treated her Romanian helpers. I had learnt that there was a limit to how much you could let the women get away with before they started to think you were a joke and lost respect for you, and explained why it was necessary. Sister Jane feels very strongly that all the children should have their own toothbrushes and used to become incensed when she found the women using one brush for all of them. Since the women probably didn't even possess brushes of their own it was not surprising that they didn't grasp the importance of oral hygiene. She also became furious and disappointed when they stole things because they were always free to approach the Sisters if they needed anything for themselves or their families. Sadly the workers don't always understand or remember this. But working for the Sisters has its plusses – since none of the workers has running water at home they are all allowed to take showers and wash their uniforms at work, which has been a great boost to them. To see the delight when they emerge, hair, bodies and clothes clean, is a joy. The Sisters also allow them one week's paid holiday a year and organise outings for them and their families.

I saw plenty of examples of their working practice in my visits and so did the volunteers I sent out. Remembering how I had felt when I returned from Romania the first time, I always contacted volunteers when they got back to the UK. It was good to hear all the news and their observations on life in Bacau. I was able to adapt my information pack for volunteers in the light of these updates and avoid possible future problems. I still didn't know the Sisters, or their ways, that well, but I was getting there!

Once a year each of the Sisters has a feast day and they all go off together. They take a simple picnic and might play tennis or climb trees or just be silly and play football, throw snowballs or have water fights. On one occasion I heard that they even tried out Russell's idea of using big stainless-steel trays as toboggans and came cascading down the hills screaming with joy. One time they returned from one of these day trips to find that all the children's toys had disappeared. 'Where are the toys?' Sister Jane demanded, stretching herself to her full four feet ten inches.

'Sister Jane,' the women crossed themselves and looked distraught, 'the children simply handed them out to passers-by.'

'You let them do that?' Sister Jane obviously didn't believe a word of it.

'There was nothing we could do. They insisted on giving them away.'

'And if people had wanted to take the children, would you have let them have them too?' she wanted to know.

'Our backs were only turned for a second and everything was gone.'

'Never mind,' Sister Jane turned to go, 'it is not a problem – we will buy new things with your wages.'

Some of the volunteers who witnessed the exchange thought this was an excessively harsh punishment for such poor women and then a 'miracle' happened. Those poor, mentally handicapped children were able to remember exactly who they had given the toys to, and even knew where these people lived. All the missing toys reappeared and the wages were paid as usual.

The Sisters, although very fond of the gypsies in the area, were aware that some of them believed the home to have endless supplies. Whenever the Sisters went in to Mass they would ask me or another volunteer to stand guard over the washing so that the gypsy women, or anyone else passing, wouldn't take it. I once made the mistake of holding the sick child of a gypsy woman who had come to ask for medicine. The Sisters very quickly made me give it back. 'Never hold the babies,' they warned me, 'or the women will run off and leave them.' While they were always happy to take in children who needed them, they believed that their first duty was to try to make it easier for parents to keep their own children and bring them up as part of normal family units. The Sisters believe that no matter how good their homes are there is no substitute for the family home.

When I returned to England I had intended to write to each child on birthdays and Christmas and maybe in between. I soon realised that with fifty or more of them it wasn't going to be possible, so I asked family and friends, people I knew would keep it up once started, to write to a specific child and send little gifts. I would then dispatch them all to Romania in one package. When the first parcel arrived I apologised to the Sisters for not sending anything for them. 'Bevey,' they said, 'the pleasure of seeing the excitement and joy of children opening presents for the first time in their lives was gift enough for us!' They told me the children were all sleeping with their presents under their pillows.

When Christmas came round we sent five hundred boxes of desperately needed basic foods such as cheese, fresh fruit and vegetables, powdered milk for the babies, sweets, chocolates and biscuits for the children's Christmas party, as well as a present for each child, a Christmas tree and loads of decorations.

The shipment arrived a week and a half late, the night before Christmas Eve. We had planned to get it there two weeks before Christmas, giving the Sisters time to get organised. They stayed up all night unpacking the boxes and putting up the tree with its lights, which also played carols over and over. Helen, who was there at the time, said that she would happily have nuked them just to save her sanity. Her every waking moment was taken up trying to think of ways to destroy those jingling tormentors.

They hung glittering decorations and balloons everywhere so that it was all ready for the children when they woke on Christmas morning. One of the two Luciens, who became known as 'Tractor Lucien' because he could only get around by sitting on a child's tractor, sat under the tree all day long, just gazing up and keeping the other children from stripping it of its finery. He was most upset when Sister Jane wouldn't move his bed there too.

For Christmas Eve the Sisters had organised a nativity play with all fifty of the children taking part in full costume. Local government officials were invited to attend, plus as many local people as they could cram into the small home. The audience was astounded that these children, whom they had previously thought incapable of anything other than lying immobile in cots, were taking part in a play. At the Christmas party afterwards Santa Claus appeared with a huge sack and one present for each child. Helen reported that the Sisters wept with joy as they watched the smiling faces of the children, who less than a year before had come to them screaming with fear, as they each received their present.

The Sisters were very keen to build a school within the grounds of the home that local handicapped children could attend along-side their own handicapped ones. They felt that if they could support those families with handicapped children at home (not all were living in orphanages) it would stop further children being sent to institutions. In some cases families managed to escape the Government's policy of putting all handicapped children in institutes – perhaps by having a family member too old to work, who could stay home and care for the child, or perhaps by simply keeping the child out of sight. The effort of looking after a handicapped child with no wheelchairs, lifting aids or zimmer frames was a terrible burden for families who had done their best to manage and they welcomed any support the Sisters could give them.

They also wanted to build a small playground to encourage the children to exercise their twisted limbs in the fresh air, to help their physical progress and their interaction with one another. Eye and body contact are vital to build confidence and to produce normal development and behaviour, and most of the children had rarely been outside before coming to the Sisters, being too badly handicapped to join me on my outings since I could only carry one at a time. The idea grew and grew and I was convinced that I had to do all I could to aid the struggle to help children who might be able to stay with their families and prevent them having to go to Ungerini.

I approached the Board at Abbey National to see if they would donate some money towards the school project. Although they couldn't donate anything from company funds, they said that I could use the branches as collection points. I got together with the public relations people and we came up with a simple photo-graph of a Romanian child on a poster, saying, 'This child is warm and well fed – what he needs now is an education.' People sacrificed many things and gave enough to build a simple school, washing and drying room and a desperately needed dispensary for the whole area, somewhere where the poorest of the poor people could come to be treated. The money came from all sorts of people from pensioners to children giving up their sweet or comic money. Some members of the Abbey's staff gave up their lunches and donated that money. The two-week campaign brought great joy to both staff and clients because they could actually see what they were helping to achieve and I gladly wrote them little progress reports once the work began.

Once Abbey National realised the size of the project we were undertaking, they suggested to the Sisters that a London-based member of staff, more experienced in money management, should take control of the project. I think they thought that I would not know what best to spend the money on and that the Sisters were bound to be too unworldly for such a task. The Sisters, however, were not to be railroaded and insisted I should continue to look after everything as I was 'knowing their ways and the needs of their poor and children'. To combat any doubts the Abbey may have had about this, I was very happy to have a Director from the bank counter-sign any cheques, and look over any accompanying paperwork. I kept a simple debit/credit book and was able to account for every penny. If only I looked after my own affairs as diligently, I would be a rich woman by now.

Throughout these weeks I had been engaged in another project for Sister Jane. I had only been back in England a couple of weeks and was still feeling deeply homesick for Romania when the phone rang and Sister Jane's voice came down the line. 'Bevey,' she said, getting straight down to business. 'We need your help. I want you to find an orthopaedic paediatric surgeon who will come out to Romania and operate on my Szuzannah for me. If that's not possible we will send her to England for the operation.'

'How on earth does she expect you to do that?' John spluttered when I reported our conversation.

'Doesn't she know you work in a bank, not a hospital?'

I knew this was a very unorthodox thing for her to ask, since she should have put a request in to her Regional Superior – then the request would be passed on to London, but I felt a thrill of excitement at the thought of getting involved once more. On reflection I wonder if she was trying to fill the void I still felt and had written to her about. Was she trying to save my marriage? Whatever the reasons, my life was about to take another extra-ordinary turn.

I soon realised that much as I still wanted to return to Romania, I could do more to help by working on the children's behalf in Britain. The Birmingham Heartlands Hospital had given me medical equipment which was technologically redundant in a British hospital, but light years ahead of anything they had in Bacau. I wouldn't have had access to this had I still been in Bacau. My heart still ached when I thought about the children, but the pain was beginning to become less intense now that my days were so full and even though I was miles away, I was still part of their struggle. And John was so supportive and understanding, of what was fast becoming my obsession, that I eventually began to feel more settled within myself, to feel at home again. About time too!

CHAPTER NINE

Answering the Call

*

*J*ust six months before I would never have had the nerve to approach a senior surgeon and ask for help, but by the autumn of 1991 everything had changed and when it came to getting things for the children in Romania I felt brave enough for anything. The question was, how should I set about finding the right surgeon? One of the people I had approached about writing letters to the children was a Catholic woman at work called Mary Cooper who'd become Szuzannah's penpal. I went to Mary and told her of the challenge Sister Jane had set me.

'Well,' she thought for a moment, 'my mother did go to an orthopaedic hospital outside Birmingham that was run by Catholic nuns. But it was years ago and I'm not sure that I would be able to remember the name now.'

'Do you think you could try to find out?' I persisted.

'Okay,' Mary agreed and, with the help of her local priest, came up with the name of St Gerrard's Hospital.

I contacted the Matron at St Gerrard's, Sister Beatrice, who was formal and businesslike but helpful. After several letters and many phone calls, during which we built up a friendship, she told me she had a number of surgeons she could call upon, but that the best for our purposes was probably a Mr Nigel Dwyer, who specialised in paediatrics. Unfortunately he was then at his holiday home in Spain, but she promised to contact me when he returned. Mr Dwyer was based in Birmingham, which would not be very convenient when it came to getting the children to appointments or visiting them in hospital, but if he was the best he was the man for me and we would just have to learn to like commuting. I knew that he was not a young man, but I felt this was good news because it meant that he might, during the course of many years' experience, have encountered similar problems to the ones our children suffered. I sent Sister Jane's medical notes, plus my own notes on Szuzannah's personality – telling how she saved me from being hit by one of the boys – along to St Gerrard's to help in assessing Szuzannah's case.

A couple of months passed before I received a phone call from the Matron to say that she had Mr Dwyer in the office and would I like to speak to him? Trembling with nerves, I said I would.

'Well,' a voice barked down the phone, "what do you want, woman?' He sounded just as grand and ferocious as I had always imagined such distinguished men to be, rather like James Robertson Justice in the old 'Doctor' films that I used to watch as a child. He asked me a number of very searching questions on medical points which I did my best to answer.

'Really,' I ventured, 'you would do better to come to Romania and see the children for yourself.'

'Are you telling me, woman,' he bellowed, 'to cancel all my appointments, my operating lists and my private engagements in England, grind my practice to a halt and just take off for a week because you think I should?'

'Well, yes,' I said, refusing to be intimidated, 'I think you should do it. Can I come and visit you?'

A few days later I received a letter inviting me to go to inspect St Gerrard's and to have lunch with the nuns. 'Oh dear,' I said to John when I read it, 'they think I know what I'm talking about and what I'm looking for.'

So much depended on my being able to get someone sufficiently interested in the children to want to help. I felt a momentary rush of panic: supposing they thought I was some batty old eccentric and didn't take my proposals seriously?

'Oh, don't be so dramatic,' John scolded me. 'You can do it for the children. It's nothing to do with you, Bev, you are just an intermediary.' This put things into perspective for me, but didn't quell my nerves.

Both Sister Beatrice and I were surprised by one another. I had been expecting someone stiff, huge-bosomed and starched, not twinkly eyed with a sweet smile, and she had been expecting a power-dressed charity queen with shoulder pads and a perm. St Gerrard's, run by the Sisters of Charity of St Paul, was a pretty little country hospital. The gardens and the chapel were full of statues of Mary and Jesus and the stations of the cross which had been carved by Polish servicemen. Matron showed me their convent and their operating theatres and asked me a lot of questions – her own Order had sisters in Romania and she was interested to hear a first-hand account of the country.

Later that morning she introduced me to Nigel Dwyer and he proudly took me on another conducted tour. There was a lovely warm atmosphere in the hospital and I began to imagine how Szuzannah might be treated there. I felt ridiculously nervous about lunch – what would I talk about? I needn't have worried. Mr Dwyer was very articulate and obviously knew the Sisters well. He was a great, booming and attractive man with thick grey hair and bushy beard, tweed suit and ripe language, who was used to being the centre of attention. He obviously enjoyed being fussed over by the nuns. I was relieved to find that he had put a great deal of thought into the possibility of treating the children and asked many questions.

After considering all my answers he said, 'I may not be able to recommend you to bring any of these children over here. The suffering and stress that the travelling might cause may not be justified by the possible benefits.'

'That's okay,' I said. 'We'll be guided by you.' This was music to my ears and convinced me that he was the right person for the job. The one thing I didn't need was a 'glory hunter', bringing children over just so that he could write up their operations as interesting cases in the medical journals.

Mr Dwyer threw up every possible barrier to going to Romania himself, from the fact that his passport had expired to his own inexperience as a traveller. Every objection he raised I dealt with. I was determined to make the whole business so easy that he simply couldn't say no.

'What do you think, ladies?' I finally asked, looking round the lunch table. 'Hands up all those who think he should go?' All their hands went up and I could see we were wearing his resistance down.

'You probably won't be able to get me a seat on the bloody plane now, anyway,' he ended lamely.

'I've already booked your ticket,' I told him. 'I was sure you would decide you had to do it.'

That afternoon Nigel Dwyer's wife, Moira, came over to the hospital for tea – to meet me and have her mind put at rest. She was a physiotherapist and so had anticipated some of the possible problems. To start with I thought she didn't like me or what I was proposing because she was so quiet. I soon realised that it was shyness and I began to see that her sweet and gentle nature belied just what a strong character she was and how dependent her husband was on her. Mr Dwyer genuinely didn't like being away from her and it was going to be a great sacrifice for them both to be apart, even for a week.

By now it was October 1991 and the earliest I could arrange for Nigel to go out to Bacau was the following January. I could not expect him to abandon all his patients in Britain overnight. He was, however, anxious to see Szuzannah fairly quickly as she was sixteen by then and if anything could be done for her it would need to be soon, while her bones were still flexible.

When Janet and Gillian had first gone out to Romania I had contacted a travel agent who arranged for a courier, a university student called Florin, to meet them at Bucharest Airport, arrange their rail tickets, take them to the station and help them on the train with their cumbersome luggage. I contacted Florin again this time and asked if he would meet Nigel. He agreed and even though he was hard up he refused my offer of payment. 'It will be my pleasure,' he told me, 'to greet and assist someone who is trying to help my beloved country.'

Moira and I worked well together because we were both equally keen for Nigel to arrive safely and to experience as little stress as possible. He suffered greatly from back trouble after thirty years of bending and stretching across operating tables, but still managed to carry five huge cases of desperately needed medical supplies with him.

'How will I recognise the driver?' he asked nervously before setting off.

'Don't worry,' I assured him, knowing that there would not be many people looking as prosperous as him at Bacau station, 'the driver will recognise you.'

The trip went smoothly and on arrival at Mother Teresa's Nigel proudly handed over the five cases of supplies. 'Oh,' Sister Jane waved them aside dismissively, 'put them over there, will you, doctor? Now, shall we start looking at the children?'

Silently doing what he was told, Nigel began by looking at Marian, the boy with very bad club feet and hydrocephalus. 'Do you think you can help this child, Doctor Nigel?' Sister Jane asked.

'Of course I ruddy well can, woman!' came the gruff reply.

He later told me that he'd noticed that as Sister Jane smiled, her eyes were moistening and thought, 'Yes, I can do business with this nun.'

The Sisters in Bacau were more than a match for Nigel's outspoken ways and introduced him both to children living in the home and to others who were carried in from all over Moldavia. Some of the people had come 150 kilometres to be there. He also worked into the early hours of the mornings with the Sisters in the dispensary, returning wearily to the priest's house, where he was staying, to write up his notes.

When I rang to find out how his trip was going I was told that he thought he would be able to help many of the problems non-surgically, but that there were about fifteen children he thought would need to come to England for more extensive surgery. The first to come should be Szuzannah. One of the reasons he was willing to take Szuzannah was because she had shown such courage in protecting me from attack at Ungerini and he believed that this proved she had the courage and commitment needed to stand up after sixteen years of disability.

'Bevey says I should hug you, Dr Nigel,' one of the Sisters told him after I had heard the news, 'but your girth is too big for me to get my arms round.'

'Good heavens, woman, you would benefit from having half your tongue surgically removed!' he retorted with the blunt good humour that is typical of him.

I was so happy to hear that there were hundreds of children Nigel felt he could help without surgery, giving them mobility with the aid of splints, calipers and walking frames. I was sure we would be able to find someone to measure and fit the equipment once we knew what was required. We had finally made a huge long-term breakthrough.

Dr Nigel (as he is now affectionately known in Romania), having settled who he could operate on successfully, decided that the next step was for all the concerned parties to sit down together and discuss which children could withstand the emotional upheaval and possible trauma of the return journey, the surgery and a long absence from home. I felt fortunate that Nigel and Sister Jane were willing to be guided by me on this as they believed that I had known the children longer than anyone and therefore understood how they might react. I was particularly pleased that he was willing to help Szuzannah. Despite her unpopularity with the other helpers at Ungerini, I had developed a very soft spot for her. I also agreed that it might well be worth bringing the whinging Patreascu to England as he had shown some signs that there was more happening inside his head than we had all at first thought and, despite the constant whinging, he had shown the sort of improvement and determination to succeed that would help in the battle to get mobile.

The Sisters took Nigel to visit Bacau Hospital. The medical staff there were very impressed that such an eminent specialist had come all the way to Romania to see those children they had been indoctrinated into believing had 'no worth' due to their handicaps. Nigel promised to help the hospital in any way he could and forged some strong friendships, both professional and personal. His visit raised staff morale and introduced educated people to the idea that the children in their institutions might just be worthy of some attention.

The Romanians weren't the only ones who thought that the handicapped children were not worth helping. When she heard that Nigel was going out to look at the children, one British doctor who had worked with the children in Romania rang him and advised him not to waste his time because they were 'hopeless cases'. He was also told that I was a 'ridiculous woman' who didn't know when to give up, had no idea whatsoever of what was needed in Romania, and was dabbling in something which was better left to professionals. She advised that any money would be much better spent on supporting Ungerini. I was worried that Nigel would be put off by this negative reaction, but he treated it with exactly the contempt it deserved.

'It seems,' he said, 'that if I don't go, the children are going to receive no help from any other quarter.'

We both realised that bringing the children to Britain was a strictly short-term solution. Nigel did consider doing some of the operations in Romania to save the children from the trauma of travel, not to mention the cost! He also offered to take some 'master-classes' for local surgeons so that they could thereafter operate on the children themselves. To prepare for this possibility he went to a local hospital to watch some minor operations. When he saw that none of the gloves or equipment had been changed after four consecutive operations, it became clear that working over there would be out of the question if he was to stand any chance of success. There simply weren't the necessary resources available.

Nigel was the first to recognise that Patreascu had contracted polio at some stage in his short life. As a result, both his legs were withered and one was six inches shorter than the other. Despite all Sister Ida's fine work with him, Patreascu still appeared severely mentally retarded and emotionally disturbed, showing no reaction to being touched or kissed. He did not speak and was still very withdrawn, whining most of the time. There had, however, been a few signs of intelligence. I had seen a flicker of life in his eyes whilst playing music to him on the cassette, and there was the painting work which he had done for Gillian. If there was something there, how could we unlock the doors and bring the barriers down? Despite the fact that it was impossible to assess Patreascu's mental abilities properly, Nigel wanted to get him up and walking so that at least he had some chance of independence.

When Nigel returned to England, we sat down together to decide on the first steps to take with those children to be operated on in England. I did not doubt Nigel's surgical abilities but I had to be sure that the children themselves would be able to channel their energies into what would be an enormous trial for them.

One of the first things Nigel said to me was that it was essential I travel out with him next time he went to Romania. He would not consider going without me. 'I need you there for your opinions, your on-the-spot information. And Sister Jane agrees!'

Both Nigel and I were keen to get a boy called Lucien Maftei over as quickly as possible. He was already fifteen and his legs were permanently locked in the lotus position as a result of his being tied up for so many years. He had also developed rickets, which made his legs bow sideways. Had he not been tied there was no medical reason why he would not have walked normally. He was a severely disturbed child and still extremely fragile emotionally. 'I think we should wait another six months before we bring him to England,' I said and was relieved when Nigel nodded his agreement.

Having discussed all fifteen children, we then put them into a rough order of priority and emotional stability and decided that we would start by bringing Szuzannah over to Birmingham. Nigel was keen to bring Patreascu to the front of the queue – keener than I was. I was worried about whether it would be possible to communicate sufficiently with him to convey what was involved in getting up and walking. Would he want to do it? He had shown little interest in much apart from his paintings and the tape player, but eventually I was won over by Nigel's enthusiasm and decided that despite my reservations about his will to walk, I could not deny Patreascu his one chance of getting on his feet.

In January 1992 we began the lengthy process of getting Szuzannah and Patreascu to Britain. The Sisters were thrilled. I was worried about how well the children would cope with the actual journey and suggested that I should bring them over personally so that they would have someone they knew with them. My offer was gratefully accepted.

There was much to do in obtaining the various permissions for the children to come to the UK. Letters from Romanian doctors and the hospital were needed, stating what was wrong with them and that the necessary treatment was not available within Romania. Government departments responsible for the handicapped and the police had to agree to their travelling. The children's parents had to be contacted, if they had any. There were also arrangements to be made in Britain. My head was spinning with all the different things I had to think about. What with my job at Abbey National and preparing the way there were never enough hours in the day.

In the course of my work in Britain, I was approached by the inmates and officers at Wandsworth Prison who wanted to help the children of Romania. I never did find out how they got hold of my name. First of all I sent out relief parcels on a lorry they both organised and had donated for the whole trip – and all free! Since I knew they couldn't get out there to see for themselves the result of their efforts I wrote regularly to tell them how the aid was received and about our plans for the school and for bringing the children to England. The prisoners and officers wrote back via Bill Robinson, the Governor, saying they had all been deeply moved to hear of the children and the poor of Romania and asking if they could do anything further to help. They suggested they do extra work in the prison donating the sweet and tobacco money they received to pay for the children's airfares. I was delighted to accept their offer, half expecting to find a large bag with 'swag' written on it left on my doorstep – the proceeds of some robbery! The prisoners asked their families to bring in spare clothes and toys; they made teddies and strong wooden toys; bought sweets and chocolate. The whole prison came alive with much needed meaningful activity – they had a purpose. They donated a huge amount of all the above to us.

The Sisters were very happy to hear of the prisoners' sacrifices on our behalf.

Sadly, not all the news from Bacau in 1991 was positive. About six months after I returned to England Sister Jane rang. 'I have news for you, Bevey,' she told me. 'Your little Costel has died.'

'Oh, no.' I immediately started to cry, I felt so upset. His life had been so short, so full of pain. He had only had a few months of love, of being wanted and cared for.

'Oh, no, Bevey,' she said. 'You should be happy for him; it is a release from his terrible suffering. We are going to have most grand and excellent funeral for our dear child.'

I knew she was right and I remembered all the nights that he had cried and screamed with the pain that we could do nothing to alleviate, but it was still an awful feeling because even though all the children transferred to the Sisters had been expected to die, until then none of them had. Gill described to me what happened.

'Sister Jane was fixing him up on a drip and she could see that he was dying,' she said, 'so she took him to the chapel to baptise him and he just didn't draw breath again. He slipped away very gently without a sound. The other children were very upset, but the Sisters were determined they should celebrate Costel's life and his death. They managed to get a little white coffin and we sat down with the children to make garlands of flowers and a crown for Costel's head. They filled the open coffin with flowers and then they put it on an open, horse-drawn cart, lifting the children who weren't able to walk to sit up beside him.

'The Sisters wanted all the children to be dressed the same but the only things they had enough of were those white Abbey National T-shirts you sent, Bev. The shirts were all the same size, so some of the children wore them tucked into their trousers and others wore them with belts like dresses. They processed to the cemetery and back and then had a party to celebrate him.'

It was eight months before I first returned to the home in Bacau.

In February 1992 the Sisters contacted me and asked if I would fly out as soon as possible because the various government departments were refusing to issue the necessary documents. Taking a week's annual leave, and organising things as best I could before departing, I mustered my courage and set off – by myself!

As well as making sure that I had all the documentation needed at my end for Szuzannah and Patreascu to fly to Britain, I took out the plans for the schoolhouse, which were now ready. It was the first time I had ever travelled alone and I was absurdly nervous. I booked into a hotel in Bucharest that I already knew, but I didn't have the nerve to go downstairs for dinner, staying up in my bedroom to eat the food that John had packed for me. Then I lay on the bed until I heard the familiar gurgling noises of water coming into the pipes and knew that I was going to be able to take a shower.

The next morning I was so worried about oversleeping that I was up and dressed hours before I had to leave. Florin put me and all my cases on the train to Bacau, asking the locals in the carriage to make sure I got out at the right stop. It was a five-hour journey and the problem with trains in Romania is that the stations are always very badly signposted. I was nervous about missing Bacau, or not getting all my luggage off in time. Russell, who had travelled the same route, had meticulously logged the length of time between each of the stops and named them so that I could work out how far I had got to go at every stage, but I was still worried.

Although the other passengers were very friendly, Romanian trains are always rather intimidating. Ticket inspectors come round very frequently, followed by threatening plain-clothes men. Beggars constantly pass up and down the carriages, most of them children with missing limbs and sad faces. I always assumed that they had a parent in the train somewhere just waiting to whip anything they were given away from them, so I used to break off pieces of chocolate for them to eat there and then. For part of the journey I shared my carriage with an old man. When I offered him chocolate he gratefully accepted it and then carefully wrapped it for his grandchildren. Seeing this, I insisted that he share some of mine. Although I still didn't speak fluent Romanian, I did have enough to make a little polite conversation.

When the train finally pulled into Bacau many willing hands helped me and my considerable pile of luggage off. As I gathered

149

my thoughts together I saw a scarf waving and was relieved to see Dom Patreascu's friendly face. He was with a girl I didn't know. He introduced her as Ana-Liese, a Swiss volunteer both Helen and Gill had mentioned in their letters to me.

By the time I reached the home it was mid-afternoon and the children were waking from their siestas. It took me a few moments of staring into their faces to see who was who. They all had hair now and their skin and eyes shone – they looked like totally different children. They were better dressed, but I had seen them in nice clothes before. I was amazed by how much healthier and calmer they all seemed. I was overjoyed to see Szulita walking, Mariana dancing and Tractor Lucien trying to make conversation. It was like witnessing a miracle and much more than I had ever dared hope for when I first saw them transferred to the Sisters' care. They actually looked glad to be alive.

I was pleased to see that I had been wrong about Valentina. She had settled in well and looked relaxed and happy, still dressed boyishly and still with a mischievous glint in her eye. The next morning I was sitting in the little parlour outside the chapel when Valentina appeared and, with great ceremony, served me a cup of tea, pouring the milk and the tea herself from a lovingly prepared tray. Her joy and pride at my surprised reaction was heart-warming. I silently thanked God that the Sisters hadn't listened to my misgivings about her.

The children had made a 'Welcome Bevey' banner and sang 'Aye Aye Yippy' in my honour. I was then introduced to a new Croatian Sister, Sister Fabiana, who had joined them recently.

I was delighted that the children still remembered me after so many other people had been and gone. I had imagined I'd been replaced in their affections. The Sisters were amused by my fear of staying alone in a hotel but understood and kindly allowed me to 'live in'. I was to sleep in the girls' dormitory. When I went in that night Valentina spotted me from her bed at the other end of the room and came leaping towards me across the beds, trampolining on all the children, bouncing them into wakefulness. They were all fascinated by the thought that I would be sleeping alongside them, because they never got to see adults asleep. I don't think they believed we ever did. They all sat down around my bed with a lot of shushing to one another and studiously watched as I tried to drop off. My mealtimes were also watched with rapt attention because although the Sisters eat the same food

Before (with 90 degree
squint)

And after (seeing *Cats* and
not double!)

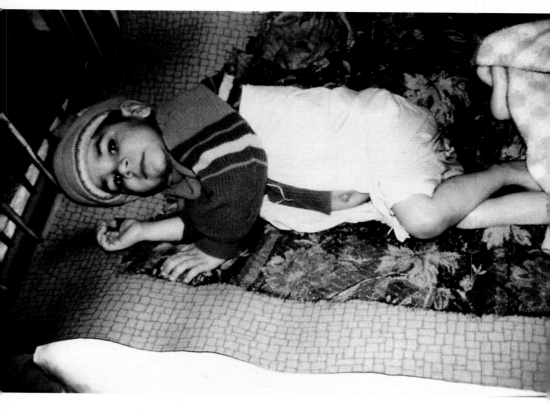

Patreascu at
Ungerini, 1990,
© Barbara Herne

Patreascu at MT's –
plump and in need
of exercise,
April '91

Patreascu with Misty and Moss – a weekend visit, June '92

Patreascu and the 'pisica' – his first word, December '92

Patreascu with John – kitchen
physio' all done

First school sports' day,
August '93

Anything you can do . . .

Patreascu and Tante Chiriac,
Bacau, August '95

With Maria Ochelari – she couldn't believe
this was Patreascu Mic!

My friend, Sister Fabiana

An overpopulated
Transit van on a
day out

John Hickman on
holiday in '94

Tractor Lucien mourning Dom
Patreascu

Valentina at Maria Ochelari's
wedding

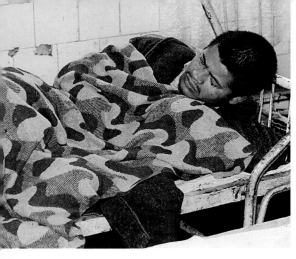

Gisteni Adult Institute

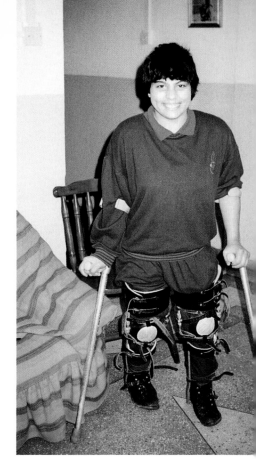

Illeana and Patreascu, '95

Szuzannah, upright in '95

Lucien Maftei, walking now, '95

as the children they always take meals in their own refectory. It is their time together and is important for them as a community; they are, after all, still a religious order. At first I used to sit outside their little chapel eating by myself, but then I plucked up enough courage to ask if I might join the children in my dormitory for meals. The children loved it and I sat at a different table each meal, chatting as best I could with my meagre Romanian.

I got off to sleep very late that first night, only to be rudely awakened the next morning by Sister Ida squeaking a toy in my ear.

'Bevey,' Sister Jane said when I emerged from the dormitory, 'come to Mass.'

'Oh, no, Sister,' I declined, not wanting to interfere in the religious side of their life, 'I don't think I should.'

'Come, just to see your children,' she insisted.

I couldn't believe my eyes as I walked into the chapel. The children who had all been so wild when I left them, still liable to pull down curtains and throw food, still behaving ritualistically and unpredictably, were now all sitting on chairs or cross-legged on the floor, concentrating in silence on the service and looking very content. They stayed in there an hour and none of them misbehaved. Many of them gave the correct responses and said their prayers to perfection. When the time came for the priest to raise the chalice, Tractor Lucien rang the handbell at precisely the right moment and the Sisters' foreheads dropped to the floor like stones. I couldn't believe that Tractor Lucien could actually be concentrating so hard on anything.

Two of the girls, Illeana mic (small) and Maria mari (large), had the most perfect singing voices and as I listened to them, watching all the children sitting so calmly, I was overwhelmed by the thought of how far they had come in the year since I had first seen them incarcerated at Ungerini and by the waste of human potential that must still be going on there. I felt the tears well up and start to flow uncontrollably. They were tears of joy and great sadness too, for so many more children were left behind at Ungerini, imprisoned in lives of sheer misery. How many of them would have been released from their emotional chains and liberated to begin their lives by just a few months with the Sisters? I felt very strange and although I couldn't understand most of the Romanian Mass, I was enveloped by a warm glow which overwhelmed me. As I gazed at a statue of Our Lady at Fatima I became very confident that things were going to be all right; that we would be able to achieve what we wanted; that our prayers would be answered.

During that visit I came to realise that it wasn't what the Sisters were actually doing that was miraculous, it was what was being done through them. I secretly went to their chapel and, in the dark, with only the dim flame of their little sanctuary lamp, I sank to my knees. I did not know how to pray according to the rules and I wasn't sure who might be listening, but I prayed until exhaustion set in. It was a simple prayer, nothing clever or articulate but straight from my heart. I just said, 'Thank you.'

Later in the first day I asked Sister Jane what they did when they went to do their Adoration in the chapel. I had often wondered in the past because I had heard such lovely singing coming out and seen the flickering lights of the candles, but I had never felt it my place to ask questions before.

'Why don't you come and see for yourself?' she asked.

'Oh, I couldn't,' I protested. 'I would feel like an intruder. Don't forget I am an atheist.'

She smiled knowingly and said I was most welcome whatever my beliefs and I went with them to the chapel that evening, watching the Sisters at prayer but not daring to join in. The first time they brought me a chair but after that I started to kneel on the floor as they did because it seemed to help me to focus my mind. It was a good opportunity to take stock of the day, to think, to meditate.

The Sisters were almost ashamed to tell me quite why they had needed me to rush out to Romania. 'A British group has been spreading rumours that you are taking the children to Britain for experimental surgery or to take parts for transplant surgery.'

'People believe that?' I was astounded.

'You have to understand, Bevey,' Sister Jane explained, 'that the local people still can't understand why such an eminent specialist as Doctor Nigel would come all the way from Britain to see such worthless and hopeless cases. This gives them an easy to understand answer. We need your help in convincing them that the rumours are untrue.'

The Sisters proceeded to take me to all the relevant Government offices, the hospital and the police. Everywhere I was introduced as the woman who would take the children to Britain, be their guardian for the duration of their stay and return them after their treatment. I suppose that my being a plump, rosy-faced, calm and honest-looking person gave all these people the necessary reassurance because they issued us with everything we needed. I felt unusually comfortable in this role, as if it was natural, and I discovered I had a new confidence without being able to understand where it came from. Our final stop was the British Embassy and none of the officials there seemed to find any cause to make things difficult for us either.

All these people had genuine fears about the situation. The Romanians were worried by the rumours they had heard. The British Embassy was worried that once we had got them into England on medical grounds the children would then be put up for adoption. We promised we had no such intentions. They also needed to be careful that once in Britain the children would not become burdens on the taxpayer and that everything would be funded by private money. I was concerned as to where I would find the money but didn't let them see it. I could not allow Nigel's and the Sisters' plans to be abandoned simply for the cost of a few hospital beds and other expenses. Something would turn up.

The officials were reassured when I was able to show them evidence that the team we were beginning to build would donate their time free and at weekends. This was important to me too because I did not think it fair that any of our children should take the place of British children who had been on the NHS waiting list. St Gerrard's was going to have to make a charge for the beds; part of this would be paid for by Allison Hall and her pupils from de Lisle Catholic School, Loughborough who sacrificed their comic, sweet and pop money and did extra jobs to pay for Patreascu's bed. Allison had read in a magazine about a Romanian child who desperately needed surgery. After contacting many groups and being dismissed as some sort of hysterical do-gooder, she finally got to Jessica at Relief Fund for Romania who gave her my telephone number. I told Allison I didn't know the child in the magazine and she asked me about what I did. A couple of weeks later she told me she had spoken to her pupils and they all wanted to help Szuzannah and Patreascu. The Sisters were extremely moved that children in Britain should care about the poor and handicapped from another country.

I was very conscious that staying with the Sisters was like being a guest in their home and so I asked Sister Jane very politely if I might be permitted to have a shower.

'Of course, Bevey, whenever you like.'

'Where should I take it?' I asked.

'Oh, take it where we do our washing.'

'Where you do your washing?' I was a little unnerved by this suggestion, knowing that they did their washing in a bathtub which was a room on the way to the kitchens – a room used as a thoroughfare by everyone. 'Someone might come in,' I protested weakly, horrified at the thought of being seen naked by anyone, let alone nuns and unstable children.

'Do it late at night if you are worried,' Sister Jane dismissed my worries. 'I promise no one will come in.'

I duly waited until I thought the house was quiet and then crept in for my shower, wedging the door with a large sugar barrel. I still didn't have the nerve to do more than crouch under the water, but it felt good to be washing. When I heard the sugar barrel move across the floor and saw the door open a few inches I thought I might just have to faint. A hand came in through the crack and switched the light off, leaving me, clutching a towel to myself, in the dark.

'What is that mad Englishwoman doing?' Sister Jane wanted to know when she discovered that she had plunged me into darkness on her lights-out round.

'She was taking a shower where you told her,' the others said.

'But I told her to do it where we do the washing! I meant where we do washing for the children downstairs,' she said, 'where there is a proper shower.' I was too embarrassed to apologise directly, or even mention it at the time but we have laughed about it many times since.

The state of the children had improved so much since I had last seen them that I could hardly believe it. After every meal they were sat down on potties, a ritual that many of the volunteers thought was too draconian, but which I thought was much better than having them soiling themselves everywhere as they had done in the old days. They had all had their teeth seen to. There was a local dentist called Johnny who used to come to Mass and the Sisters asked him to have a look in the children's mouths. Most of them had breath so rancid that when I first arrived at Ungerini I used to think they had soiled themselves every time they breathed on me. Most of them had terrible abscesses and needed painful extractions without the help of much anaesthetic, bringing back fearful memories of the brutal way they were treated by the medical staff at Ungerini. One of the most difficult jobs which Russell had had to do while out there was to hold children down while the dentist worked on them. Johnny the Dentist is a lovely man who does his very best for the home with the limited materials he has. I very much wished I could find a British dentist whom I could persuade to come out and help Johnny, or at least to send supplies.

After returning to Britain in 1991 I seemed always to be on hectic 'scavenger hunts' with lists of urgently needed supplies to take with me on my visits. The Sisters do not ask for anything; it is not their way. They are, however, happy to accept whatever God sends to them: all sorts of things were offered by would-be donors, ranging from a wing mirror for the ancient Transit van to medical supplies or bras and knickers – 'pretty and colourful,' the Sisters told me, 'but not the breasties hanging out and bottie cleavage showing types please, Bevey'. Whenever I went out to Bacau I usually had at least ten large cases of stuff for the home and just a small holdall for myself – thankfully nothing was ever stolen, despite widespread need and people would always help me lift stuff on and off the trains.

During that first year other charities were very helpful, offering us room in their transport. One gave me half a lorry-load of space going out in the first week of every month, so I could fit in things like food, particularly fresh fruit and vegetables, medical supplies, clothes, therapy toys and toiletries. One of my earliest tasks had been to get each of the children a 'best outfit'. The Sisters didn't mind dressing the children in average clothes during the week, but their dream was for each child to have their own special outfit, with good shoes, for Mass and special occasions.

Whenever I went out in '92 and '93 I would fit in a visit to Ungerini and was always made to feel very welcome despite often arriving unannounced. The children would remember me and smile when they saw me, running up and wanting to hold my hand, smiling and shrieking their excitement, 'Bevey! Bevey!' All the workers went wild too and it was good to feel they remembered me with happiness. Not very much seemed to change there after I left. They did build a new laundry room which brought a little light into the corridor downstairs, and they built a nice house for the British volunteers to live in until the time came for them to hand back the work to the Romanians. The corridors had murals painted on the walls and each room has a sink with running water, and a cupboard for clothes and shoes.

I was saddened, though, to see that most of the children were still sat on one or two beds in each room or in their cots. The lack of occupational therapy was just the same as when I arrived.

CHAPTER TEN

Bringing the First Children Out

*

When John had first heard that I was planning to bring two floor children, or 'bottom shufflers' as they were affectionately known, to Britain on my own he was aghast. 'You can't do that,' he said. 'They are bound to be frightened and need special attention. Then there is the luggage and all the documents. Supposing one of them needs the loo, who will look after the other one? Would you like me to come and help you?' For a few seconds I resented the idea of him coming. At that stage Russell hadn't been out to Romania yet and I was still reluctant to mix my two lives. I thought it might spoil the mystique of my experiences in Romania for me if John had been there too.

I was desperate for John to like Romania, the people and especially the children. I felt like I wanted to show off something I was proud of. I really wanted him to feel the same way about the people as I did. Everyone I spoke to who knew what we were doing told me that they were praying for us and for Szuzannah and Patreascu. I got a lot of comfort from this news. I was beginning to find that if I prayed things tended to go right. At first I tried to rationalise this, telling myself that it was because I was taking time to stop and think that I had a clear head and made better decisions. I can't say that I totally believed at that stage, but I couldn't totally discount it either. There just seemed to be too many coincidences as our plans fell into shape, like the Wandsworth prisoners coming up with a cheque for our children's airfares just when we needed it. I wondered if I was finding faith after all these years. I had so many questions and was still too concerned about seeming dim to ask the obvious things. I was thirsty for knowledge but had no one to ask.

Eventually all the necessary documents were ready and we set off in March 1992. We were going to be arriving in Bucharest too late for the evening train to Bacau and would have to spend the night there. I contacted Florin and asked him to meet us and purchase our rail tickets in advance.

A friend of John's, Roger Phillips, who, along with his family, had already been very helpful in filling relief lorries for us, came along to handle our luggage, leaving us free to look after Szuzannah and Patreascu. We accepted the offer gratefully.

On our arrival Florin insisted on taking us on a tour of Bucharest, and told us a lot about recent Romanian history. I wished I had met him when I first arrived in the country. John and Roger were surprised by the hotel, expecting something less grand, and by how many staff there were, none of whom seemed to be willing to do anything. The porters didn't even bother to help us with our bags.

On the way to the station the next day John was fascinated by the sight of the crowds of peasants with their livestock, and horrified by all the beggars and street children everywhere, some looking as young as three or four.

'They are the sewer children,' Florin explained. 'They have either been abandoned by their families or they have escaped from the orphanages. They live underground. When the central hot-water plant is working they huddle around it under their rags and bits of cardboard. When the plant is not working many of them freeze to death.'

'How can the authorities see these children and do nothing?' John wanted to know. His face was white with shock and I could see his eyes were moist. By now the children were surrounding us, holding out their hands and trying to cuddle us. Some were trying to talk.

'Are you my mama?'

'Are you my papa?'

Romanian people shouted at them to 'leave the foreigners alone'.

Suddenly one of the children shouted something and they all rushed off, returning with chunks of bread and pieces of salami which two elderly but sprightly nuns were dishing out with mugs of milk. We went over to talk to them and they explained that this was the only food and drink most of the children received all day.

'We are going back to Britain for two weeks' retreat,' they told us, 'so we wanted to make sure they had one last meal before we went to the airport.'

'What will happen to them while you are away?' we asked.

'Some of them will surely perish,' the nuns said sadly.

'Are you from the Order of the Sisters of Charity of St Paul?' I asked, remembering the nuns at St Gerrard's.

'Yes,' they smiled sweetly, 'we are. We were both called from retirement because our Sisters heard about the sewer children. Our work is no more than a drop in the ocean, but someone had to begin somewhere.'

Meeting them was quite a coincidence.

Dom Patreascu met us at Bacau station and drove us to Mother Teresa's. As the gates were opened there were suddenly children all around us. The noise was incredible and I looked anxiously across at John and Roger. John was smiling shyly at Sister Jane, who was introducing all the Sisters and children to him. They were all crying 'Johnny' excitedly, recognising him from the photos I had shown them and stories I had told about my husband back in England. They were fascinated by his height and his width and they all wanted to hold his hand or swing on his jacket.

The Sisters quietened the children down and they began to sing, 'We love you, love you, Johnny. We love you, love you, Johnny. We love you, love you Johnny, with all our hearts.' John could not stop himself from weeping. He had expected to be standing in the background while the children welcomed me; he had not expected to be so warmly embraced.

We discovered that Sister Fabiana had moved to the Bucharest house. I was disappointed not to see her and to think John wouldn't meet her. Had we known she was there in advance we could have visited while we were in the city but by then it was too late.

I slept in the girls' dormitory and John in the children's dining room, on a mattress which Tante Magda, one of the helpers, insisted on making up for him each evening and putting away again in the morning.

The children all took to John immediately, thundering past me to get to him whenever they spotted us. They particularly liked it when he took his teeth out for them. None of them had ever seen false teeth before and they were amazed. To this day the poor man has to drop his dentures down each time we visit and the children and workers rush off in all directions, shrieking and screaming with mock fear and delight. The workers love it when there is someone new who doesn't know John and he can give them a shock with his teeth.

The workers have hard lives, working all the time at the orphanage or their homes, only eating what they have grown themselves, drawing their water from deep wells, cooking over fires which they have to light with sticks they have previously had to chop. There is not much time for leisure or laughter and I think that's why they appreciate the bit of light relief which visitors like John bring – something different, something fun. John had a huge snowball fight one day – him versus the workers and children – which they all enjoyed, and the helpers were amazed to meet a man who was willing to do 'women's work' like washing up, making tea or helping the children. Whenever they saw him doing such chores they would rush to take over, not believing his assurances that if was quite normal for him.

Sister Ida became cross with him for picking up the children so much. 'Who,' she wanted to know, 'is going to pick them up when you have gone home, John? You would be helping them more if you encouraged them to be independent and walk for themselves, that boy you are carrying is nineteen!' John only needed telling once and from then on he was the most successful of all of us at getting the children onto their feet when they needed physiotherapy.

At first John was nervous about getting the children out of their cots – their legs and arms were so deformed he was afraid of hurting them. But he was so gentle with them that soon they were crying out to be lifted every time they saw him, wanting him to play with them.

At first he kept a respectful distance from the older girls, having been told how they had suffered at the hands of men in the past, but soon they came to realise that this gentle giant wouldn't do them any harm and began to play football and join in the games which he proved so good at organising. One boy of eleven, a worker's child, was able to talk to John immediately, crossing the language barrier as they swopped footballers' names. John asked him if he had a football of his own. The boy looked amazed.

'He says,' Sister Jane translated, 'I could never afford a football – only rich people and foreigners can afford them.'

'It is good for our children to get to know another man,' Sister

Jane said approvingly. 'There are too many women around them all the time.'

As well as providing an extra pair of hands wherever and whenever needed, the Sisters asked me to start doing some speech therapy with the children.

The Sisters could not understand why the children were not beginning to speak and wanted me to help. I started speech sessions with Alena. She had become a firm favourite with Tante Magda and it was noticeable that because of the extra little bit of attention she was coming out of her shell amazingly quickly. Then I moved on to a group of five of the children. I used to get them all to pull faces and then we would begin to put out our tongues, to the left and to the right – anything that would exercise facial muscles. Of course it must have looked hilarious to anyone watching and we all laughed at each other. Hearing all the noise many more of the children joined us until I was sat in the middle of a horseshoe of chairs with most of the children trying to sing and speak. I didn't know whether it was the correct way to encourage speech – but it was the only way I could think of.

I called each child by name, clicking my fingers to get their attention if they did not show a reaction or look at me. We practised animal noises – I would ask them what each picture was and then what noise the animal made – and clapped rhythms. I thought that maybe if they got the idea of copying this then they might copy speech. We sang scales; we sang selections from *The Sound of Music*, from *Annie* and those scales. Pavarotti it was most definitely not – but it was fun and most importantly it kept the children cheerfully occupied.

We also threw ourselves into the day to day work of the Sisters, helping to unload a forty-foot lorry which arrived one day, forming a human chain in a blizzard of snow to get everything down into the cellars below the house. The Sisters had heard that there had been terrible floods up in the mountains, destroying all the crops, and so John, Roger and Dom Patreascu took the ancient Transit van out to distribute foodstuff, skidding up the mountain roads, loaded down with clothes and toys and sacks and boxes of milk powder, powdered soup and biscuits.

'The villagers were so excited to see us,' John marvelled on his return. 'People calling out to one another and rushing out of their cottages. We ended up with a crowd of about two hundred around us. They were so careful not to leave anyone out. One small boy was sent to run right across the valley to fetch an old lady. When she came she was walking through the snow with no shoes. By that time all the shoes had gone. The look on her face was so pitiful I hunted through all the bits and pieces left over and found a brand new pair of football boots, studs and all. She politely, but very firmly, snatched them out of my hand. Her face lit up with glee as she sat down on the tailgate of the van and pulled them on. She paraded proudly around, showing how the good the studs were for gripping in the ice. The villagers all applauded her as she danced about.'

'Your visit will be talked about for years to come,' Dom Patreascu told him. 'They will pass on stories about the day the foreigner came with gifts from people in Britain who had never met them. It makes them all feel special, just for a moment.'

Dom Patreascu explained that these people have nothing but all look out for each other. If someone is wealthy enough to own a pig, then when that pig is killed for its meat the family will make sure that the elderly, or perhaps a widow with young children, all get a share. Nothing is wasted.

On a visit to a local school, John found eight pupils shivering in a freezing cold room, watching the teacher writing on a blackboard which had long since lost its black. There were no books and there was no heating. The teacher told them, in broken English, how proud the village was to have a school because it meant these children might one day be able to get jobs and earn money to help their poverty-stricken families. John found some books, pens and paper in the van and gave them to the teacher. There were also a few toys left which John handed over.

'Excuse me,' the teacher asked shyly, 'my wife has just had a new baby. Do you think you have anything for a baby?' John remembered seeing a Fisher Price Activity Centre which he gave to the man who was as thrilled as if he had received a thousand pounds.

When John met Patreascu he was initially rather concerned at the amount of noise he was making. John is quite self-conscious and never likes to draw attention to himself. Patreascu had no such inhibitions and still liked to whine at the top of his voice all the time. John decided that he would have to do something about this if he was going to have to sit on a plane for hours with the boy. Every time Patreascu grizzled at him. John would grizzle back in just the same tone of voice. To begin with this puzzled the boy, then interested him enough to test it a few times and finally it bored him. He stopped whinging for the first time in his life.

Sometimes Patreascu would just sit, so deeply withdrawn within himself that someone might drop something right next to him and he would not flinch or show any reaction. I wondered if he might be partially deaf, and that perhaps that was why he wasn't speaking. Perhaps whinging was the only sound he could hear and imitate. Years of lying flat on his back and tied up might have affected his vocal chords. I was also beginning to appreciate even more the importance of the children eating and chewing proper food. It was difficult to persuade them to try anything that didn't have a smooth, puddingy consistency. If the food had any bits in it they would instantly spit it out.

On Patreascu's and Szuzannah's last evening before departing to the UK, we had a magnificent party with lots of little fairy cakes and trifles made with the ingredients I always brought with me from England. One of my claims to fame in Bacau is that I taught them all to dance the hokey-cokey, which we did that evening until I thought I was going to drop with exhaustion.

The Sisters made up a bed for Patreascu and Szuzannah in the back of the Transit van, with plenty of blankets as the temperature had dropped to minus 20. At 11 p.m. they roused the two children and dressed them, but all the others woke as well and straight away we were surrounded by well-wishers. The Sisters had been saving their very best clothes for this trip so that the children would not look out of place in Britain, but for some reason they had Patreascu dressed in three pairs of shocking pink tights, two pairs of trousers and several jumpers. Apparently they were frightened he would be cold shuffling on the floor in Britain. On the way out through the hall the Sisters paused in front of their statue of Mary and sang a little adoration which was very moving indeed. We all cried because the Sisters were so sad to see Patreascu and Szuzannah go from the home. They gave us their blessing and suddenly all my fears welled up; would the children travel well, would the operations be all right and, above all, would they be happy? The day before we had had a special Mass and Szuzannah had wept afterwards. She was enjoying all the extra attention but was also sad at leaving the Sisters and workers whom she had grown to know, love and, above all, to trust.

'Bevey,' Sister Jane said as we prepared to go out into the cold, 'I entrust our children to your most beautiful care.' All the workers held hand-made garlands above the children's heads, their faces streaming with tears because they feared for them so far from home and with the prospect of painful surgery ahead. I felt all my fears evaporate and I knew that everything would be all right. As I gazed at the statue of Our Holy Lady of Fatima, I felt such confidence. She almost seemed to smile at me, but I dismissed it as imagination and over-tiredness. If it wasn't that, I must have been cracking up!

The Sisters were also very concerned for Szuzannah's moral welfare because, although she had the figure of a grown woman, she was still an innocent. They were terrified that she would become pregnant in Britain, despite the fact that I assured them the nuns at St Gerrard's Hospital in Birmingham would keep a strict eye on her. As the van turned out of the gates I shouted back to Sister Jane, 'Start knitting – for twins!'

'If that happens,' she shouted back, 'Szuzannah and the twins shall come to live with you and John.'

Little Sister Ida, the four-feet-six Indian ball of energy, came with us on the six-hour drive to Bucharest to help keep Patreascu happy. She prayed all the way, only stopping to give directions like, 'Our father, who art in heaven – take a left here – hallowed be thy name.' She also sang, so compellingly that we all joined in. It was a very spiritual time, despite the fact that we were driving through blizzards all night and Szuzannah was continually sick. Patreascu had been given a sedative but it didn't seem to be having any effect on him: his eyes were wide open and he seemed to be taking an interest in everything that was going on around him. When we arrived at the airport we waited in the van while the authorities tried to find us wheelchairs. Failing in their search they brought out an army ambulance instead. They didn't want us to walk through the main area of the airport in case the sight of the children frightened or upset other passengers.

As we loaded the children into the ambulance a young soldier absentmindedly dropped the tailgate down onto Patreascu's legs. I could see what was about to happen and managed to put my arm out to protect him, but unfortunately the gate came down on my head which frightened the children. I am usually such a wimp and I wanted to cry, or at least lie down, but I had to appear to be quite brave about it. I could really have done with a few stitches. After we had been driven round the airport I was told by the soldiers to get out of the ambulance. I was terrified to leave the children but they insisted and much to their annoyance I refused to go away, hovering about outside, determined not to let them out of my sight as we worked our way towards the departure gate.

I felt very real pains in my heart when I saw Sister Ida with Patreascu. She loved him so dearly and knew that once he left for Britain he was bound to be away for many months, by which time her three years in Romania would be over and she would have moved to her next posting. In the early hours of Monday morning, standing in slushy snow, the wind howling round us, she said her final farewells to him. I looked into her eyes and saw a momentary flicker of pain. She blinked away the tears and said, 'Now, Bevey, you take him to Mass and keep up his religious instruction, and always remember this little prayer, "Mary, Mother of Jesus Christ, be a mother to Patreascu now." Use it whenever he needs it.'

I hadn't warmed to Patreascu during the past four days, but John, who had him on his lap on the plane most of the way back, said that he agreed with Sister Ida and thought Patreascu was brighter than everyone else believed. I've always found John to be a good judge of character, so I looked forward to seeing what would happen in England – perhaps with new surroundings and more stimulation Patreascu would learn to speak and become a bit more sociable. It would be good if we could return him, walking, as a role model for the others. We had been worried about how the flight would go for him because he had a habit of doing some pretty wild gruntings, but he seemed to be enjoying every minute of it, despite having been wide awake all night. The only time he let out a very loud noise was when he unexpectedly discovered the joys of real orange juice for the first time and swallowed it with a long moan of pleasure. He ate all the food that was put in front of him without a murmur.

Szuzannah found her first flight very frightening. I started singing, 'Oh, Szuzannah' to calm her and John joined in. Other passengers turned to look; they must have thought we were some sort of weird religious cult but it did the trick and she was fine after that.

As the plane landed I had Patreascu on my lap and told him what we were seeing through the window. I noticed his eyes shone when he saw cars and he made little excited noises which were a marvellous change from all the grizzling. Even if the children show no response I always speak to them as if we are having a two-way conversation and I chatted on to him about everything we were seeing.

An ambulance organised by Wandsworth Prison was waiting on the tarmac for us at Stansted Airport, complete with a couple of teddy bears which the prisoners had made. Roger, who had been a wonderful help throughout the journey, left for home after saying a sad farewell to the children. Poor John had to go straight to London for an urgent business meeting, so I headed off towards Birmingham and the hospital with the children. It had been arranged that I would stay with them for the first few days to help them settle into their new lives. A fine one I was to look after the children – I was the only one who was travel-sick on the final leg of the journey.

Szuzannah was sixteen by now, but she still had the mental age of a very young child, and there was little hope of progressing much further. She suffers from cerebral palsy and for many years her legs had been bound to her chest and had been broken in that position. I had first seen her at Ungerini during one of the frantic feeding sessions which the older children had to endure. I remember watching her on all fours, desperately scooping up whatever food she could find. She had been particularly badly treated because she was a gypsy. The Sisters were the first people to really be kind to her. Even the gypsy workers were cruel to the gypsy children. Most gypsy girls ended up working in the streets as prostitutes or cigarette sellers, the Sisters having to treat many of the locals for venereal diseases.

Many of the British workers hadn't liked Szuzannah because she would sulk if you didn't hold her hand when she asked, but I was fond of her despite her moodiness and I suppose it was because I had shown her friendship that she had saved me from that punch. Many of the children became extraordinarily loyal and protective towards anyone who showed them any friendship.

It was only after she had arrived with the Sisters that Szuzannah had started trying to speak. Though her Romanian was very basic, she had a little English too by the time she got to Birmingham. She became a great favourite of the nurses at St Gerrard's who loved to spoil her. Both children had the most wonderful nursing care while they were in hospital and none of the miracles which happened subsequently would have been possible without all the people who worked so patiently with them.

Szuzannah and Patreascu were initially in an open room at the very end of a ward until Patreascu found a little push-along train which he pulled himself up onto. He was spotted setting off down the corridor toward the X-ray department and the chapel. It was decided they should be moved to a room at the other end of the ward, next to a room where a priest, Father Gerrard, was recovering from heart surgery. That way, if Patreascu made another bid for freedom he would have to go past the nurses' office and all the side wards. I found it very hard when the time came for me to leave them there and go home to John. I knew they would be in perfect hands because the Sisters and nurses had already gone to great lengths to make them feel loved and at home. Their room was full of toys and the nurses would often spend their spare moments in with them. Patreascu didn't respond well to the nurses' efforts, but Szuzannah was beginning to flourish and showing her enjoyment at all the attention. She wept uncontrollably when I had to leave and clung to me as if I was abandoning her. I worried all the way home on the train and as soon as I got in I phoned the nurses. They told me she was fine, sitting up and trying to do some colouring. I was partially relieved by this news but still very much looked forward to seeing her again at the weekend.

The only problem was that Szuzannah was very good at getting everyone else to do everything for her and it was hard for the nurses to always remember that she needed to be encouraged to do things for herself. She also treated Patreascu badly, beating him furiously if she thought he was stealing her limelight and shouting and screaming at him. Although she was my favourite of the two I did feel sorry for Patreascu. Szuzannah seemed to see it as her job to keep an eye on him in place of Sister Ida, but sadly she took as her role models the women at Ungerini, not the more enlightened Sisters.

At the same time Szuzannah often showed a very gentle and caring side to her nature; she had a great capacity for helping with the elderly and respite care patients. She would make sure their tea was cooled down and then tenderly help them sip it, carefully wiping any spills off them. She was never harsh with these poor patients, never raised her voice. Her instincts told her exactly what to do and with these little kindnesses she seemed to satisfy her own need for someone to depend on her, fulfilling her hunger to love and be loved. It was beautiful to watch.

When John and I suggested taking Szuzannah home for week-ends, Nigel Dwyer was delighted because, apart from walking, the greatest gift we can give the children is their independence. It is always tempting to satisfy our own needs rather than theirs by doing everything for them, and it is certainly much quicker but they really need to learn to manage on their own. One of the main reasons for getting them upright and off their bottoms is so that they can get themselves to the toilet and clean up after themselves. Those sorts of things make all the difference to a child's self-esteem and self-respect.

Getting her from Birmingham to Milton Keynes could be quite an adventure. I would finish work at the Abbey at 5 p.m. on Friday evenings, get a taxi and then a train and then another taxi to the hospital. We would then take another taxi back to the station or, if I was lucky, Matron would give us a lift to save me a bit of money. Szuzannah would be guffawing happily in double legplasters and I would have our Intercity seats booked in advance. Matron, a British Rail porter and I would then have to winch Szuzannah onboard because of her double hip dysplasia. She would invariably play to the gallery and get the giggles as we tried to straighten her out. Both her feet were turned in and, because Nigel had operated on one leg, there was a danger the cerebral palsy would make the other leg and foot turn in more. So it was necessary to plaster both legs in order to try to straighten them. Nigel did consider doing both her hips but there was no guarantee that this would work. Because of the length of time her hips had been out of place, the operations could have led to terrible problems with arthritis later in life.

We would find our seats in the carriage, usually in the dining car where she had room to stretch her legs out, and British Rail would not start the train until she was seated. The carriage would always be full of business people on their way home after a week's work and they would start out attempting to hide from us behind their newspapers while Szuzannah tried to make eye contact with them. Suddenly she would bang her crooked fist down on the table with the most enormous explosion, making all the cutlery and newspapers rattle in surprise.

'Hey,' she would shout at them, 'not beautiful!' And she would insist that they all crossed themselves and said grace before they took another mouthful of anything.

By June 1992 Nigel got her calipers so she was able to get up off her bottom and walk for the first time. Her gait was very strange, with wobbly legs and bottom crouched down, but it was a long way away from bottom shuffling and looking up at people from the floor like a sad old dog hoping for a pat.

At one stage Nigel became so frustrated with the nurses in Birmingham who let her use a zimmer frame, instead of the crutches she was meant to be using, that he threw the frame through the window. 'Lucky there was an open window for you,' I said to him afterwards.

'I didn't f......know it was open,' he growled. Many times he would shriek things like, 'Nurse, do you have your dinner in bed, chopped up and fed to you? No, so why the f...ing hell should Szuzannah?' Hearing these outbursts, Szuzannah would crook her finger and say, 'Naughty, naughty Dr Nigel!'

The first thing we did when Szuzannah came home to us was to put the wheelchair away in the dining room. The next was to get her crutches out. At first she was terrified of the dogs, telling us she had been bitten at Ungerini and how the women had laughed at her pain and fear, but she quickly grew to love Moss and Misty, and Sweeper the cat. Often when I popped in to check she was all right before going to bed I would find Szuzannah curled up in bed in a space the size of a mouse, surrounded by the animals who were luxuriating in this normally forbidden treat. It also made it easier to get her out on walks – if the dogs were going she wanted to be there too. She would make them shake her hand before giving them biscuits from her mouth, her fears completely conquered.

The physiotherapist told me they wanted her to stand as much as possible, so I would give her bowls of vegetables to peel and things to wash and dry up, conveniently forgetting that we had a dishwasher machine. We were working towards helping her to lose her fear of being upright and at the same time I hoped she would show the people in Romania that it was possible to give the children little jobs to do. I had to teach her to close the door when she was on the toilet or in the bath, as John or Russell might be about and I thought it would give her more dignity. She also had very bad breath, like all the children, and I thought she might benefit from some teeth-cleaning lessons. So I decided I would clean mine with her so that she could copy me. I was just about to put the brush in my mouth when she shrieked, 'Bevey, close the door! Johnny or Russell may see you!' I decided not to bother to explain but shut the door and thanked her for reminding me.

She loved to bake cakes with elaborate and distinctive decorations. The best of the batch always went to the dogs, followed by Johnny, then Russell, then me. I knew my place.

Every time I went to see her in the hospital after the operations she used to like to play the same game. She would pretend to begin her journey home with plenty of action; packing, getting on the train and the plane. She would then imagine arriving back with the Sisters in Bacau, her case full of presents for everyone. Then I would have to pretend to be each one of her friends and all the carers in turn – it was not a short game. She would knock on the door and one by one they would come to see who it was. Each of them would look down to the floor but would be unable to see who it was because now she was standing. They would call out, 'Szuzannah, where are you? We cannot see you,' which would result in her becoming helpless with laugher.

Eventually the friends would become so exasperated they would call out for Sister Jane who would also be unable to see her on the floor. Sister Jane would then proceed to look on and under all the beds (with a great deal of overacting on my part) and then suddenly Szuzannah would say, 'But, Sister Jane, look up here, I am tall and walking and it is very beautiful up here!' Whereupon Sister Jane would shriek with delight and say, 'But, Szuzannah, I can hardly believe it is you, you are so tall and beautiful now!'

I'm sure the people at the hospital thought I was completely potty but it was a good way of talking about home, reminding her of her friends, and it gave her a boost and practical encouragement at the thought of being able to return and show off her new abilities. We were very fortunate that Joyce, the Assistant Matron, took a great shine to Szuzannah and had her home for several weekends. She also spent a great deal of time with her while on duty and it was a terrible wrench for her when Szuzannah had to return home. It was lovely for Szuzannah to have someone she was special to.

Sister Maria, the physiotherapist at St Gerrard's, would tell us what she wanted us to try and encourage the children to do. She was a great inspiration, spending hours coaxing and encouraging Szuzannah into walking, never giving up or despairing even though Szuzannah's twisted feet began to look as if they would never be straight. Sister Maria was also wonderful with Patreascu. Firstly in his wheelchair and then with the aid of a little zimmer frame he used to come down in the lift by himself, dark glasses on, and suddenly appear in Sister Maria's office, where they would share a cup of tea and a biscuit.

Patreascu and Szuzannah would come home to Milton Keynes with me and John on alternate weekends and we had to do lots of physiotherapy with them. I tried to make it fun, spending hours walking backwards, pointing a broom handle to where Szuzannah's left foot should be, then her right foot, and making a great pantomime of bumping into things because I wasn't looking where I was going.

My Romanian vocabulary was pretty small but I would encourage her to get up and walk by saying, 'On the floor is for dogs. Try and stand and be up here. It is very beautiful to be upright, you know.' If I have any talent it is a gift for getting kids to believe they can do things, making things that might be a chore seem fun.

Finally Szuzannah was upright and, with the aid of calipers on both legs, walking. Her boots posed a huge problem. The pull of her spasticity meant that no matter how tight they were, her feet would force their way out and she would be walking on the backs of the boots. We tried everything, but to no avail. The fact that she had confounded the doubters by dragging herself off the floor at all, however, gave us hope that she could overcome this next hurdle as well. We decided that although it was tempting to keep Szuzannah in Britain as company for Patreascu, she might well progress more quickly in her normal surroundings. She was missing the Sisters, her friends and her favourite worker, Doamna Anna and wanted to go home. She'd been away for ten months in all. Many people in England thought I was very hard to take her back. I kept explaining that she was not going back to an institute but to a loving home which she missed, but I could see they were not convinced.

Joyce was very concerned that the sudden separation would be too much for Szuzannah and decided to travel with us, bringing her friend Val, too.

Szuzannah wept when she said goodbye to Patreascu and all the staff at the hospital. She had been attending Brays Road School and her teacher, Lucy Danyi, organised a special farewell. The most painful parting was from Moss and Misty; her tears plopped onto their furry coats as she hugged them. The Christmas season was starting and whenever I heard carols being sung I felt very sad that we would not be sharing the festivities with Szuzannah.

Maricica, who had been in Norwich short-term, undergoing surgery on a very bad cleft palette, was also ready to go home. Helen Wilkinson, whom she had been staying with, thought it would be a great idea if we went back together. Helen had offered help with children with ear, nose and throat problems – and the services of an ENT surgeon. We all met at Stansted Airport, Maricica rushing up to me, leaping up and clamping her legs round my waist, chattering excitedly about going home. She was a little disappointed that John wouldn't take his teeth out at the airport.

Janet Stevens had warned me about Maricica's flight out. Apparently she had been so frightened of flying she had pulled her jumper right over her head, only coming out to be sick. Armed with this knowledge, I had plenty of plastic bags and Wet Ones. Szuzannah cried bitterly when it was time to say goodbye to John and Russell.

Because we were such a large group we tied yellow ribbons on our luggage so we could recognise it more easily at Bucharest Airport. As we came through Immigration and Customs I noticed a man disappearing carrying a large case with a yellow ribbon on.

'Oh, don't worry,' Joyce assured me. 'That nice man offered to take it for me,' pointing to an unshaved old gypsy man.

'I'll bet he did.' I said. 'Look, get the girls on the pavement, please, keep the luggage together with them. I'll be right back,' and I tore off after the man, only just retrieving the case.

I staggered back with it to find a huge crowd milling around our group. One of our number had taken their dollars out and was counting them. People were offering to change dollars into lei, taxi drivers were trying to pull us and our luggage into their cars and suddenly, in the distance, I saw the glorious sight of the Sisters' orange Transit van.

We sang all the way from Bucharest to Bacau, finally arriving at ten at night. Joyce had kindly paid for herself, Val and Szuzannah to have one last night together at the Hotel Dumbrava, so that they would be fresh when they arrived at Mother Teresa's. Unfortunately, when we arrived at the hotel they had given the room away and were completely full. Joyce seemed so disappointed that I suggested we try some of the other hotels. By now it was 12.30. Thankfully the Hotel Moldova had a room to spare – but their lift wasn't working. So we winched Szuzannah and all her luggage up five flights of stairs, gamely helped by the hotel porter. Once I was sure they were happy and secure, Maricica and I raced downstairs, jumped into the van and headed for Mother Teresa's. We tip-toed into the girls' dormitory and crept up to the beds which had been left ready for us.

'Cica! Bevey!' shrieked Valentina from her bed at the very end of the long room as she leapt out and trampolined down the dormitory from bed to bed. Soon everyone was up, touching Maricica, talking to her and kissing her. I felt happy, but exhausted and keen to catch a few hours' sleep. Just three hours later Sister Ida woke me and I saw Maricica was already making the beds, desperately wanting to get back into her comfortable and secure routine. All the children were up and the atmosphere was electric. Maricica had only been away for two months but Szuzannah had been away for ten. Everywhere there were children blowing up balloons or colouring cards or helping to make garlands. The Sisters could hardly contain their excitement. The whole place was alive – they couldn't wait to see Szuzannah.

I had arranged that we would go to collect her at nine. When we drew up at the gates of the home we could see Valentina, who was Szuzannah's best friend, bobbing up and down on the other side impatiently. When the gates were opened every child was out there, with all the Sisters and the carers and the neighbours. There were hundred of balloons, a big banner and flower garlands. They were singing, banging tambourines, beating drums, shouting and screaming – the whole scene was vibrant, like a tribal welcome in some remote African village.

Joyce was overcome with emotion and the realisation that Szuzannah was home for good hit her forcefully. She wept and clung onto her, hugging her as if for the last time. I was afraid I was going to be overcome with emotion, too, so I opened the van door and gently pulled Szuzannah away, allowing her to be engulfed by her family. Szuzannah's favour carer, Doamna Anna, was weeping very loudly and everyone wanted to touch her, to see her legs in their calipers and to kiss her. I was able to blend into the background while I tried to recover my composure. I could see that she didn't need me, that I had done my job. She was not dependent on me and I felt very proud.

The welcome turned into a party for the evening with Joyce and Val making cakes for everyone and me making trifles and leading the hokey-cokey. Sister Jane even gave a rare display of Indian dancing which she had enjoyed before she became a nun.

The Sisters couldn't understand why Szuzannah's Romanian had improved while she had been away, and then it dawned on us. As I have a small Romanian vocabulary I tend to repeat the same words, especially the verbs. I had used them all the time in conversation with Szuzannah. She had, of course, been having plenty of one-to-one conversations in both English and Romanian during her stay in Britain, and her confidence and eye contact had improved dramatically. The differences in her behaviour did not go unnoticed by the Sisters and served to reinforce their belief and encouragement of the workers to 'talk to the children as if they are your family'.

Joyce Val and Helen wanted to see Ungerini while we were there so a few days later we drove up the winding roads in a thick fog. When we arrived they were as appalled as I had been by my first sight of the place. I did my best to explain that things were better than they had been but they were deeply shocked. By the time we came out the fog had grown impenetrable and we had an eerie journey back to Mother Teresa's, forced to continue because we were due to leave in the early hours of the morning for our flight back to England. There was a deep silence in the van, each of us lost in terrible thoughts. Joyce's impending and probably final parting from Szuzannah was weighing her down and even in the darkness of the van I could see her lip trembling. We finally made it back. Joyce said a very moving and sad farewell to Szuzannah and went back to the hotel for a few hours' sleep. When it was time for us to leave, Szuzannah wept and I felt a huge wobbler coming on. My eyes filled with tears and I had to put on an act of being mega-jolly, walking around with my hands on my hips doing exaggerated Rik Mayall impressions. 'Well, aren't we a load of silly billies!'

From the moment we left Szuzannah became an expert on walking and told everyone that, 'On the floor was for dogs. Being upright is beautiful – Bevey says so!'

CHAPTER ELEVEN

Patreascu's Ordeals

*

Once Nigel returned to Britain he sent me detailed medical reports and asked me to go up to Birmingham to discuss them.

'Patreascu,' Nigel explained, 'has had polio in one leg. The other leg is withered through having been tied, knees to chest, for so many years and not used. The leg affected by polio is even more withered and is also six inches shorter than the other one; the muscles are completely stunted.'

He then, with the aid of detailed diagrams, showed me what he intended to do. Patreascu was going to have an operation to lengthen his shorter leg and was probably going to have to spend a total of a year in hospital.

'After enduring all that,' I asked, 'will the legs be equal and will he be able to walk?'

'Of course he ruddy well will – I wouldn't put the dear chap through all that if the end result wasn't walking!'

I was wondering how Patreascu was going to cope with such prolonged pain. As it was he whinged if anyone even lightly touched his stunted leg, or if another child just came near him. What would he be like after all this?

'Although the leg muscles are all wasted,' Nigel went on, 'the nerves are all there and will be highly sensitive to pain, probably more than average.'

Poor child, I thought to myself. But what were the alternatives? A life of shuffling about on his bottom? A life of never being able to get out?

Nigel estimated the operation was going to take five and a half hours. 'You can come and watch,' he told me cheerfully.

'Oh, no.' I was horrified. 'I'd be sick. I've never been good around anything to do with blood or medical matters. I can't even watch operations on television.' I hoped that would close the subject.

'For God's sake, woman, I tramped all the way to Romania for you,' he roared. 'The least you can do is watch an itsy bitsy operation for me.'

'Okay.' I took a deep breath and tried to block the details of what was about to happen from my mind. I didn't want to upset him and I was flattered that he felt he wanted my support in the operating theatre.

'Good,' he grinned. 'I've invented a new anaesthetic, specially for you.'

'That won't be necessary,' I told him sniffily. 'I'm quite capable of walking out if I feel it is too much.'

'It's not to calm you down, woman, it's to stop you ruddy well talking while I'm working.'

Nigel said that the operating theatre at St Gerrard's was not sophisticated enough for an operation this complex. 'BUPA Parkway Hospital in Solihull could handle it,' he told me. 'Why don't you write to them and ask?'

'Wouldn't the letter be more impressive coming from you?' I ventured.

'Look – ' he sounded exasperated ' – you must have realised by now, the persuasion bit is what you are good at!' I hadn't realised, but I wrote anyway. I composed a long letter explaining all about Patreascu, and the hospital management agreed to give everything absolutely free. All the staff then said they would donate their time and stay on for whatever extra hours were needed. If we had been presented with a bill it would probably have been around £20,000.

I shyly offered to stay with Patreascu again as his 'mum' because he knew me and it would be less traumatic to have me doing his painful dressings after surgery than a stranger. I was rather afraid that I might be attaching too much importance to my presence, but Nigel was ecstatic at the idea, having hardly dared to ask me as he knew I was on annual leave from Abbey National and running out of time. I still felt very squeamish about the idea of attending the operation but I didn't dare to say anything else to Nigel.

The morning of the surgery I got Patreascu up and he had a long, luxurious bath. I put him into the sweet little operating gown they had left for me. A nurse came to keep an eye on him whilst I went to get ready myself. By this time he was fairly relaxed by the pre-med, so the nurse didn't worry when she was called away for a few minutes. When I returned to his room I discovered that Patreascu had locked himself inside. We tried talking to him through the door but there was no response. The only thing we could do was take the door of its hinges. By the time we had found a carpenter to do that Patreascu in his terror had crapped from one end of the room to the other. It was like a stable and I had to clean up everything before we could take him through to the theatre. Retching and heaving rather loudly as I tried to clean off the little push-along train he had been sitting on whilst evacuating, it did occur to me that there were better ways to spend a Saturday morning.

The sight of the trolley terrified him because he couldn't work out what was happening. He didn't understand enough words for me to be able to calm him or explain that it was all going to be okay.

'It won't work,' I told the theatre staff. 'I'll have to carry him.'

He was wearing a pair of dark glasses which he loved and they covered the tears in his eyes. He also had Russell's Walkman over his ears as I carried him down to the prep room. There he finally allowed me to lay him down on the trolley, squeezing my hand tightly in his little fingers.

The Sisters in Romania were going to start a special Mass at exactly the time Nigel was due to make his first incision. He had been delighted by this news but told me, 'Tell them to begin an hour earlier. I want them up to full steam by the time I start!'

To my utmost surprise I found the operation fascinating and managed to stay upright throughout. Sister Valerie, a theatre nurse and one of the nuns, had come with us from St Gerrard's as an observer and she gave me a whispered commentary at the moments when Nigel was concentrating too hard to talk. Once Patreascu was fully anaesthetised and I could prise his fingers loose from my hand, I stood back, Nigel stepped forward and they started cutting. He then took his bone hammer and broke Patreascu's tiny leg in four places. The plan was to drill four holes in the thigh bone and five in the tibia, between the knee and the ankle.

The most crucial hole was the one at the top of the thigh, and an air of tension built as Nigel continued to work in grim silence. Eventually he straightened up. 'F...... hell!' he exploded 'I'm going to have to abandon it. I can't get a hole through the bone. I'm sorry, everyone.' At that moment I felt a great spiritual uplifting, something I had read about happening to other people but had never experienced myself. It was like the room was full of a tremendous air of excitement and exhilaration, as if some sort of positive energy had entered it.

'Dammit,' Nigel said, 'I'm going to keep trying.' He went back to work and twenty minutes later, dripping with perspiration, he had made the ninth hole. 'So, Bev,' Nigel said at last, 'when can we book you in for your leg operation?'

'Don't bother with a pre-med, just shoot me,' I said. 'I would never be able to tolerate that.'

Nine steel bars were screwed into the holes Nigel had drilled. The ends stuck out through Patreascu's flesh, the thigh ones on the outside, the lower ones on the inside, so that he looked like a human television aerial. As we came out of the operating theatre I asked Sister Valerie if she had felt anything unusual at that moment when Nigel had been about to give up and she described exactly the feeling I had experienced.

'You know, it's a funny thing,' Nigel said a little later as he was disrobing. 'I felt the oddest sensation when I was about to give up. It was like a rush of excitement filling the room. A very strange feeling.' He shook his head in puzzlement.

After the operation I stayed with Patreascu in the recovery room. I wanted him to see a familiar face when he woke up. Sister Valerie stayed too. I was alarmed by the way his body was twitching but she told me there was nothing to worry about; this was normal. Once he was conscious we took him back to his room and, with the help of a nurse, lifted him gently onto his cot. I was still in my theatre clothes and rushed back to the theatre to change, anxious to return immediately to his bedside. BUPA had very kindly provided a nurse who specialised in children but I wanted to be there to comfort him with a few words of Romanian, even though I wasn't sure he would understand.

Nigel had other plans. 'Stop fussing, Bev. The poor mite will be asleep for hours yet. Come and have some lunch and tell us your thoughts.' It was a command, not an invitation. Moira had provided a wonderful picnic, which Nigel and his team ate ravenously.

'He's always tense before difficult surgery,' Moira confided. 'Now he can relax for a while.'

After lunch we rang the Sisters in Bacau to tell them all had gone well and before Nigel and Moira left he looked in on the still-sleeping Patreascu, tenderly lifting up his little hand and feeling his pulse. Nigel's eyes were wet with tears. He suddenly looked absolutely exhausted from the sheer physical strain and emotional stress of the operation. 'Poor little Patreascu,' he said. 'You'll have your work cut out now, Bev. He'll be even more of a whinging little bugger, but with reason. Oh, by the way, you're invited for Sunday lunch tomorrow. Moira will be offended if you refuse.'

'Oh, I can't,' I said. 'I couldn't bear to leave him. He needs me and it's my duty. Anyway, I promised the Sisters I would stay with him.'

'Look,' he interrupted, 'I am speaking to you as a doctor now, Bev. You'll be no ruddy good to Patreascu if you are worn out. You have to have breaks. If I thought you being away for a few hours would harm our precious patient I wouldn't have asked you in the first place. For God's sake listen to me, woman. I have to listen to you often enough.' I gave in.

I sometimes felt sad for Szuzannah, Patreascu and the others when I looked round the hospital wards and saw groups of excited families visiting their loved ones. They had no mums or dads to visit them or worry about them, just the Sisters waiting for news on the other end of the telephone line. It made me all the more determined to be there for them – I neglected many of my old friends and I know that some of them felt hurt and rejected but I just couldn't do anything else. I couldn't let the children down; they were my first responsibility and I loved them. I rarely discussed my trips here and there with John, but he always supported me and helped. Occasionally he would get worried if the phone kept going and I didn't get a chance to relax and he was surprised by how many things were going on at once, but he never wavered in his support. When I had doubts about myself before meetings it was always him who told me, 'Look, this has nothing to do with you, Bev Peberdy, it is the children you are going to talk about. You can do it.' Contrary to all my fears our marriage had become even happier than before. I was content, busy, fulfilled. My faith was increasing daily and I found prayer a great help. It felt like discovering a very good friend – someone who never lets you down, never forgets you and someone who isn't frightened to let you see your own faults.

Both Patreascu's legs had been useless because there was no muscle, and now the shorter one had these bars sticking out which, if he ever knocked them against anything, were agony for him. Even lying in bed could give him unspeakable pain if he turned in the wrong direction. He frequently went into spasm during those first few weeks and the nurses would try to inject the legs with painkillers, but it was hard to find enough flesh to put the needles into. Throughout the nights he twitched and rocked and never seemed to sleep for more than ten or fifteen minutes at a time. I wished I could explain to him why he was suffering, assure him that he would walk one day.

After two days the dressings which were packed around the savage-looking pin sites had to be changed. We soaked them as much as possible before attempting this but they were encrusted and stuck fast. I cannot describe the agony Patreascu endured and how I hated to inflict this appalling additional suffering on a child who had been through so much in his few short years, but it had to be done. I wondered if he would become frightened of me; after all, I was torturing him no matter how hard I tried not to. I used to wrap him in a blanket after each session, cuddle him and try to comfort him until his little body stopped shaking from the sobbing and the pain. It was a miserable time for him and must have seemed endless.

A week after the operation he was given a hero's welcome back at St Gerrard's. I stayed overnight and the next day to settle him back in and then I had to leave to go back to work. I was surprised how hard I found the parting. I thought it was probably the best thing for Patreascu – it would be unkind of me to allow him to become too reliant on me. Although I felt miserable at abandoning him in the hospital he didn't seem the least bit bothered. Unlike Szuzannah, who had always cried whenever I left her, Patreascu was so institutionalised that it didn't seem to affect him. He still had the vacant look that I had grown so familiar with in the eyes of the children of Salon One. He was sadly all too used to having people come, do painful things to him and go again.

Two weeks after the operation the next phase of treatment started. Four times a day a key was applied to each of the steel bars sticking out of his leg and they were turned, prising the bones a little further apart, causing internal bleeding of the bone, with the aim of encouraging the formation of calcium and ultimately new bones. It had to be done to an exact timetable. The first few times Patreascu screamed in terror. I felt sick with horror and I am ashamed to admit that I turned on Nigel accusingly while he was showing the Sisters how to do it and shouted, 'Surely you can give him something for the pain? Look how he is suffering!'

Nigel's face was livid with anger as he swung round on me. 'I am not in the business of causing children unnecessary pain. We cannot give him painkillers four times a day for the next eight months. He will get used to the discomfort. Most of his crying is not pain – it is fear of the unknown. Look,' he pointed at Patreascu, 'he is already calming down.'

In the end Patreascu became very adept at unscrewing the external fixators, the two big bars which the individual pins were screwed into, himself. After eight months of this slow torture, Patreascu's leg had grown an astonishing six inches and matched the other one. As the bars went through the flesh, leaving open wounds, he was very susceptible to infections which antibiotics seemed to have little effect on and the flesh wounds were often more painful for him than the pins themselves.

He started coming to our home for the weekends as soon as he was strong enough, alternating with Szuzannah, and John and I would try to visit both of them in hospital during the week, if time and work allowed, but not as often as we would have liked. I would also go to all the doctors' appointments with them both as their legal guardian. At first I was frightened to have Patreascu to stay. Nigel suggested he show me how to turn the pins but I didn't feel confident enough to do it and waited until they were being turned only every second day. Nigel was totally against Szuzannah and Patreascu coming at the same time, feeling they would be in competition with one another when both of them needed individual attention. I did worry that the one left behind would not get a visit and thankfully Joyce Jones stepped in to have Szuzannah to her home and various other volunteers were happy to visit from time to time. The nurses were also generous with their time and one lovely girl called Maureen, who was from a large and musical Jamaican family, shyly asked if she could take Patreascu home with her on a Saturday. Her father had an electric organ and I'm sure that listening to Maureen's family singing was what fostered his love of music. Patreascu also befriended another patient, a good-looking young man called Neil. One day Patreascu went missing and the nurses eventually discovered him sitting amongst Neil's female visitors, enjoying a can of Coca-Cola with Neil's Walkman on his ears and his baseball cap trendily turned the wrong way round on his head. He was quick to pick up Neil's ways of speaking, greeting everyone with, 'Hey, my man,' and 'Give me five.'

Father Gerrard Jackson, the elderly priest who was recuperating after a valve replacement in his heart, was a lively and charming man. His love of God and of life positively shone out of him. He had to rely on a walking stick to get about and we both horrified to see Patreascu cower away in wide-eyed fear at the sight of it when Father Gerrard popped in to say hallo. Patreascu's arms came up to protect his head and he tried to hide under the bed or in the cupboard. It took weeks to persuade him that in Father Gerrard's hands the stick was nothing to be frightened of.

One Sunday I heard excited laughter coming from the children's room. I found Father Gerrard sitting on the bed with Patreascu beside him. They were putting an old yoghurt pot on the end of the stick and Patreascu was flinging it across the room. It was the first time I had seen Patreascu laugh and truly enjoy himself. It was a heart-warming sight.

When the children were resting I would pop in to see Father Gerrard to ask some of the many questions I had about my growing faith. He was endlessly patient and interested in helping me. His room had lovely patio doors opening out onto the gardens. He used to hold Mass in there and I brought the children along for the services. We became firm friends and eventually, in the summer of 1992, I plucked up the courage to tell him that I was thinking of converting to Catholicism myself.

'No,' he shook his head after a moment's thought. 'I don't think you are quite ready yet.'

'When will I be ready?' I asked.

'You will know when the time is right,' he said. 'This is a commitment for the rest of your life. You need to be sure.'

I had come to know, by seeing the Sisters in Romania doing God's work with their own hands and by watching the pain of the children, how even the most appalling suffering can draw people together and help them. I was starting to understand the joy of faith. Although I knew I could probably never shake off my anxieties about life, I realised that by praying I was releasing myself from the fear of what to do and about what might happen. When I prayed everything seemed to begin to happen, maybe not exactly on request or precisely as I wanted, but happen none the less. I began to wonder how I had managed before and to see how difficult life had been without this great warm blanket enveloping me, giving me confidence.

In September 1993 I started to take instruction at my local church. I was certain that this was the path I wanted to follow. By seeing their work and allowing me to share it, and by never preaching to me or trying to convert me, the Sisters had shown me that Christianity was the faith for me. All the time that I had been 'meditating' in Romania, thinking about things that I wanted to happen, I realised I had actually been praying. And too many of my prayers had been answered for me to believe it was just a coincidence any more.

Spending so much time with him over the course of his treatment, I slowly came to realise that Patreascu was a highly intelligent little boy. I had noticed that many of the children in Ungerini who had seemed to respond most readily to attention didn't always continue to progress. I think that perhaps the more intelligent ones, being more aware of what was happening around them, had in fact retreated further into themselves, put up more barriers, and were more reluctant to risk lowering them at the first sign of kindness. Some of the children who had seemed the most retarded might well be the ones with the most potential.

Patreascu was slowly emerging from his self-imposed prison. Little things began to give him pleasure, like having a good soak in his baby bath. His face came alive, if only temporarily, filling with mischief as he loaded a syringe with bath water and drenched us all. His eye contact was still not good but he was beginning to take a real interest in what was going on around him. His powers of observation surprised me. It took him only seconds to work out how to use the channel changer and video at the hospital. He used to copy Nigel and very quickly knew how to take pulses and blood pressure. He used sneak down to Rita the receptionist's office to help sort out and staple documents, put things into envelopes and lick stamps. He needed to be occupied and stimulated all the time.

He became very determined to walk, although it was hard at first with all the metalwork on his left leg and virtually no muscles in the right one. He saw other children getting up and moving about and he wanted to do the same. Every new experience filled him with terror, but once he overcame that fear he took to almost everything with gusto. Changing from the wheelchair to a zimmer frame was a major step forward and eventually he began to develop a little muscle in his right leg and buttock. Nigel explained that he would never develop any in his left leg, that it would simply act as a prop, like a wooden leg except that it was part of him and could still feel pain. The little bit of muscle that was beginning to function in his left hip allowed him to begin to swing his left leg around and position it to support himself.

The whinging child who had been unpopular with everyone in Bacau had now developed into a favourite of the Sisters at St Gerrard's. Sister Beatrice, the lovely Matron who used to hide her mirth and joie de vivre behind a serious-looking façade, would let him sit on her knee in her office, when no one was watching, wearing her veil and glasses. She would whip them back off him and compose herself the moment anyone knocked at the door. A sweet faced, eighty-year-old nun, Sister Marianna, reprimanded me when I told Patreascu off for pushing his head up her skirts with a joyful, 'Haloooooo!'

'Don't scold the boy,' she chided. 'Hasn't he suffered enough?'

John and I began to notice big changes on Patreascu's weekend visits. He was hard work to start with, partly because of the bars in his legs, but also because he still wasn't communicating and had virtually no control over his bowels or his bladder. We spent most of our time cleaning up after him. It was like having a large one-year-old around the house. I must admit we dropped him back at the hospital on Sunday evening with a sense of relief because we were so exhausted.

Patreascu was not particularly interested in toys, but loved to be wherever there was something to be done, assisting me in the kitchen or the garden. The eyes that had been so dead at Ungerini were now alive, sparkling and curious, his little fingers getting into everything and sometimes breaking things in their impatience to discover what was happening in every nook and cranny of the house. He helped me with the weeding and the planting of bulbs for the spring, watering them carefully and lovingly. I became increasingly sad that he wouldn't be there to see them bloom. Every new experience seemed to fascinate him and I realised that my feelings for him were growing stronger. I started to miss him during the week and to dread having to take him back to the hospital after weekends. I was pained at the thought of returning him to Romania, but I realised that I was just being selfish because that was his home.

At first it was difficult to have Patreascu to stay because like Szuzannah and all the children at Ungerini he was afraid of dogs. He began to stroke our collie, Misty, but would still scream if she turned to look at him. He would crawl over to Moss but before Moss showed any signs of aggression he would crawl away again. Moss would almost immediately show his teeth. It was as if Patreascu sensed danger before there were any visible signs. The dogs were equally unsure about the unpredictable little animal who had been introduced into their home.

Because he didn't want to play with toys like most children it was sometimes hard to occupy him, so I often took him out in his wheelchair to the woods with Misty and Moss. We would meet up with my sister-in-law, Joy, and her huge German Shepherd, Strauss, and after a while Patreascu would hold the leads of all three dogs, allowing them to pull him along the woodland paths. One day the dogs spotted a deer and took off like rockets, with Patreascu rattling along behind like something from *Ben Hur*. Although I had strapped him in I was terrified he would crash and undo all Nigel's brilliant work and I panicked. By the time Joy, who was much fitter than me, managed to catch them and bring them to a halt, Patreascu was shrieking with joy and waving a finger at the dogs.

I used to take him to the playground a five-minute walk away from the house. It would take Patreascu an hour to cover the distance with his zimmer frame and I used to think I would die of boredom; waiting, coaxing and then waiting some more. I had to force myself not to think of all the things I should be doing around the house and garden. Then, after playing, we had the slow walk back.

Nigel and John used to tease me, 'Poor Patreascu,' they would say, 'a captive audience for Bev's talking. He'll probably go deaf.' It was true that I used to talk to him a lot, not knowing if anything was registering really. I used to point out flowers or cats or birds or anything of interest, but it remained a very one-way communication. He had a concentration span of seconds, never wanting to play or give the television more than a fleeting glance. He just wanted to be with us, like a small baby. I spent hours sitting opposite him, pulling faces for him to copy, hoping he would develop throat and facial muscles which would help him to speak. But I knew his silence wasn't just a result of physical problems. He still wasn't ready to talk. It was as if he was soaking everything up and storing it like a computer, waiting for the time when he might decide to put it all to use.

I was chuffed when Russell, who had been very patient with the children who came to the house at weekends, announced that he would like to go to Bacau. Russell and his friends at Rotaract have helped lots of elderly and handicapped people at home. They raise funds and have fun while they are at it. I've been very grateful to have had their help in collecting, sorting and transport for aid to Romania many times, but I really appreciated Russell's desire to get out there and see it for himself. I felt confident that he had seen enough of the children to know what he was in for. Patreascu had had to learn the meaning of the word 'no' very early on, especially when he was caught crawling towards Russell's room, attracted no doubt by the music centre and computer equipment. Sometimes when Russell had friends round Patreascu would drag himself into the room and sneak onto a bean-bag, pretending to join in their chatter and imitating their laughter. On one occasion he even downed a lager and became extremely merry, falling about even more than usual. The next morning he had a king-sized hangover which did nothing to improve his whinging. Russell, an adult, was entitled to his privacy and I'd been careful not to force the children on him.

I often used to take Patreascu to the toy department at our local John Lewis where the staff would kindly allow him to use the cars and tractors. He used to get into a Little Tikes car and then bomb around the limited floor space, screeching happily at his new-found freedom, his leg with all its equipment stuck out of the roof at a very strange angle. The Alliance & Leicester was another stop. They used to wave to Patreascu and he used to love to go in and play with the toys they have for customers' children, or to sit on the counter watching the computers. He was always fascinated by computers. These were treats at the end of long walks to exercise his muscles!

John's elderly parents, like many other people, had not understood why I had gone all the way to Romania when I had never shown any interest in helping children at home. One day we had to call in on them and took Patreascu along. When they saw him trying to walk with his little zimmer frame they visibly melted and made him very welcome. Bert (John's dad) produced an ice lolly and indicated that Patreascu should keep it safe for him. Licking it, Patreascu gave a puzzled shriek at the unexpected coldness and then as the taste hit him his face lit up. Bert returned and made a big joke of, 'Where's my lolly, you cheeky monkey?' none of which Patreascu could understand but they both seemed to enjoy the pantomime equally.

Though still not speaking, Patreascu was noticing everything. He was constantly asking for jobs to do; as with Szuzannah, physiotherapy at our house was to empty the bins or stand doing the potatoes. The hardest thing was to allow him to do things for himself. Slowly but surely we were giving him his independence and he loved it.

He was becoming much more sociable. Walking around the corridors of the hospital he would wave his arms in greeting to everyone who passed and managed to get replies from even the frostiest-looking consultants. When the staff brought him meals, he would get them to set up a little table outside his room so that he could wave to passers-by.

To begin with it didn't seem to trouble Patreascu to go back to the hospital after our weekends together, but one Sunday night in November he started to cry when I passed him to the nurses. I stayed with him and got him into his pyjamas, then sat on the bed with him and felt impotent and desperate as he sobbed himself to sleep. Eventually I had to go home. On the two-hour train ride back I felt terribly miserable and wondered if John and I were doing the right thing in letting him grow so attached to us. Were we actually going to cause him more unhappiness by giving him a glimpse of family life and then whipping him away from it again?

The next day Dr Mike Tarlow, who was Patreascu's blood doctor and was also an eminent paediatrician and psychologist, rang to make an appointment for us to talk about the result of some anaemia tests and I told him how badly things had gone at the hospital the previous evening.

'Excellent!' he exclaimed to my surprise. 'You should be grateful; it means he is starting to form relationships, make choices and show some normal behaviour. This is a major breakthrough for him.'

'But it was heartbreaking,' I protested.

'He'll soon realise that although you have to leave him, you always come back for him. The fact that he actually cares about something is an enormous step forward. He is becoming de-institutionalised.' Although I felt cheered to think of it that way, it didn't lessen the sadness I felt at having to watch him go through such unhappiness.

The prospect of taking each of the children in turn back to Romania excited mixed feelings in me. It was good to imagine them triumphantly walking in on their own legs and Szuzannah's return fulfilled all my expectation. Their ability to endure complicated surgery was always a worry, no matter how many tests were done in advance. At the same time I did feel sad at the thought of losing them. Coming to England was a frightening and exciting experience but Szuzannah especially was very keen to get back to the Sisters and her friends and carers in Romania, eager to show off the new skills that the doctors in England had given her. In contrast, even after he had been at St Gerrard's for many months, Patreascu hadn't seemed bothered where he was.

People who thought I must be very hard to be able to take the children back to such poverty didn't realise that the Mother Teresa home was a lovely place, and that to be with the Sisters and all their friends was what the more aware children looked forward to most. While they enjoyed the extra attention and different experiences in England, they all missed the Sisters dreadfully and were overjoyed if there was ever a chance to speak to them on the phone or if they received a little note or gift. Whenever they reached a new stage, like standing or walking, they would say, 'Tell Sisters,' or, 'What did Sisters say?' If they saw a photograph of the Sisters their faces would light up and sheer joy would shine through. Szuzannah would ask, 'Home soon, how is my Sister Jenny?' because she could never say Jane.

After several months, while I was in Romania with Szuzannah, Patreascu had his pins taken out, an agonising experience for him. Shamefully and selfishly, I felt relieved that I had been away and missed the event. He was put into plaster from the tips of his toes to the upper thigh. A huge hinge joined the leg plaster to a body plaster which ended up under his arms. The plaster, which was to protect his fragile new bones until the screw holes had healed up, had to be changed several times because the doctors needed to see how the painful, open wounds of the pin sites were doing. At last the wounds had a chance to heal and the continuous infections ceased. Dr Tarlow had told us that Patreascu's severe anaemia would almost certainly go if he were with a family, eating a normal child's diet. A year in hospital was much too long to be healthy for a child. I vowed to find a better alternative to extended stays in hospital for any children coming from Bacau to England in the future. Although the care at St Gerrard's was excellent and the love Patreascu received was exceptional, I knew in my heart that hospital was the wrong place for him, but it was too late to do anything about it.

When the plasters finally came off, the wounds were still sensitive but, joy of joys, Patreascu could go back to having baths at last. He stayed in the water so long he came out like a little white prune.

Once he had overcome his fear of dogs, Patreascu grew so fond of Misty and Moss that on a Friday night I didn't dare to feed them until he arrived home with John, no matter how late. It was always his first job, the second being to check if the bins needed emptying. Whenever we were sorting out boxes and black bags for Romania, he would be in there tying them up, putting the labels on, pairing the shoes and tying them together, knowing that he was doing it all for his friends back home in Bacau.

I was giving more and more thought to the things I had learned from the Sisters. I felt pretty sure that Sister Jane had deliberately given me this job in England to show me that I could keep my old family life and still be fulfilled by my new work helping the children. I was praying for Patreascu's legs to mend enough for him to be able to live a near-normal life. He had also contracted an infection in hospital because the constant intake of antibiotics had left his resistance to germs low. I was in Romania with Szuzannah when Nigel rang to tell me that Patreascu was seriously ill. I prayed on my knees in the Sisters' chapel, 'Please help this poor child. He has endured so much.' Finally, I prayed that someone would come forward to adopt him.

What I really wanted was to keep him for myself but when I broached the subject of adoption with John he was adamant that we were 'too old, too fat and past our sell-by date' for such a venture. We ended up having a terrible row. I suppose that it reawakened the longing for a child of my own that I had suppressed for so long. I already felt almost as if Patreascu was mine and the thought of losing him was awful.

On the other hand I realised that I had to be fair to John who, at fifty, had built himself exactly the sort of life he enjoyed and that I had been happy with before going to Romania. He was already making big sacrifices to help me ferry the children around and having them to stay with us. He was always kind and patient and spent hours helping them to walk or do whatever exercises Nigel wanted. He had been wonderful, even having Patreascu on his own one weekend when I was in Romania with Szuzannah, washing his wounds when they were at their most unpleasant and clearing up the results of his incontinence. I couldn't find fault with anything he did and it was quite understandable that, now Russell was grown up and independent, he did not fancy the responsibility of taking on another small son whose capabilities were far from certain. But I still resented the idea that he had set his mind against the adoption without even talking to me about it or considering my feelings. Inside I was deeply unhappy about not being able to adopt but I knew that it would only work if John truly wanted it as well. Once I had got my anger off my chest I let the subject drop and went back to saying my prayers.

Nigel rang me again in Romania a few days after telling me about the infection. 'It's a bloody miracle, Bev. Young Master Patreascu is clear of infection. We have double-checked and re-done the tests and he's fine. Scientifically there is no explanation. Did you by any chance ask the Sisters to pray for him?' I thought he might laugh at me if I confessed that I had been on my knees myself, so I remained silent.

Nigel told me that the progress on his legs was another miracle. He said he had never in his wildest dreams imagined that Patreascu would get so far so fast. Sister Beatrice suggested that Patreascu might benefit from going to St Edward's Catholic School, next to the hospital, just for a little recreation. We had discussed Patreascu's future and our hopes that he would be adopted by an Italian family. Mother Teresa insists the children are put forward for adoption to Romanian families. If no Romanians come forward then the children go for adoption to Italy as she has an agreement to this effect with both governments. It seemed a brilliant idea to get Patreascu to a normal school for a few weeks in preparation for this eventuality. The Headmistress, Jill Owen, was delighted to take him in and the whole school took him to their hearts. A few weeks later I was approached by a family who had grown so fond of him that fostering and eventual adoption were mentioned. Oh delight of delights! This would mean that Patreascu could stay in England and I might be able to go on seeing him as he grew up. I was so happy for him and immediately phoned Sister Jane with the good news that all my prayers had now been answered. I did feel a pang of sadness that it wasn't to be us, but I couldn't be selfish and deny him his one chance of family life and happiness.

'I absolutely forbid you to encourage this adoption,' Sister Jane said with extraordinary firmness when she heard the news. 'We cannot allow it.' No matter how much I argued she wouldn't hear of it, firstly saying it would contravene our arrangement with the Home Office, which stipulated that Patreascu could only stay with us, and then saying they had a family in Italy designated for him. I felt very sad.

The Sisters always hoped to find families for all the children in their care, but they were ruthlessly realistic about which of them would be suitable. Just because a family was willing to change nappies and clear up after a cute five-year-old didn't meant that they would have the same attitude to a lumbering great fifteen-year-old. Some children, they knew, would always be better off staying with them. It was good that they now considered Patreascu to be a candidate for adoption at all, because he certainly wouldn't have been when he first went to them.

During this convalescent period Patreascu started to talk and to call us Mummy and Daddy. I felt a surge of joy every time he said those magic words, followed by a wave of panic because I knew that I could never be his mummy. The realisation made me weep many times. We were shocked by his use of the words because we had never mentioned to him that we were his mummy and daddy. At first we thought he might be copying Russell, but Russell always calls us Mum and Dad. We then thought it might be learnt from the few other children at St Gerrard's but he hardly ever mixed with them. So where had he got it from?

I used to love giving him his bath, massaging cream into his little body, putting baby powder on and then taking him downstairs for a bit of time together before bed. He used to sit on my lap, cuddling in, his head resting on my chest – which he later called 'Patreascu's pillows' – and I sang to him. I began to experience a tingling glow of contentment and fulfilment. I asked a friend of mine, Janey, who had a young child, if this was normal, because I had never experienced anything like it before. With

Russell it had been different because he was already independent when he came to live with us and very active and athletic. He had never physically needed me in the way Patreascu did. Janey said I was describing exactly how she felt about her own child, Andrew.

Russell, always a clever boy academically, was also a good all-round sportsman, winning many cups and medals and enjoying all the same things his father had as a boy. I did wonder if this was at the back of John's mind, knowing that none of that would be possible for Patreascu.

One day I went to do something for him and he said, 'No, Daddy do it,' and it seemed so right, so natural, so beautiful and for one moment I allowed myself to think how wonderful it would be if we could all be together as a family. Then John laughed and said, 'No, I'm John, you little rascal,' and I couldn't tell what effect the word Daddy had had on him. The harsh reality hit me and for a few seconds I hated John for depriving me of this wonderful feeling of being wanted, of being unconditionally loved. To Patreascu I was not fat, not ridiculous, not garrulous and not boring – all he saw was someone who loved him and whom he loved back. His face used to light up when I arrived at the hospital to collect him and he used to race down the corridor, his little rucksack on his back, his crutches flying, not looking back at the nurses who so tenderly and kindly looked after him all week, launching himself into my arms. It was such a deep joy for both of us and I now knew that we were what he needed; we had all the skills necessary to be his parents. There was no therapy needed, no experts, nothing but the best medicine in the world, love.

How could John deprive Patreascu and me of this shared miracle, this beautiful journey of discovery? How could he tear us apart? How could he be so unfeeling? Deep down I knew the answers to all these questions but I still kept on asking them inside my head.

I had tried so hard to put the thought of being parted from Patreascu out of my mind, but it didn't often work. My last thoughts at night were always of his sweet little face, now so very much alive; his little body, disabled with the gammy leg but always quivering to be active. He was so brave, so desperate to please, so ready to give his trust and love. I would wake in the early hours of the morning with the cold realisation that it was not a nightmare, it was real: he would not be staying with us. I worried so much about the possible effects on him. I was going to have to reject him, abandon him. We had come through so much, grown so close, shared so many experiences. How could all that be discarded without doing him untold damage? I vainly tried to console myself with the prospect of the big, loving Italian family.

At one of Patreascu's appointments, Nigel sat back and beamed. 'Well, Bev,' he said proudly, 'I think this young man is just about ready to go back to Romania.'

His words were like a dagger piercing my heart. I felt the air rush from my lungs, my temples were pulsating, my face was flushed and my heart racing. I realised my jaw had dropped. 'Are you sure?' I croaked.

'Absolutely,' he beamed, knowing nothing of my dilemma. 'He's done wonderfully.'

By Christmas 1992, Patreascu had been in England for ten months and he was wanting to do things with John rather than just me, following him around, wanting to help with the tree, the lights and the decorations. Although he was not speaking very much he used to point to things and say, 'Me do!' and show such joy when John included him. He made John laugh. John would have mock fights with him and generally encourage him to get up and use his legs, while having fun at the same time. It was the best Christmas John and I had ever had together. It must have been then that John began to think about Patreascu returning to Romania, realising that we might never see him again. He noticed how much Patreascu was progressing when he was able to enjoy one-to-one attention. I watched all these signs, hardly daring to dream that John would change his mind, but always hoping and praying that he would. Then, on New Year's Day, he spoke the immortal words that were to change our lives once more: 'Look, this is probably a ridiculous idea – I still believe we are too old, too fat and past our sell-by dates – but I think we should try to adopt Patreascu, if they will let us.'

Now I was truly convinced about the power of prayer to change things. I stared at John in disbelief, sitting down quickly before I fell down, a thousand fireworks going off in my head. 'We'll have to check it with Russ,' we agreed. So, plucking up our courage, we sat Russ down and cautiously broached the subject with him.

'Russ,' John began, 'you've probably realised Patreascu will be going back home to Romania soon...'

'What?' Russ looked surprised, as if this was the first time he had considered the prospect. 'That's ridiculous. Why don't you try to adopt him?' We couldn't have been more gob-smacked!

When I told Sister Jane about John's change of heart, I was nervous about her response in case she became angry again but she was overjoyed.

'But what about the family in Italy he was designated for?' I asked.

'Foolish child,' she chided. 'We always had him designated for you and John, but we had to wait for you both to want him.' I heard her passing the news on to Sister Ida, who them came onto the phone.

'I knew you would,' Sister Ida panted breathlessly, 'ever since I saw that photograph of Patreascu in your home. The look of love on his face. I have prayed to Our Lady so often that this would happen.'

We had to contact Mother Teresa herself to obtain official permission to begin the adoption process. I telephoned a number in Calcutta which Sister Jane had given me to leave a message for her. A soft but strong voice came on the line, 'Mother here.'

'What?' I stuttered foolishly. 'Mother Teresa?'

She laughed kindly. 'Yes, that's me. How may I help you?' I told her briefly about working in Romania and about Patreascu, how we had grown to love him and wanted to try to adopt him.

'Oh, such good news.' She sounded so warm, excited and happy. 'God bless you and your husband and son for wanting to give a home to one of our dear handicapped children. God will reward you. But,' she added, 'you must promise Mother one thing – everything must be done legally!'

She promised to write the necessary letters to the Romanian authorities and asked that I let her know how things were progressing. Most importantly, she wanted to know personally all news of how Patreascu settled in. 'You must bring this dear little man to meet me in London – I will be there soon. Please tell him that I want to see him walking.'

I promised I would. I couldn't believe that with all the thousands of people she was responsible for, she would spend so long chatting to me. I didn't dare to think what the phone bill was going to be.

'We will remember you in our prayers,' she said. 'Now I must go and tell the Sisters this good news,' and then she was gone.

Nigel did not react quite as well. In fact he was furious. I had always known that he would disapprove of the idea of me adopting any of the children, believing that it would make it very hard for all the others I knew and loved and who knew me, and that it would make it impossible for me to continue my work in Romania. He also thought that Patreascu should go back to Bacau as an inspiration to the others, a figurehead to show them what was possible. 'Adopting him will not solve any of the big problems,' he had argued in the past, 'and it will look as if you bring them here to fix and once they look decent we decide to keep them.'

The last thing we wanted the Romanian people to think was that once we had patched the children up, and they began to look a bit normal, we would keep them for ourselves. Of course, this was a logical and professional attitude. What happened between us and Patreascu was totally illogical, unplanned and exactly what I had promised the British Embassy in Bucharest would not happen. It had taken us by surprise, totally and absolutely. Our lives were stable, organised and we could go to London to the theatre or to a concert at the drop of a hat without worrying about the consequences. For many years we had been able to go abroad annually for a holiday and then have a week's walking in the Lake District too. The thought of having a young child in the house again, with all the associated mess and restrictions couldn't have been further from our minds. However, we had not accounted for Patreascu, how his love for us would give rise to our love for him.

I was so scared of Nigel's likely reaction that I made John ring him with the news. He exploded just as I expected he would, and I heard John trying in vain to get a word in edgeways. Eventually I heard him say, 'But, Nigel, we love him.' The voice at the other end of the line fell silent. He continued to make his unhappiness known about our decision for weeks afterwards, and many of his arguments were very sensible, and were what I had believed myself before Patreascu came on the scene. We finally managed to convince him that we were doing this for the right reasons. One very relevant point he made was how the other children would feel if their 'Tante Bevey' just wanted to adopt one child, rejecting the rest. We both liked Nigel tremendously and valued his opinion. We desperately wanted him to understand and approve. I had already given a lot of thought to the children who would be coming to the UK in the future and praying very hard for a solution to present itself. Nigel was due to retire in a couple of years and it was important to get the children to England for surgery just as soon as Patreascu was discharged.

In the summer of 1993 I heard that Mother Teresa had decided to open a house in Birmingham later that year. What joy. Maybe if I continued to pray hard the Sisters at the Birmingham home would be able to have the children from Bacau to stay with them. That would get them out of the hospital and allow them to be amongst the familiar white and blue saris. They would receive love and care in a similar environment to Bacau.

I knew without any doubt that I would carry on helping, for each time I go to the Adult Institute at Gisteni I look into the faces of the young, the old, the men, the women, the boys, the girls and I see Patreascu's face.

I see him in each and every one of them. I see their suffering, their pain, their misery and I know that would have been Patreascu's life, or death. He would have lived there, as they live; he would have suffered, as they suffer; he would have had the very life drained from him and died, as they surely will, unloved, broken, lonely and forgotten. I have heard their cries and cannot now become deaf to them. I have seen their despair and I pray I shall never become blind to it.

'Despite your disapproval of what we're doing,' I said to Nigel eventually, 'please, please, will you continue to look after Patreascu?'

The moment I saw the sad, hurt look on his face I realised I had said something very stupid and wounding; he would always care beautifully for all the children I brought to him. I could only apologise for my careless words.

Moira Dwyer took the news of the adoption quite differently from her husband and independently rang to congratulate us.

We had to work very hard at keeping Patreascu working on his physiotherapy. I used to take him down to the town centre and put him through his paces, making him walk. Passers-by thought I was being cruel to him, driving him on when he was begging to stop. Some of them would come up and ask me to let them carry him. 'No, no, I'm his physiotherapist,' I lied. 'He has to take the exercise.'

My other main pre-occupation in 1992 was the building of the school and dispensary in Bacau. I was anxious not that they should be showpieces but that they should be built well and would last. Care had to be taken with the design and planning of materials to be used because north-eastern Romania does sometimes suffer from earthquakes. The Sisters could not afford expensive upkeep and repair bills so it was important to build to as high a standard as possible at the beginning.

Who could we trust for such a long-distance project? Then I had a brainwave. I remembered when Sister Jane first showed me round the home in Bacau she had proudly told me that all the heating and water systems had been installed by an Englishman, a co-worker of Mother Teresa's called George Bushell. George was a builder by trade but also organised the shipping out of clothes and medical supplies to Mother Teresa in India.

'What about George Bushell?' I suggested to the Sisters. 'He is known to you; he will do an excellent job—'

'And he is trustworthy.' Sister Jane finished my sentence for me.

They then had to put the proposal to their Regional Supervisor who in turn needed the direct permission of Mother Teresa herself. She approved the idea immediately and George went out to Bacau to draw up preliminary plans even before I knew for sure that I would be able to raise the money. I felt a puzzling certainty that everything would be all right and George believed me. The money duly came in – every Abbey National Branch must have given money, if not every customer – and a few skilled men from George's home in Bridport, Dorset, heard about George's work and offered their services free if we could fly them out. Our only problem then was that the men could only spare two weeks of their time and would therefore have to work fast. We did not want them to have to waste time worrying about where their meals would be coming from. How could we look after them while giving the Sisters minimum inconvenience? Jessica, who I had come to know through her work with the Relief Fund for Romania, had met George Bushell and they had become close friends. She offered to come out as their cook and washer-up so that they could concentrate on the work they were most skilled at.

We were now ready for action. Ready to take things one step further. The children were already well fed and warm. The next thing they needed was an education. I was going out every couple of months on some errand or other, either picking a child up or taking one back so I was able to report back to all the people who had made donations and sacrifices on just how well things were going. Russell went out to help the Sisters dig the foundations, shifting tons of shingle and rubble for the hardcore, using ordinary garden tools. It sounded from his description as if they had a great deal of fun and every day there was a rush of excitement as the children came out to see the progress of their school. George and his team worked tirelessly from first light to late evening in the scorching heat of summer.

It had been a long struggle getting all the plans and materials organised, but the results were worth it. With the money which had been donated we were able to make the building three times the original planned size, which meant that there was plenty of space for the children to run and crawl and for a variety of toys to be left out to play with each day. It was wonderful to watch them painting and making things and being taught to read and write. Apart from the skilled tradesmen, we had also employed many local labourers to bring some employment into the area, and encourage the sharing of new skills.

The building is very simple, with a verandah running all the way along the outside so the children can sit out in the fresh air for their lessons during the summer. Desks and chairs renovated by prisoners from High Down prison in Surrey were put to very good use. When Nigel came out to see it, and watched the children playing, he broke down and cried.

We were also able to build a proper dispensary and examination room onto the side. We needed a room where drugs could be kept under lock and key and away from the children, and it also gave the Sisters somewhere better to see their four hundred or so patients a week – the poorest of the poor.

Half the front garden was concreted over to make a hard-standing play area which could be used in all weathers. The other half has been grassed and some shrubs and flowers have been planted. There are two big old trees which are very good for shade and also have swings and ropes hanging from their branches. The first time I visited the new playground I witnessed a pretty wild water fight, started by Sister Jane throwing a bucket of water from the balcony onto everyone below.

Mother Teresa came back to Romania in the summer of 1992

to visit her four homes. This brought all the local dignitaries out to see what the Sisters had been doing and prodded them into helping with things like providing some extra trained teaching staff. They were all amazed by the progress that the children had made and at the wonderful warm atmosphere of the homes.

It was decided to combine the official opening of the school with the baptism of the children. Initially, the Catholic priests in the neighbourhood refused to baptise the children, claiming that they were 'sinners' and that because of their handicaps they were unable to 'renounce their sins'. The Sisters were very disappointed but managed to prevail upon the Bishop to change his mind. He came to the home with ten priests to bless the school officially and baptise all the children. There was then a huge party with all the local people.

At last people in Romania were beginning to overcome their prejudices about the mentally and physically handicapped and those who have been rejected at birth. But at the same time wars in Africa and the former Yugoslavia were claiming the attention of the international media. People in other countries like Britain seemed to be forgetting Romania. We were no longer on the news and so the aid was beginning to dry up. It was becoming harder and harder to drum up support for lorries bringing goods out. It was as if people thought that the Romanian orphanage 'problem' had been solved now and they could turn their attention to the next disaster area.

The Sisters wrote to tell me all about their big day and I wished so much I could have seen it, but I had run out of money for airfares and annual leave by then. My father was also in the last throes of life and I needed to be with him. He had to struggle for every breath and in the early hours of 17 August he slipped away.

I had known for some time that his illness was terminal, although I had prayed that the doctors were wrong. I had even asked the Sisters to pray for his recovery. 'Oh, no Bevey,' Sister Jane had said, 'you should pray that your father will be released from suffering and that he may go to heaven to be with our dear Lord in paradise.'

Although my faith was becoming stronger, I was not quite ready for such a reply. With Dad gone I suddenly felt much older. Nigel rang to say that he had just heard. 'Oh, Bev, love,' he said,

'Moira and I are so sorry,' and the line went dead. I began to sob, wondering if I should have spent more time with him at the end of his life and less with the children. I prayed that Dad and his widow, Margaret, would forgive me.

CHAPTER TWELVE

The Others Follow

*

By the time Szuzannah returned home, Tractor Lucien was seventeen. He was thrilled to see her up on her legs but began to cry uncontrollably. I asked him why he was crying.

'Szuzannah said that you got her to walk,' he sobbed. 'Please will you do the same for me?'

I told him that it was the doctors, not me, who had done the work, but he still believed it was me. The more I explained the more he begged me to help him walk. I told him that he was to be number four on the doctors' list, but as we talked I realised that he expected to be able to get a pair of donor legs in Britain; that he would be six feet tall and this would mean that his family would come back to get him and they would all love him. He believed they had only rejected him because he was small and deformed. With new legs he would not only go home, but be able to play football for Romania.

I was so tempted to lie to Lucien and give him some hope for the future, but I knew that it would be unforgivable to have him go through so much only to be disappointed at the end. I told him that he would not grow much more, but that he could be upright. I told him that he would always have to wear calipers, but that we would make sure they were out of sight under his trousers. He imagined he would be playing football like a 'campion' (champion). I told him that he would be able to walk very well and would manage to run a little and play football, to see out of the windows and many, many other things like being able to reach up higher, but that he would never be in the Olympics.

In the end we played a game together, imagining him returning from Britain like Szuzannah, knocking on the door and calling out Sister Jane's name. She would bring his tractor to the door and he would laugh and say, 'No need for that, Sister Jane. Look at me, I am walking now.'

Illeana also begged to be brought to Britain. She needed operations on her eyes to correct the two ninety-degree squints, which meant that virtually all you could see were the whites of her eyes, making her look strange and self-conscious about going out because of people staring. She had implored me to help her, saying, 'But, Bevey, you help the children to walk; help me to see properly, I beg you.'

She had already had so many let-downs and disappointments in her short life that I had to be very careful not to make matters worse by promising something that might not come about. I promised her that I would *try* to find someone who would examine her to see if an operation might be possible. I explained that I might fail and that even if I succeeded the doctors might decide the problem was too severe or that she was too old for the squints to be corrected. I was desperate to do something for her, and equally desperate not to get her hopes up in vain.

Various people recommended eye surgeons and a couple had written to me, offering their services. I was not sure. I rang Nigel to see if he knew of anyone very special who might help. He put me in touch with a distinguished eye surgeon called Gus Sutton who offered to look at any children I brought to him – without making any rash promises that he would always be able to help. Mr Sutton would see Illeana at the Birmingham Eye Hospital and Bob Dalrymple, the Hospital Manager, wrote to say all costs would be met from the private sector. Wandsworth Prison offered to pay her airfare. Everything was in place except for one thing – where would she stay? There was nowhere suitable. She wouldn't be able to stay with us because I was working full-time. It was a major stumbling block. Illeana waited patiently, happy in the belief that I was doing everything I could on her behalf. Every day she would go to the chapel and pray, then ask Sister, 'When does Bevey come for me?' I prayed for guidance and the answer became obvious. It was time for me to give up my job. I tentatively sat down to discuss it with John, knowing that it would make a big difference to our lives. Not only would we lose my salary, we would also lose the big mortgage subsidy which we received from the Abbey National. We couldn't afford it; it did not make financial sense, particularly with our new responsibilities as Patre-ascu's parents, but neither of us could bear to think of Illeana not coming to Britain. We decided we would face the financial problems as they cropped up. For now the important thing was to get Illeana to Britain before it was too late. We didn't tell the Sisters of our decision and I wondered how we were going to be able to afford my airfare to go and collect Illeana.

I rang Sister Jane to make the final arrangements. Illeana was so happy she rushed to the chapel to thank God for answering her prayers.

'Illeana asked me to thank you for remembering her,' Sister Jane told me, 'and asks me to tell John that he will not have to draw a single drop of water from the well as long as she is staying with you; that she will happily do all his washing and his chores for him.'

Everything was happening at once. Patreascu was about to be discharged from hospital to come and live with us; Illeana was due to arrive for surgery and I was trying to work out how we would manage without my income. There were boxes and sacks to be packed, lorries to be organised, volunteers to be interviewed, vetted, checked and organised. My fridge had begun to look like the north face of K2, my cooker like the Black Hole of Calcutta and the garden like a jungle.

We had made the first tentative steps in the procedure for adopting Patreascu by approaching the Social Services for advice. They warned us that we might be considered too old to adopt. The uncertainty was almost too much for me to bear. We decided to bring Patreascu home from the hospital anyway, even if it was only for the few weeks before the authorities made up their minds and insisted we take him back to Romania.

'Should we tell them at the hospital that we are hoping to adopt him?' I asked.

'I think it would be better not to get their hopes up yet,' John counselled with his usual wisdom.

'They'll be so unhappy to see him go,' I warned, 'and they'll hate us for being so cruel as to send him back to Romania. I can't face them.'

'That's okay,' he smiled. 'I'll go; you get everything ready for him here.'

As John walked down the long ward to collect Patreascu there were huddles of people snuffling into tissues everywhere. John's eyes filled with tears – he felt like a monster. He went down in the lift to the Physiotherapy Department where Patreascu was wearing his favourite dark glasses and sitting on each of the Sisters' laps in turn, sharing a last rich tea biscuit and cup of tea, puzzled as to why he had been unable to raise their spirits as usual.

'John,' Sister Maria implored him, 'surely there must be something we can do to keep him in Britain.'

'There must be someone who could adopt him,' Sister Beatrice joined the entreaties.

John made some noncommittal comments about families in Italy.

'But that is so far away; we would never ever see him again,' cried Sister Rita.

'Surely something can be done, John. We have been praying so hard,' Sister Maria insisted.

In the face of so much despair John threw caution to the wind. 'Well actually, Sisters, there is a possibility that someone will adopt him.'

'Will it be in Britain, John?' they all wanted to know.

'Oh, ummm, yes, they are a British couple.'

'Do you think they would allow us to stay in contact with Patreascu? Are they a nice couple?'

'Oh, yes, I'm sure they would love you to stay in contact,' John replied, now abandoning all hopes of keeping our secret.

'Is it anyone we know?'

'Well, actually, yes, you do. It's Bev, Russell and me.'

There was a few seconds' silence and then the Sisters leapt up, weeping even more now. The news rang round the hospital. People were rushing around crying and laughing. Patreascu didn't know quite what was going on but enjoyed the carnival atmosphere all the same. The Sisters carried him to the chapel, pushing John along with them. Candles were lit and they sank to their knees in front of the altar with Patreascu in the midst of them, thanking God for answering their prayers and praying that the adoption would be allowed to go ahead.

I was very worried about going away to Romania to pick up Illeana just as Patreascu was coming home to us. 'Look,' my sister Karen said, 'while you are away Patreascu can come to us for two weeks' holiday. John can join us at weekends.' Despite the fact that I wanted to be with Patreascu more than anything, I could see this was a very good solution. They had a big garden and lots of toys which he could share with my nieces, Becky and Claire. I tearfully kissed him goodbye at Stansted although he appeared completely unmoved, apparently still unaware of what was going on around him and more interested in pulling John out to see the planes.

Despite missing Patreascu, it was wonderful to see everyone in Bacau again and to spend Easter with them. My happiness, however, was tinged with sadness at the realisation that soon Sister Jane and Sister Ida would be leaving Romania and moving on. The thought of not seeing them again was almost unbearable. They were very close friends and had been such an inspiration to me.

When Illeana first went to the Sisters I had explained all about Gabriel and their lost love for one another. Sister Fabiana had given the matter careful consideration. Wondering if Illeana still had strong feelings for Gabriel, she decided to try re-uniting them, to see if their love would flourish, perhaps even leading to marriage with the Sisters helping them to set up home together. The Sisters and Romanian friends of the house go to the Adult Institute, twenty miles away, twice a week, so they took Illeana with them one Sunday. The two young friends were very shy with one another to start with and afterwards the Sisters gently enquired whether Illeana wanted them to help her be with Gabriel. She had decided, however, that she didn't want to leave them. Occasionally I would see her green eyes lost in thought and I would wonder what she was dreaming about.

Once on the plane Illeana clung to my side like a limpet. Her terror increased on take-off. 'Oh, Lordy, Lordy,' she shouted in the Indian accent she had learnt from Sisters Jane and Ida, 'Oh, my Jesus Christ!' When we landed at Stansted she was frightened of everything, keeping her head down and not daring to look up. It took me ten minutes of gentle coaxing to get her onto the escalator but when we leapt off the other end she thought it was hilarious. Everything must have been so much more frightening viewed through quadruple vision.

When Illeana spotted John she leapt joyfully onto him, even though she hadn't seen him for a year. On the way home John decided to stop at a Little Chef. Every detail of it thrilled her – the little packets of sugar and ketchup, the serviettes and most of all being able to choose exactly what she wanted to eat for the first time ever. 'American hamburger!' she exclaimed, 'just like *Dallas*!' Apparently she had seen the programme once at a worker's house and it had made a big impact on her. We visited the Ladies and I showed her how everything worked. The only thing that panicked her was the hot-air hand-drier. She tried to save me by pulling my hands out from under its roaring air.

On examination, Gus Sutton said Illeana should ideally have the surgery required on both eyes in five different stages. Each operation would be very delicate in order to ensure that he did not overcompensate and make the eyes point the wrong way. Since Illeana was terrified of everything to do with doctors, Mr Sutton asked everyone at the Birmingham Eye Hospital to take off their white coats. She was also scared of the idea of giving blood until a handsome young doctor turned up to do the job and then she suddenly became very brave!

At the last moment Gus Sutton said he had changed his mind. Although we had assured him that she could stay with us for as long as it took, he had thought long and hard and was going to attempt to do the whole job in one go.

To get Illeana used to what would be happening I would bandage her eyes and she would pretend to wake up after having had the operation. I didn't want her to panic and tear the bandages off when the time came. We practised her telling me when she had pain and I showed her how quickly I would get her tablets to ease it. The hospital set up a bed for me next to hers, although I had been expecting and would have been happy to sleep in the armchair.

In reality she was an absolute cat when she came round from the anaesthetic, and she kept wanting to rip the bandages off, despite all our rehearsals. In the end I had to threaten to telephone Sister Jane if she didn't do as she was told – that threat had the desired effect. A few days later Gus Sutton came in to take the bandages off. I could see that he was very nervous because if he had overdone the work he would never be able to put it right, having cut away too much nerve tissue. As he unwound the bandages I held Illeana's hand. There was a frightful silence for a few moments as he stared into her face. 'Illeana,' he said, 'you have the most beautiful eyes,' and I could see that his eyes were wet with tears. 'Excuse me,' he coughed and left the room, returning a few minutes later having composed himself.

Illeana peered into the mirror, slowly focused and then blinked. Her mouth began to curl up in the corners and she let out a shriek, blinked and focused again and said, 'Lordy, my eyes are straight, Bevey, my eyes are straight!' She had indeed got the most beautiful green eyes.

'Thank you, Gus,' was all I could say before I too dissolved into tears.

'Take her home,' Gus said. 'Hospital is no place for a beautiful young lady like Illeana.'

We said our thank yous and goodbyes and headed home, Illeana's head held high. As we came into the house Patreascu looked into her face, then looked again, breaking into an enormous grin. He had no words to describe what he wanted to say. Instead he mimed, pointing to Illeana's eyes, crossing his two fingers and then pointing both fingers out straight in front.

While she was with us Illeana learnt to do everything, how to do the washing and peg it out, how to prepare dinner, how to clean and how to iron. We thought these skills would be useful to her should she ever have her own home and she took pride in every task, revelling in our praise and amazement at each one completed. It was her seventeenth birthday a few days before her return and we decided to give her a party. First I took her to Dickins and Jones to a young hairdresser called Mark. He lavished attention on her and when he finally turned her to look in the mirror she exclaimed, with obvious joy, 'Ah, Pamela! *Dallas*!'

She learnt a lot of practical and social skills in England. She still sulked, sometimes for hours, but no longer for days or weeks at a time. She was far more tolerant of other children. She seemed softer, more at peace, less on edge and less inclined to lash out over any minor incident. At first Illeana was very impatient with Patreascu because he couldn't move very fast – she believed he was stupid. But once he began showing Illeana how to do things that were new to them both – putting music cassettes or videos on, turning on the central heating – it dawned on her that being physically disabled didn't necessarily mean mentally disabled. This being a still widely held belief in Romania, the Sisters were very happy to see that Illeana knew differently on her return and passed her knowledge on to others.

Illeana had led a very sheltered life in a lot of respects and now she was getting used to meeting people and talking to them. She was happy to be able to do things like make cups of tea and walk the dogs. She lost her hunched, haunted look and her personality began to develop. It was lovely to watch her looking in the mirror, having suddenly caught sight of herself, and the resulting smile. She was happy with what she saw now.

We sent photographs of Illeana with her beautifully straight green eyes to Sister Jane and Sister Ida, and telephoned so that Illeana could say goodbye to her friends. I did feel sad that they wouldn't see the results of her operation for themselves, see Illeana's newfound confidence and happy outlook. The Sisters would have moved on to their new three-year posting by the time Illeana returned home to Bacau. When I expressed my sadness that after going to so much trouble on her behalf, Sister Jane would not see Illeana, she said, 'Oh, no, Bevey, it is Illeana's joy now to see – not mine. My joy is to know of my child's happiness.'

Illeana was desperate for a family and when she discovered that we were going to adopt Patreascu she took the news very hard. She felt we had rejected her and there was nothing I could say to make it better. The truth was that although she hoped we would adopt her, that had never been our intention and we knew she was too old for the authorities to agree to the adoption anyway.

'Why can't you adopt me as well?' she asked.

'Would you rather we didn't adopt Patreascu?' I asked.

She thought about it for a long time. 'Is it possible that he will get better if he stays with you?' she wanted to know.

'Yes, very possible,' I said.

'Then you must adopt him.'

I tried hard not to cry with her, biting my lip and looking away, but I couldn't stop the tears falling.

'Oh, Bevey,' Illeana said, 'I thought you weren't upset about me going home, but you are really upset.'

'We love you dearly, Illeana,' I explained. 'You will always be extra special to us and we hope you will always remember us too.' Nigel had been right. The other children would always think, Why Patreascu? Why not me? and I would always feel guilty about that.

I had talked to Illeana and became convinced she had lived at home before going to Ungerini. There seemed too many details for her to have made it all up. She even remembered the name of her teacher, Cristy. I told Sister Fabiana and she promised to check Illeana's records at Ungerini.

The sisters were very understanding when Illeana went back to them and Sister Fabiana told her that she planned to write to all the children's families. 'Would you like me to try to find your family, Illeana?' she asked.

Illeana was ecstatic – all the years she had been telling us that she had a family and someone believed her at last. Some days later Sister Fabiana found out which village she had come from. She decided not to wait for a reply to her letter but to take Illeana for a visit.

'Imagine our dear child's excitement,' Sister Fabiana told me later. 'She dressed in her best outfit. Valentina did her hair for her. Szuzannah lent her a necklace. Maricica insisted on making her bed for her. They were all so happy that she would see her family again. All the house was at the gate to see us off.

'When we arrived we did not know which was her family house. People were glad to guide us and then suddenly we were at the house of her mother. Illeana stayed in the van, suddenly shy. I called out and a middle-aged gypsy woman came to the fence. She was Illeana's mother, surrounded by her younger brothers and sisters. Her mother came to the back of the van and opened the door. She looked at Illeana, put out her arms and pulled her to her, hugging and kissing her, weeping and calling out her name, "Illeana, my child, my child, my child." Illeana wept too, calling, "Mama, Mama." They all moved to the house. Sister Bartholomeo and I did not want to intrude on such a private occasion but Illeana pulled us in as well.

'The mother explained to us, "I have six children. My husband left me to bring them up alone. Earthquakes had already devastated this region. When Illeana was nine years old floods came too and swept away our house and our crops. We had nowhere to live and nothing to eat." Apparently Illeana had a teacher called Cristy, the woman she had talked about to us. Cristy took pity on the girl and, in the true belief that she was helping her, took her to the authorities in Bacau so that she could be found a home and continue her education. It was very unusual for a gypsy child to receive education and her teacher must have been fairly exceptional to have accepted Illeana.

'Her mother and Cristy were unable to trace what happened to her after that. They wrote numerous letters and Cristy even went to see the government department responsible, at great danger to herself. No information was forthcoming. They hoped that she had gone to a good place with good food and a good education, which would lead her to a better life than theirs.

'Her mother confirmed that at that time Illeana had a slight squint in one eye. That must have been enough to get her classified as handicapped.'

I could only imagine what Ungerini can have seemed like to a bright nine-year-old girl. It must have felt like her world had ended. Her grandparents arrived at the house while the Sisters were there and as Illeana told them all the awful truth of what had happened to her they all began to cry. After that first visit Illeana decided she wanted to stay with the Sisters to complete her education, but now she visits her family regularly and knows she can go home as soon as she is ready.

There was a school next door to the home in Bacau where some of the more able children used to go to have lessons before the new school house was built. While she was in England Illeana told me that there was an oaf in the school who used to take pleasure in teasing, pushing and taunting our children, encouraging others to join in and calling them 'handicapart'. She also told me that the teacher who was supposed to be looking after them was setting them work and then going out shopping. I rang Sister Jane and passed this information on. She said she would deal with it and the next time I rang she told me what had happened.

'I found the boy,' she said, 'a boy so big I had to bend him double to reach his ear. I was booting and beating him all the way to the Principal's office. I had one such fine temper on me I made the Principal call all the children together and I told them they should be helping our children, not ridiculing them, and I told them if I heard of such a thing again I would be booting them all the way to their parents' houses.'

When Illeana went back, looking so beautiful with her eyes straightened, several of the boys in the school asked her out. 'What did you say to them?' I asked her later.

'I told them to remember that I was "handicapart".' She grinned mischievously. 'I don't want to go out with nasty boys like that.' The straightening of her eyes had changed her whole personality. She was suddenly tolerant and serene, a truly beautiful person. She began to see herself as someone, not just a label, 'handicapped'.

Not all the operations were so successful. Petrutsa was a young blind girl who used to beat herself furiously in her frustration, sometimes laughing as she whacked her head against the floor, and only stopping if a worker picked her up. She seemed to have some reasoning powers but it was hard to know what to do for her. Sadly, Gus was unable to do anything to restore her sight. 'There is no possibility of sight,' he said. 'I could re-attach the retinas but she still would not see. I could take off the cataracts, which would make her look better,' he said, 'but that would only help the rest of us; it would do nothing for her and I am not prepared to put her through so much pain just for that. Please get her back to the Sisters' tender loving care.'

I felt such grief for Petrutsa and, rather discouraged, rang the Sisters with the news that her condition was irreversible. They too were disappointed for her, but reminded me that we must have the courage to try, even if the result is not what we hoped for. Mr Sutton confirmed Sister Jane's suspicion that Petrutsa's handicap was a result of her mother contracting German measles when she was pregnant.

All the children had become great fans of Status Quo after the discos at Ungerini, but none more so than fifteen-year-old Daniel. When he came to England, Status Quo's guitarist, Rick Parfitt, agreed to meet him at a London hotel and – delightfully and refreshingly – insisted on no publicity before we could even mention it. Daniel managed to spend two and a half hours with his hero the day before returning to Romania. I was desperate to go along myself, as I am a great fan of theirs, but I felt that Ashley, the young English co-worker from Mother Teresa's who had been so good to Daniel, deserved the treat as thanks for all he had done.

Daniel's bones produce too much calcium and this accumulates on the outside of the bones, causing abscesses and eruptions on his skin. It is all very painful and gives him limited movement in his arm. He is highly intelligent and attends high school in Bacau, but can't live with his family because he needs constant medical attention. Ashley hoped that by bringing him to Britain and taking him to Great Ormond Street Children's Hospital, something could be done to help him return home.

Daniel spent one week with us in Milton Keynes in the late summer of 1991, not long after I had returned from my first trip to Ungerini (Ashley desperately needed some time off, he gave constant care to Daniel for five weeks in all). During that week Daniel became alarmingly ill, running a high temperature and suffering a great deal of pain from infected abscesses. I rang our doctor, Dr Prisk, to ask his advice about what best to do. I was scared to lift Daniel since I couldn't move him without causing him absolute agony.

Dr Prisk came out immediately and when I opened the door to the lounge where Daniel was bedded down on the couch, the doctor rushed in ... 'Ah, Daniel, now what's the problem, young—' But before he could finish, disaster struck and Dr Prisk let out a piercing, 'What the—'? Moss, having seen a strange man rush into the house and sensing Daniel's vulnerability, had decided a 'seeing-off' was called for and bitten Dr Prisk abruptly on the bottom! Despite his discomfort Dr Prisk continued to minister to his patient. Daniel wasn't over-impressed with his skills, however; when the pills prescribed didn't work overnight he told the doctor, 'I do not think those antibiotics you prescribed are strong enough. The ones Sister Jane gives me would have worked by now!' Dr Prisk good-humouredly suggested sending all his patients to Sister Jane and retiring himself!

Sadly Daniel was told the results of the hospital tests showed there is nothing that can be done, but he didn't really understand or take it in – maybe he didn't want to. When I explained to him that his condition was irreversible and that he would never walk he wept and became very depressed. Then, after a few days, he told me that he was going to snap out of it, organise the rest of his life around his disability and stop making himself miserable. I admire him so much. Now he is painting icons on glass quite beautifully and plans to sell them to help support his parents and family.

After their meeting, Status Quo contacted us to find out the time of Daniel's train into London and sent a limousine to meet him at the station the next day, packed with T-shirts, hats, sweatshirts, cassettes and a huge ghetto blaster for all the other children. The chauffeur then drove Daniel and Ashley to Heathrow and escorted them, with all their luggage, to the departure lounge.

Whilst Patreascu, Szuzannah and the children who followed were in England they were able to spend some time at Brays Road School in Sheldon, a very well equipped special needs school; it gave them a chance to get out of the hospital for a few hours each day. Nigel was a governor of the school. The first time I went along to see what was happening I went into the staff room at break time and found myself standing on my own, unable to make a move, not daring to encroach on the groups huddled together and talking. Seeing my discomfort, a very attractive older man with lovely, wavy white hair and kind, hazel eyes came over and introduced himself as John Hickman.

'You are with the Romanian children, aren't you?' he asked.

I said I was and he asked me lots of questions about what I was doing.

'I would love to go there and do something like that,' he said.

'Why don't you?' I jumped at the possibility of recruiting a fully trained special needs teacher! 'I'll make all the arrangements for you.'

He proved to be one of the most successful volunteers I had found so far and has been an invaluable help over the years.

The other person I met at Brays Road was a gentle, grey-haired man called Bob Vicarage. He was an orthotist, a person specialising in the design and manufacture of mechanical devices to support or correct weakened joints, things like calipers and splints. He worked closely with Nigel at the various hospitals, clinics and special schools Nigel was associated with. I started talking to him about something I had seen at Brays Road called a standing frame. It was basically a box which went up to under the child's arms and was almost impossible to tip over. It gave badly crippled children the sense of what it was like to be upright, supporting them securely and encouraging muscle growth.

'Would it be possible to get the designs for something like that,' I asked him, 'so that we could ask carpenters out in Romania to make them?'

He said he thought it could be arranged and suggested a lot of other things we might do. I asked why he didn't come out with me to see what really needed doing and, after some initial hesitation, he agreed. I told him to forget all his anxieties about getting out there – to leave all the arrangements to me. I may not be able to do any of the clever medical bits but, by golly, I can make great arrangements. The children called him Doctor Bobby, which they thought was hysterical because one of the dogs at Mother Teresa's was also called Bobby. He proved to be the most wonderful ally, persuading his firm, Salt and Sons in Birmingham, to donate thousands of pounds' worth of splints, calipers, special shoes, boots and appliances, with many of the staff working through their lunches and after hours to get rush orders completed for us. He came to Bacau with the Dwyers and me to meet the children and see the problems for himself. His expertise, advice and guidance were invaluable in getting many of the children on their feet and he has been back several times since to help the children in the home and others in the surrounding areas.

Our ultimate aim was for Dr Bobby to teach the local people how to make some of the simpler appliances, so that they would not have to rely on donations from other countries. I would like to build a small workshop and to employ local handicapped people to make calipers, crutches, splints and false limbs. During his first visit we saw dozens of children with the most painful stumps; their lives could be transformed with the right equipment.

Moira Dwyer agreed to come out to Romania with us on the condition that nobody expected her to do any physiotherapy, saying that she had not worked with children for thirty years and that it would be reckless to begin working on such severely handicapped little ones now. My job was to take notes.

One of the children, a frail little girl called Cristina, was obviously highly distressed. Putting her back in her cot still didn't calm her but I had to leave her to go back to my note-taking. I glanced up a few moments later and saw Moira smiling reassuringly at Cristina, their fingers touching through the bars of the cot. Cristina stopped crying. I went back to my notes, panicking at the unfamiliar terminology, realising how unequal to the task I was. A few minutes later I saw Moira totally absorbed in doing physiotherapy on Cristina, who was no longer protesting. She then went on to work magic with many of the children during the week.

Most importantly, Moira was able to work with the Sisters and carers, gently encouraging them to have the confidence to do what she was doing. Her work carries on, and that of Sally Braithwaite, the physiotherapist from Brays Road School. Their visits offer not only short-term relief but inspire long-term work.

After the first day's clinic, whilst everything was still fresh in my mind and I could still read my own writing, I sat down at the Sisters' antique typewriter to get the day's notes typed up. After hours of consulting *Black's Medical Dictionary*, I realised that I couldn't make any sense of anything I had written. I despaired, weeping with frustration as I stared at all the words which looked so similar. The notes were so vital. I headed for chapel but even praying made no difference. I had to face facts. My notes were complete gibberish; the one useful contribution I might have been able to make and I had failed miserably.

Next morning Nigel, Moira and Bob arrived early to start another packed clinic. Parents and children had been queuing for hours again and the Sisters were giving out bread and milk – all they had to share. Nigel went straight to work and didn't stop to look at the notes until he took a lunch break. I went off and busied myself in a remote corner, wishing I could make myself invisible. A strange rumbling noise began to reach me. It got louder and louder and then the awful realisation hit me. Nigel was laughing. My humiliation was about to be total and public. Nigel was sitting on a small stool, tears pouring down his face. He had lost all semblance of control; he had 'corpsed'. I didn't know whether to laugh or cry. I was on the borders of a king-sized wobbler. My bottom lip was quivering and Nigel tried to compose himself. 'It's all right, Bev,' he spluttered, but then lost control again and fell off the stool. That made everyone laugh and I began to feel better. When he had recovered himself enough to speak he told me that the notes, although hopelessly misspelt, would serve to remind him which patient was which and his brilliant secretary, Cathy, would fill in the correct medical spellings later.

As my faith increases, so does my confidence, but I still hate getting up and speaking in front of people. When the Sisters asked me to read the lesson at a very special Mass I politely said 'yes' then panicked seconds later and told them I couldn't do it. 'But you will be amongst friends,' they said, completely puzzled by my attitude.

'I'm truly sorry. I am just not the kind of person who gets up in front of everyone. Please, please forgive me.'

I rang Nigel at the hotel, fairly hysterical and abandoning any sense of pride, and begged him to help me out by reading the lesson himself. Nigel laughed and laughed but this time I didn't care.

'Oh, Bev, you are priceless,' he managed to say at last. 'Here is a woman who terrifies half of Birmingham – and probably most of Britain – a tigress and protector of children who can talk anyone into doing anything and you can't even read a little lesson to a group of friends, most of whom don't speak a word of English anyway.'

I allowed him his moment of gloating and then he agreed to read the lesson. He did it beautifully, his rich voice echoing round the little chapel. He gently placed the Bible back on the lectern and the whole thing fell to the floor in pieces. I raised my eyes and said a silent prayer of thanks that it hadn't been me up there. Valentina started to laugh, then the other children, then Nigel and the Sisters and even the priest joined in.

Getting to know the children so well over the years, I gradually learnt more about the horrors that had been perpetrated on them at Ungerini. As they grew to trust me they told me things they had forgotten or had been bottling up inside. The evidence came in tiny little pieces, sometimes from the children and sometimes from other people working or staying in the Ungerini home. The bigger girls, I discovered, had often needed to have abortions. To start with I assumed it was just because they were left unsupervised with the bigger boys, but gradually tales emerged about how a small number of the women carers would dress them up, paint their faces and then bring the older boys up to their rooms and encourage them to have sex so they could watch. The women also brought male workers into the building at night when the managers and volunteers were not there and let them loose on those girls least able to protect themselves. One 'medical worker' designed himself a special table that he could lie the girls on; it held their deformed bodies and limbs in exactly the right positions for him to have his way. Two girls separately told me how they had performed oral sex on one of the medical workers. When Madam Augustina found out about him, after an investigation, she dismissed him. This was a very brave action because he could have caused her problems with the authorities or spread rumours. Thankfully we did not hear of any repercussions.

Other workers became very angry when they found out about this, but it was always hard to discover the truth of what was happening because most of the victims couldn't speak coherently. Lucia was instrumental in finding out about and stopping some of the worst excesses. Luckily, enough of the perpetrators were sufficiently frightened of her to take some notice.

The damage done to the children by this sort of behaviour was incalculable. One girl I grew very close to gave me detailed descriptions of her own abortion, details she could only have known if she'd been fully conscious throughout. She believed her baby's death to be her fault, that because of her sins he was condemned to hell for eternity. I gently explained to her that it hadn't been her choice to abort the baby. She hadn't understood what was happening to her until it was too late and therefore it couldn't be her fault.

First someone had told her she was going to have a baby, then a couple of weeks later she had been bundled into a van, dragged into hospital, undergone a painful and public indignity, only to be rushed back to Ungerini in terrible pain, with blood pouring down her legs. She hadn't realised that this had anything to do with her baby until she missed the feeling of the child moving within her.

'Oh, Bevey, he would have been mine. I could have loved him as no one loves me. I could have given him the things I do not have. I would have bathed him and dried him, and now he is with the Devil in hell, and it is my fault!'

I tried to remember what I had learned as a child. 'Jesus said, "Suffer little children to come unto me." That means that your child was innocent and will be right now sitting in the arms of Jesus, happy and loved. Loved by you on earth and Jesus and all the angels in heaven. He will not be forgotten.' I wondered how she knew about heaven and hell, given that she was supposed to have lived at Ungerini all her life – there was no religious teaching there. How I wished I spoke more Romanian, that we knew more about the children's backgrounds.

I hope I gave her a little comfort, but her sad, haunted look, and subdued yet agitated demeanour, will stay with me forever.

Many times after we spoke about her child, that he might be walking or talking, whether he would have looked like her or his father. Such was the girl's understanding of what abortion really means – a terrible curtailing of life, and the awful suffering and mental anguish of the mother – that I came to the conclusion that there was no reason for her to have been sent to Ungerini at all. Her baby's life had been wasted before it began, and hers was wasting away too. Both seemed equally tragic to me. I began to think about what abortion truly meant, the ending of life before the infant had drawn breath independently. How could it ever be right to do such a thing to someone so small, vulnerable and unable to defend themselves? We held the children's lives in our hands and it wasn't only their physical and mental welfare we should cherish, but their moral welfare too.

I don't ever think about this girl and her terrible experience without feeling I could have done more to protect the children in my care. I pray she will fall in love one day and have a much wanted child, fulfilling her dream to have a family, a home and someone to share and return the huge amount of love she has to give.

CHAPTER THIRTEEN

Our Son – the Prodigy

*

December 1992 brought Patreascu's sixth birthday. I had just returned from taking Szuzannah home and Patreascu was still not speaking at all. We decided to take him to see the West End show, *Cats*, and were given the best seats, right where the actors came from under the stage. Initially he was terrified when the cats came up to him, and I began to think I might have to take him home. The actors, however, must have sensed his fear. Staying completely in character, they began to gently wash and stretch in front of him, putting their paws against their faces. He reached out and touched a pure white one, rubbing his face in her fur as she cuddled him. From that moment on he was entranced. Every time a cat passed it made a fuss of him and he thought it was brilliant. There was a rowdy scene where the dogs had a loud fight in the park. Patreascu was shaking his finger at them as if to say, 'Naughty, naughty,' which the actors on stage thought was hilarious. They were all coming very close to him at the edge of the stage.

Before the performance the stage hands had had to weigh down Patreascu's seat because he was so small, he kept disappearing through the back of it, and in the interval we were invited to go behind the scenes to meet the cast. They were wonderful, letting him touch their fur and explore their microphones and make-up, encouraging him to show them how he walked with his little crutches. I had been very nervous about meeting such interesting and arty people, but they were a complete joy and I made a vow to bring all the children to the show in future.

On our way back Patreascu spied the orchestra and rushed in to have a go on all the instruments. The musicians loved him and wanted him to stay but the show had to go on and the audience was returning to its seats. Back in our seats for the second half I could see that his eyes were dancing with excitement. He was completely lost in the make-believe of it all. He suddenly saw his favourite character, Rum Tum Tugger, who he had spent most of the intermission with, and pointed, shouting with glee, 'Pisica!', his first ever spoken word. Old Deutoronomy came off stage and gave him a massive hug and said, 'God bless you, Patreascu,' and Patreascu gave him a broad grin and a thumbs-up sign. Although he did not understand the language, which is all in song, or the story, his powers of observation were amazing and he followed the plot from their mimes and body language. When all the cats were unkind to Grizebella, a very old, grey and tatty cat, he turned to me, pointed to Grizebella and began to weep, burying his head in my chest.

After the show we were asked backstage once more. The actors had a hat, T-shirt and tape of the show for Patreascu. As soon as he saw Grizebella he ran over to her and hugged her, stroking her gently and comforting her as if telling her he understood the pain of rejection.

When we got home at about 8.30 that evening we thought Patreascu would be more than ready for bed, but he rushed straight to the lounge, changed into the T-shirt and hat, put the cassette into the player and proceeded to boogie until about 11 p.m.

Richard Oriel, who set up and ran *Cats*, and had been our host at the London show, was very interested to hear about Romania. I told him that all the children would love to see the show in Bacau and he wondered if it would be possible. 'Why not?' I replied.

Some weeks later Richard joined Bob Vicarage, Roger Wolsley, our orthotists, and me on a short visit to Mother Teresa's. Richard wanted to look around and assess whether it would be possible to stage even a 'pocket' version of *Cats*, given the limited facilities available. He is a very lively, kind and gentle giant of a man, six feet five in his socks, and all the children were very taken with him. I was surprised, but pleased, when he asked me to sit in with him at his meeting with the Sisters. They expressed delight at the prospect of a show for the children, not only their residents but all the local kids, and a plan was set in train for bringing the show to Bacau.

Richard had shown the Sisters photographs of the London production and they had only one problem with it – the costumes. 'What about the costumes?' Richard asked. 'Oh, Bevey will explain,' they said, disappearing. Will I? I thought, looking puzzled.

I ran after the Sisters and asked what they meant and they giggled and said, 'Bevey, have you no eyes, girl? Men's private parts so prominent we could hang our umbrellas there! Local people would be most shocked.'

Richard went on to set up and run *Sunset Boulevard*, then *Oliver* and now works directly for Cameron Mackintosh. Sadly he was inundated with work and unable to work any further on getting *Cats* to Bacau after that first trip – but we still harbour a dream of taking the show to Bacau one day. I know it will happen!

Having said his first word, Patreascu came on in leaps and bounds with his talking and worked constantly on his walking and dancing. I spent hours giving him speech coaching but made a silly mistake, getting him to copy everything I said. If anyone said, 'Hallo,' that was fine because he replied, 'Hallo'. But if they then said, 'How are you?' he would repeat that too. Everything I learnt with Patreascu I am now using with the children at Mother Teresa's and slowly they are beginning to speak too.

At first we feared Patreascu might be deaf because his speech was very unclear and he never finished words. I spoke to Nigel about it, asking whether it was a physical problem. He humoured me by recommending an ear, nose and throat colleague of his who, after a lengthy examination, said he was fairly certain there wasn't anything physically wrong although spending four and a half years flat on his back in a cot staring at the ceiling certainly hadn't helped Patreascu. He told us that he was almost certain there was nothing to worry about – it was just part of the learning process. He confirmed my suspicions that lack of chewing and other exercise of the facial and throat muscles had been a major contributing factor in the children's inability to talk. Patreascu and I spent many hours together, pulling faces to exercise his speech muscles, singing scales, anything to encourage movement. Gradually his speech became clearer and his vocabulary increased, but he was still not using long sentences and if he was excited by something his speech tended to become garbled again.

We worried that the fear, aggression and misery he had experienced in his early years would leave a mark on his personality, but no sign of this has appeared; he only ever shows kindness and gentleness to everyone. For a long time he suffered from terrible nightmares which left him sobbing, fearful and bathed in perspiration, but as his speech improved he was able to tell us about them as we rocked him back to sleep. 'I was tied up in a cot, a big white octopus comes and all its arms are hitting me but I can't move. Then I saw a white sari with a blue stripe and Sister Ida with her wooden spoon and she beats the octopus and unties me.'

Patreascu's mental processes were hard to assess those first few months after he left St Gerrard's, and we were not sure whether he would ever catch up with his peer group or be able to read or write or achieve complete independence. All this had to be taken into account as we prepared to adopt him. We knew that at our age (I was in my early forties and John was fifty) we would not necessarily be around for as long as he needed us and we did not want him to be a burden to Russell, who was then only twenty-five.

Some of the family had been very nervous about meeting Patreascu at first but my sister, Karen, and her husband, Les, were very helpful. They had invited us for a weekend in Kent some months before, but we had to decline as we were having Patreascu home from the hospital.

'Is he free from disease?' Karen asked.

'Absolutely,' I assured her. 'He is more likely to catch something from other children because of his poor general health than to give them anything.'

'Bring him too, then,' she said.

Both Karen and her husband are in the police force and they have two daughters, Becky and Claire, who we had always said we would have if anything happened to Karen and Les. We have spent many happy holidays with them, a practice which has regrettably stopped due to my commitments in Romania. As we set off for the weekend we were a little worried about how Patreascu would interact with two robust and very 'normal' children. We needn't have worried, though. At one point we found him, plaster cast and all, on the top bunk bed, having been helped up by Becky and Claire. All the work Nigel had done and all Patreascu had endured flashed before my eyes. If he had broken his leg then it would have shattered in about thirteen places. Thankfully he came safely down. Everyone was enchanted with him and Karen and Les took us to one side. 'He is so divine,' Karen said, 'that we want you to know that if you do adopt him and anything happens to you, we would be more than happy to take him on completely.'

By April 1993 Patreascu insisted on trying to dress himself. His first attempt took him two and a half hours. I am not a patient person and I wasn't sure I was going to be able to cope with it so I left him alone and went downstairs, returning every few minutes to encourage him. Patreascu was so happy when he managed to complete the whole process himself and one of his favourite sayings for the next few months was, 'No, me do it.'

Initially, Patreascu had to have two crutches, then he moved to one and finally he threw that away as well, preferring to make his way about with a sort of rolling gait, swinging his feeble leg around confidently. He would often fall over but always got straight back up without making any fuss. He had really started on the road to independence now. Before long he was washing himself, doing his own hair, choosing his own clothes, making his own bed and dressing himself every day. He became totally toilet-trained. He took to dancing in a big way, using the kitchen as a disco and the lounge for ballet. I sometimes shudder to think what Nigel would have said if he could have seen Patreascu's leaps across the room, often with one of the dogs grabbing his leg in mid-air. (Misty never really recovered from the shock of the first time her teeth encountered the unaccustomed hardness of his leg plaster.)

He also started painting again, loving to get himself in a mess and then helping to clear up afterwards. Gillian had told me how his paintings in Romania had been dark and disturbing but now he was using lighter, happier colours. Patreascu never buys cards from shops, always insisting on making them himself in bright and cheerful colours, with glitter plastered all over them.

Our next problem was finding a school that would suit him. We wanted somewhere where they would not be bothered by his problems and wouldn't molly-coddle or patronise him. We went to see a lot of different ones before we found the one which we thought would be the best for him. St Monica's is a local Catholic primary school and they didn't seem to think that his disability would be a problem. They were extremely keen to discuss his abilities, not his disability. There was a wonderfully warm and happy atmosphere, which we felt immediately we entered the school, and a great deal of emphasis was placed on sociability as well as academic standards. At first John thought me mad, as I don't drive and St Monica's isn't within walking distance so getting there would be a problem. I knew it was not the most sensible option in lots of ways, but the school had seemed so right that I really prayed he would be accepted. There were some stumbling blocks initially: he had not been baptised; John and I were not Catholics.

One night, shortly after our visit, I overheard Patreascu saying his prayers, 'Dear Jesus,' he said, without prompting, 'please, please let me go to St Monica's.' Suddenly I just knew that he would be accepted, that everything would be all right, and the next day we went out to buy the distinctive uniform in readiness. Reckless? Foolhardy? Certainly, but he and I knew this was his place, that these were his teachers and that it would only be a matter of time before he was accepted.

Every morning Patreascu went to the cupboard where his little school uniform was hanging and enquired hopefully, 'School?'

'No,' I would have to say, 'not today, but soon.'

We were going to Mass at several different churches in our area. One Sunday we went to the Church of Christ the King. Father Sean welcomed us and asked who we were. We told him and he said he recognised the name Patreascu because he was one of the governors of St Monica's and had seen our application. During the service Father Sean asked the congregation to 'give each other signs of peace'. Patreascu rushed out in his caliper, nearly falling over in his haste to get to the altar and said, 'Peace, Father – nice church.' I think it was at that point that he won a place at St Monica's. I heard from another governor that Father Sean and Mrs Helen Finkenrath, the very active Head Teacher, had both spoken at the next governors' meeting but that it was the words of Adam Gawronski, a parent/governor, which had moved them all to make their decision. 'This child,' he said, 'so desperately seeking an education, is a gift from God. We must surely accept him.'

It was really Patreascu who decided, after visiting many different churches, that we should celebrate our regular Mass at the Church of Christ the King with Father Sean. It is an unusual church shared by the Baptists, United Reform Church, the Church of England and the Catholics. We liked the idea of Patreascu being able to mix with such a wide variety of people and he has been warmly welcomed by all the various congregations. Patreascu refers to our priest as 'my beloved Father Sean' and they do indeed share a tremendous repartee!

Once his attendance became a reality, we were very anxious about how he would cope with the daily routines. How would he know where to go for the toilet, for PE or lunch? Would he be able to follow instructions when he was still only speaking a few unclear words? We were terrified that someone would call him over to the school gate and take him away because he was so trusting of everyone and unaware of the possible dangers. Our fears were soon allayed by the practical common sense of Marion Shires, the school secretary, and Mrs Finkenrath, who was always available and proved a very positive and spiritual guide, both to Patreascu and to John and me. Whilst having to stop herself from breaking into helpless laughter on many occasions, she managed to encourage Patreascu in many ways. I am sure that a lot of his personal skills, his communication and general confidence when talking to people, are due to her persevering with speaking to him, even when she couldn't always understand his replies.

When Patreascu finally started school, in late June 1993, his attention span was about five seconds and we were nervous as to whether he would sit still long enough to join in anything, and worried he would be disruptive just because he did not understand what was going on. We need not have been concerned. His very first teacher, Mrs Binks, took him firmly and kindly in hand. Care assistant Pam Cunningham was appointed to work with him for one hour every day and they formed a wonderful relationship. I felt quite envious, especially when he came home one Friday evening and began to sob, 'Won't see Pam now!'

After his first two weeks I nervously approached Mrs Binks and apologised for all the extra work which having Patreascu in her class must mean. 'Yes,' she replied, 'he is extra work but what he brings to me, to this class and to the whole school, more than compensates; we are all enriched by his presence here.'

Each evening we would sit down together and try to do his homework. Patreascu had a tremendous thirst for knowledge. He was a child of a thousand questions and his inability to express himself often made him frustrated.

A month after he started we went to school sports day, wondering if Patreascu would be able to compete at all. We should have known better. Though greatly inhibited by his giant caliper Patreascu was determined to do what the other children were doing. Mrs Binks was anxiously following him around on all the apparatus, giving him a little lift as and when needed, but he whizzed round everything. The sight of John gamely doing the hurdles with his son raised a great cheer, which made Patreascu stop dead, laughing and waving to the crowd – as always the showman. After that a cheer went up every time he did anything and I don't think there was a dry eye in the school.

The following year he went on to Mrs Brooks, with mornings spent with Mrs O'Brien, who taught the new five-year-olds, in order to catch up on the many things he had missed. After a few weeks it was decided that this was unsettling for him and he should remain with his own age group full time. Mrs Brooks is a very lively teacher and they formed an instant bond. When she was ticking off one of her pupils one day Patreascu said, 'Brooks not happy?' whilst staring into her eyes and grinning hopefully. He cannot bear to see anyone sad, ill or in pain.

Sports day 1994 showed us just how far he had progressed in a year. He was now able to rush around by himself. The only problem was the high jump but as he tried to jump two bigger pupils appeared, as if by magic, grabbed an arm each and assisted him over the bar.

Each year Patreascu wept at the thought of leaving one teacher and moving on to someone new. His next teacher was Mrs Tholen who had lots of beautiful long blonde hair and played the guitar and, as with the others before her, he immediately formed another extraordinary bond. Throughout this time he continued to be encouraged by Pam Cunningham and by us at home. The academic work was becoming harder now and Patreascu used to return home from school exhausted. Just walking required ten times the effort of another child and Patreascu was having to absorb so much else at the same time too. I used to make matters worse by thinking I had to be 'Supermum' and always be doing things with him. Mrs Finkenrath tactfully told me that her own children used to come in and just sit watching television in order to relax after a hard day and I realised that I needed to give Patreascu a little more space to behave like his new friends.

On his first day they had put Patreascu in the charge of a little blonde Norwegian girl, called Ida, who looked after him and became his best friend. She and the other children had to stand guard over the gates when they were in the playground in case Patreascu wandered off and disappeared. When Ida had to leave because her parents were moving on to Thailand, Patreascu was heartbroken, but he soon formed a deep attachment with two other little girls, Emily and Rebecca. His other great friend is Christopher Gavagher whose footballing skills Patreascu admires and whose fighting and protection skills have come to Patreascu's rescue on more than one occasion.

He has had to face up to a little bullying in the form of ridicule about his left leg being so thin and scarred, having a caliper and a splint, not being able to run, the fact that he fell over a lot, even that he had to wear orthopaedic boots, nice as they were. This hurt him terribly and puzzled him because he was usually so naturally kind to everyone less fortunate than himself. The school was as upset to hear about it as we were and immediately set in motion procedures to make sure it stopped. One unfortunate side-effect is that Patreascu will no longer wear short trousers. He feels embarrassed and nothing any of us can say will make him change his mind.

When Emily saw that Patreascu was being bullied, this delicate, feminine little girl advised, 'If they hurt you again just punch 'em. Punch 'em in the tummy then there's no blood and you won't get into trouble.'

'I can't do that,' a surprised Patreascu responded. 'It's not right to hit people.'

'I'll do it for you then,' she told him firmly. 'I can't bear to see you hurt.' They then continued with their cushion fight.

When he started school Patreascu still needed to wear a very heavy-duty caliper on his leg and Nigel warned us that he would probably have to wear it for the rest of his life. Patreascu, however, had other ideas and insisted on discarding this uncomfortable old thing and wearing his lightweight 'night' splint all the time. We asked Nigel's advice fearing it would do him no good at all.

'I'm not sure,' he admitted, 'but the boy has a pretty good sense of self-preservation and seems highly capable, so let him have a try.'

We did and within a few months Patreascu was walking about, albeit with a limp, but able to go up and down stairs with more ease than when his leg was held completely straight and rigid in the caliper.

'I am good,' Nigel told us when he saw the result of this for himself, 'bloody good. But what has happened to Patreascu is a miracle.'

When he had been with them a year the school told us that although he was one year behind his age group in language and reading, he was actually two years ahead on intelligence and memory. The only thing that had been lacking for him in Romania had been input and stimulation. Because the teachers were keeping such a close eye on Patreascu at the beginning, they were also able to tell him off when he misbehaved. We did not want him to be given any special treatment which might lead to jealousy. They were soon telling us that he was by far the kindest and most helpful child in the school. If another child was hurt in the playground he would be the one to cuddle them and take them to the medical room, where he would lavish them with healing creams and plasters. He was always smiling and bringing a sparkle to the eyes of the teachers with his innocent cheek, complimenting one teacher on her new hairstyle and another on her new perfume. At the beginning they would always push him to the front of the lunch queues but before long the other children were treating Patreascu just like everyone else. It was the nicest compliment of all!

In the Nativity play he strode confidently about the stage in a false beard, gently coaxing the shyer children to wherever they were supposed to be and taking the instruction to 'sing loudly' very literally indeed, even when he didn't know all the words. 'Away in a manger, no ... for a bed!' Mrs Finkenrath turned to Father Sean and said, 'Just look at Patreascu, what an extraordinary difference in only one year.' At the first Nativity play he had been unsure and nervous, now he was not only taking an active part, but encouraging others too.

Patreascu's first invitation to tea came from a schoolfriend who we found lived quite close to us, Paula Gawronski, a rising ballet star who was quite a bit older than him. Mary and Adam (the parent/governor who had pleaded so effectively for Patreascu to join the school), her mum and dad, Jan and Ronan her older brothers, and Anna her older sister, all made him so welcome that all our fears about little things like how he would ask for the loo or know to change out of his school uniform just evaporated. The whole Gawronski family have since been invaluable in my work. Mary told me that she would dearly love to work in Romania but was too committed to her family. In order to give me the freedom to go there, however, she offered to have Patreascu after school and to give him tea whenever necessary.

Remembering Patreascu's interest in music I enrolled him for some violin lessons and after the first few the teacher became tremendously excited. 'It is early days yet,' he told me, 'but considering his background his ability is extraordinary. It may well be that he is a musical prodigy.'

He also went to dancing classes with Paula. Mrs Woollard, Paula's ballet teacher, while more used to training potential stars for the Royal Ballet, formed a sparkling friendship with Patreascu. Though appreciating Patreascu will never be another Nureyev, Mrs Woollard has been teaching him ballet and tap, greatly increasing his balance and co-ordination.

By sports day 1995 he was still putting everything he had into competing. 'Oh, Mum and Dad,' he said sadly, 'if only I could come first in one of the races.' We felt so bad for him but realised he was going to have to face up to his limitations more and more as he grew older.

Patreascu has also begun to be naughty from time to time: a great relief to us and the school – another longed-for sign of normality. He was told off one day by the Deputy Head, Kate Harper. He had been talking in Assembly and she sent him out, telling him to go to her office and 'face the wall until I return!' When Kate did return, having survived a reproachful look from an adult witness, Patreascu turned to her with sad eyes. 'Darling Harper,' he said, 'me very sorry!' She said that in thirty years of teaching no one had ever dared to call her that before.

Now he has been at school for a couple of years John and I catch ourselves being disappointed when one of his school reports say that in some subjects he is just 'average'. We have to kick ourselves and think back to the child we first came to England with, a child who was little more than a vegetable and who certainly couldn't have been considered 'average' at anything in a Romanian orphanage for the handicapped, let alone amongst a class of mainstream English schoolchildren.

All the governors, teachers, staff and pupils at St Monica's have had a positive impact on Patreascu, so much so that really he is a little piece of them all. It is impossible to single out any one person for they have all guided him to where he is today – a happy, normal and enthusiastic pupil at an exceptional school.

CHAPTER FOURTEEN

A Holiday, a Wedding and a Funeral

*

When Illeana was in Britain in 1993 she and Patreascu were invited to London to meet Mother Teresa. Illeana was particularly excited because we were told that Princess Diana, her greatest idol, was going to be visiting at the same time. But when we arrived at the Sisters' modest mission house in Kilburn Mother had been whisked off for a meeting with Princess Diana at Kensington Palace, because the crowds of press and television were too big at the mission house. We were told that Mother Teresa was coming back to see us as soon as she could. We managed to get inside the building but the crowds outside were so great that they were forcing the doors down. John had to lean all his weight against them to keep the reporters out. Suddenly, unannounced, Mother Teresa was there amongst us; it was well worth the one and a half hour wait! She saw Patreascu and cupped his face in her hands.

'Child,' she said, 'you are truly beautiful. What is your name?'

'Patreascu.'

She indicated his school uniform, which he had proudly insisted on wearing. 'What are these fine clothes you are wearing?' Falling over his words in excitement, Patreascu answered her questions. 'You must walk for me,' she said and watched as he wobbled across the room. 'You walk wonderfully.'

She pinched his face and then turned to Illeana and said, 'Child, your eyes are beautiful,' and spoke for a few minutes with me translating her English into Romanian as best I could for Illeana. Then she turned to John. 'And who is this fine big fellow?'

'This is the husband of Bevey,' one of the nuns told her.

'Thank you, John, for helping us,' she said, shaking his hand.

'I haven't done anything,' he protested.

'You allow Bevey to help us,' she said. 'We are very grateful.'

Then she told me that she had heard about my work and wanted to know everything we were doing. She asked me to keep in contact, sending bulletins on Patreascu's progress, his school reports and photographs, because she wanted to know how he was getting on. After that I talked to her as often as I could afford to, or wrote, and she told me that she was taking the photographs around with her to show people just what a family's love can do for a child.

It is Mother Teresa's policy to move the Sisters on every three years, which can be very hard for them and for the children with whom they form relationships, but is all part of their accepted way of life. In July 1993 Sister Jane was moved to Sri Lanka and I missed her a lot. I knew that she had been unorthodox in the way she involved me in life in Bacau and I worried that with her departure all that might stop. I couldn't bear the thought of not having so much contact with the children I felt so close to.

By the time I was due to take Illeana back to Bacau at the end of July, 1993 Sister Fabiana, the Croatian sister, had taken over from Sister Jane as Sister Superior and she came all the way to Bucharest to meet Illeana and me. She greeted us warmly and told me she had prepared me a bed in the girls' dormitory. 'All the girls are hoping you will stay with them,' she said. I was so relieved to know that things were going to continue as before. They still do, and I feel very much part of the Bacau home.

I love staying with the children and being part of the house, despite the savage hours and the sixteen people snoring, calling out and getting up to pee in the night. Whenever I visit Maricica always makes my bed, with her by now traditionally perfect hospital corners. She loves it when I come out of the bathroom and feign total surprise every time, thanking her profusely. Each night my pyjamas are laid out and the top cover pulled down for me and a little teddy hidden within. I always have to leap up and pretend finding it is a great shock. I'm sure the children are bored with doing this every night but keep it going just to humour me.

Sister Jane had dreamed of all her children visiting the seaside and asked me if I would consider taking all the children to the Black Sea for a holiday. She warned me that I wouldn't be able to bring Patreascu because I might not be able to get him back out of the country again afterwards due to the bureaucracy surrounding the adoption. I also knew that his British medical visa had expired and that we would not be able to get him back into England without it. I was very loath to leave him but I thought it would be lovely for the rest of the children to get a chance to see the sea and Sister Jane said that unless I was willing to go it wouldn't happen because they had no one else to call on who was experienced enough to handle all fifty children and the carers. Put in a corner like that there wasn't much I could say except, 'Okay'. Cecilia, the dentist's wife, went to immense trouble to try and make the best possible arrangements.

By the time we came to take the holiday Sister Jane and Sister Ida had left Romania, but Sister Fabiana didn't want to deny the children this longed-for break so we went ahead. I felt torn in two – was I going to make a good mother if I could so easily abandon Patreascu for three weeks for these other children? I wondered.

I knew I was going to need all the help I could get so I asked John Hickman to join me. He was the volunteer and universal grandad whom I had met at Brays Road School and who I thought was particularly good with the children. He agreed. As well as being a special needs teacher he was also a swimming instructor, which would make him doubly useful at the seaside. Then I rang whacky Helen, who I knew had been such a success on her previous trips to Bacau.

'Would you consider coming back to Romania with me for a couple of weeks?' I asked.

'Can you give me a little more idea what it's about?' she said, cagily.

'We're taking the children on holiday to the seaside.'

'Count me in.'

It was decided we should take the children in two groups so that we had enough people to ensure their safety and proper care. The first group consisted of twenty-six children, three of us from Britain and seven Romanian carers, including Johnny the dentist and his daughter Delia who would translate.

So we set off at the end of July from Bacau for Constanza, in two van loads with so many children in each van that we all had to sit on the floor. I had Valentina on top of me for most of the trip and the heat was incredible. The driver in our van insisted on keeping the windows shut because he was afraid he would get a chill from the draught and when I took my shoes off Maricica was sick in them, and continued to be sick throughout the twelve-hour journey, despite having been dosed up with travel-sickness pills. Then one of the big boys got severe diarrhoea and we discovered that we had packed a thousand sanitary towels instead of the Pampers nappies that we were going to need. Somehow, however, we managed to contain him and continued on our way, sweating profusely, smelling disgusting and singing merrily.

We took an open ferry across the Danube, feeling rather nervous that some of the children might try to jump over the side. The ferry operators agreed to take us free when we explained what we were doing and I decided from then on to ask for everything free, on the principle that if you don't ask you don't get.

Constanza is the most beautiful place with long sandy beaches and warm blue sea, but our joy at arriving was dented by finding that none of the beds in the hostel were made up. It was a bit of a struggle settling every one in, but we were soon set up, and the holiday started in earnest the next morning. The town was clean and neat with plenty of fruit available in the markets and, a great treat for the children, ice-cream.

Apart from children like Szuzannah and Illeana who had been to England for operations, this was the first time many of our charges had been outside the Bacau or Ungerini areas. And it was certainly the first time they had seen the sea or beaches. There was a fair right on the beach and Tractor Lucien's face lit up, a picture of joy, when he saw a little train roundabout. Although he was twenty years old, he had never seen anything like it. Nor had the other children or the carers.

This holiday outing was the first time I had been in sole charge of so many women workers and I found I had to be firm with them from time to time. I wanted to go on the evening outings together, all of us, and they were unhappy about this. In the evenings they wanted to put the children to bed early so that they could clear off and really enjoy themselves. I could see that they would want to get out, but this holiday was intended for the children; the women were being paid to work not to party. I wanted the children to get out and about as much as possible. There was a lot of grumbling but they eventually went along with me. They wound up watching one another like hawks and complaining furiously if they thought someone else was doing less than them, or had easier children to deal with. Most of the bedrooms were allocated one carer to two children, but I made it one to one for a particularly difficult child. This, however, meant that some of the women had to have three children, which caused terrible arguments. I had three children myself and chose ones that I knew the women didn't like or found too temperamental or difficult. I wanted everyone to have as nice a holiday as possible, with the least possible ill-feeling.

After a couple of days some of the women came beating on my door, crying and wailing and crossing themselves. I had learnt that whenever they started crossing themselves something was afoot.

'Oh, Bevey, Bevey,' they cried, 'it is terrible. Six of the children are terribly ill. We think they are going to die.'

I asked which six and they told me the names of six gypsy children.

'Oh dear,' I said. 'Well, give me half an hour and then come back and I will have arranged picnics for you to take with you on the train.'

'The train? Us?' They seemed puzzled.

'Well, I am just so grateful that I have you women here to escort the children home,' I said, 'and that you are willing to give up your holiday by the sea. I could never send sick children all the way back with just some village girls in charge of them. So go and prepare yourselves and the children to travel and I will organise the food.'

The women disappeared, muttering amongst themselves and returned half an hour later, rejoicing and shouting hallelujahs to the Lord because the children had been miraculously cured. I had to agree with them that God, indeed, was great.

Our routine was much the same each day, since we chose to keep to the same timetable as the home in Bacau. We would get up at the normal time and head down to the beach and play there until about eleven-thirty. On our two return trips in the van we were always singing and banging tambourines, making our own fun. Then we would come back for lunch and a break while the sun was at its hottest, returning for another beach session in the afternoon. In the evening we went out to places like the local dolphinarium and fun fair and a boating lake. Dom Patreascu had come with us and insisted on rowing vigorously on the lake, despite the fact that he was fitted with a pacemaker. The Romanians were always very proud of their surgical adventures and he would insist on not wearing a shirt so that everyone could see his scar. To show off his strength he went rowing off into the middle of the lake, so I jumped onto a pedallo, beckoning Valentina to join me, and we set off in pursuit, laughing fit to burst. Halfway across I realised that I was doing all the work and had to encourage my partner to put a bit of effort into it. But once we got close enough, we scooped water up in cups and sprayed Dom Patreascu and his crew and she didn't hold back then. Comparing an evening like this to the way the children had been when they were incarcerated in the gloomy dungeons of Ungerini, seeing them in the fresh air in such beautiful surroundings, laughing and shouting, their stomachs full and their skins tanned, was miraculous. I wouldn't have believed it possible jut three short years before.

The people at the dolphinarium and the beach fun fair very kindly didn't charge us, but unfortunately for the other holidaymakers, once our children got on the rides at the fair we couldn't get them off. They would sit for twenty minutes at a time, just going round and round. The gypsies running the rides enjoying seeing the obvious fun the children were having, were happy to give them extra time. I noticed that other people were taking their children away when they saw our children. To begin with it made me angry, but then I decided it was just a good opportunity to fit more of our children onto the rides. I suppose they were frightened their children might catch something or would be upset by the physical ugliness of our children – they were the ones suffering from their ignorance, not us.

I used to tell them not to be frightened, that their children could not catch anything from ours, but my words fell on stony ground so I decided to ignore them and look on the bright side. The carers thought I was wonderful, sacrificing all my turns on the rides to look after the bags – little did they know that just watching made me feel travel sick.

Johnny the dentist had asked at the hotel about other activities available in the area, and Doamna Victoria had rung a horse-breeding farm owned by a very rich family of gypsies (who looked as if they would slit your throat if you turned your back on them for a moment). Our evening at the farm turned into the most memorable outing of the whole holiday. All the horses were brought out for rides and demonstrations and the children were given carriage rides around the beautiful estate in the warm evening air. An enormous thoroughbred appeared and I was offered a ride, but I didn't want the responsibility of breaking the poor creature's back and so declined. Many of the women carers had a go and thoroughly enjoyed themselves, however.

At the end of the evening I went to the head man and asked him how much I owed him for our evening's entertainment. Very formally and very emotionally he refused any payment: 'It is I who should be paying you,' he said, 'for the most beautiful evening of my life.' He then started to weep and gave me money to buy the children ice-creams and drinks.

For the mornings and afternoons, we colonised a beautiful, secluded piece of beach. A few people came up and warned us not to let the children too far out into the water – there was a deep channel nearby through which the fishermen took their boats out to sea – but we felt there were enough of us to stand guard and we needed to find a fairly uncrowded area to spread ourselves out in. I have to say that once we arrived and started to organise ourselves we usually found that the surrounding areas cleared pretty quickly.

There were always a few curious onlookers who would come and stare. Helen, resplendent in her bikini and Doc Martens, joked that they were staring at me in my bathing costume because they thought I was a beached whale, but it was obviously the children who excited their interest. Helen was very brave and used to sit herself down cross-legged in front of these people and stare straight back at them until they felt so uncomfortable they got up and left. I never had quite that much courage.

There were those who wanted to practise their English on us and would ask us the usual irritating questions: 'Who's paying you?' and, 'Why don't you bring nice children to the beach?'

'These children have no one else to bring them,' I replied, as reasonably as I could, 'and they *are* nice; they're just handicapped.'

If anyone hung around too long we would give them a child to hold and sadly that got rid of them pretty quickly. There were some people who were very kind, though. One man bought a kite for the children and others bought them ice-creams.

When the sun was particularly strong we would use the van and a few sun umbrellas to provide shade for the less mobile children, and I encouraged the more able ones to lay the towels out and look after the ones who needed watching over. We ate melons, which Johnny the dentist and his daughter Delia got from the market each morning. I wanted to get the children working as a team as much as possible, helping one another whenever they could. For the first time they were not having everything done for them; they were having to do things for themselves and each other. I even got them saying 'please' and 'thank you' for things. They seemed to enjoy it all.

I constantly worried about the children drowning or wandering off, and so I would arrange the volunteers and women into a triangle with John Hickman out at sea to catch any who ventured too far out. He was wonderful at coaxing the more timid ones into the water, gently splashing their faces and getting them used to the waves. They all loved being smothered in sun cream and after-sun lotion. We did, unfortunately, manage to burn poor Shanti because I hadn't realised she had a condition which meant her pale skin burned at the slightest exposure. She got burnt only on our last day and the Sisters were furious with me when we took her back in that state. All I could do was apologise to her and to them.

In the hostel dining room, where we would eat lunch and supper, we regularly met a group of perfect-looking Russian children, visiting gymnasts. I had noticed that they were ridiculing our children but lacked the courage to do anything about it. Then one mealtime Szuzannah had one of her classic falls, tumbling inelegantly off her wobbly, duck-like legs, hitting her head on the table and knocking over a chair. It was a hard job getting her back up because her feet turn in so much and she is always shaky after a fall. The Russian children were all screaming with laughter and imitating her fall. I became so incensed with anger that anyone should mock Szuzannah after all that she had endured to be able to walk at all that I stormed over to their table and started shouting at them in English, telling them they should have helped instead of picking on someone who was obviously in trouble.

Their teacher turned on me and wanted to know how I could expect them not to laugh when our children were so handicapped. That merely made me angrier and I began listing all the defects of the Russian children and ended, rather grandly, saying, 'At least our children don't eat like pigs at a trough!' They didn't laugh at us any more after that.

The Sisters made me promise that I would keep the children's religious observance while they were away from their care. This meant sprinkling holy water on the beds each night in the sign of the cross as many Catholic families do, a kind of daily baptism, and saying prayers with them. We took it in turns to say grace before each meal. It was a wonderful holiday, although such luxuries are not the Sisters' usual way of doing things – it is hard to justify a seaside holiday when the poor are banging on your door and begging for a slice of bread for their starving families.

Sadly, the following winter, Dom Patreascu died and his widow, Doamna Patreascu, insisted that I should go to the funeral with her – I was in Romania at the time collecting Lucien and Marian to take them to England for operations. I felt honoured that the family should want me there, and grateful to have the opportunity to remember the life of this very special man. Dom Patreascu's was the first Romanian funeral I had ever been to and I was not prepared for the level of emotion I would encounter. The funeral was held on the day before we were due to return to England and a howling blizzard had set in. The local women and family members set up a shrieking and screaming like I have never heard before. The body was put on display in an open coffin on an open cart. Dom Patreascu was all dressed up in his best Sunday suit and shiny shoes, but as I looked at him I couldn't find the tears to express my own sadness. I looked down at the children and saw they were all watching me, solemn-faced and dry-eyed, waiting to see what I would do. The sight of their sad little faces, thinking how they had lost such a good friend, their 'Grandad', was enough to set me off and as I began to weep they all followed suit.

'Please, Bevey,' his widow asked me, 'say a few words to Dom Patreascu.'

I started to protest but realised it would mean a lot to her and, praying my Romanian was up to it, went up to the coffin to thank the old man for being a grandfather to us all. 'Dom Patreascu was the first and only family the children have ever known,' I said, 'and he was family to me too – thank you for sharing him.'

When the time came to put the lid on the coffin the screaming and moaning reached new heights.

'Let my lips brush the lips of my husband one last time,' Doamna Patreascu wailed. 'When they put the lid down I will never see his sweet face ever again.'

'Let me touch the hand of my father,' his daughter cried, beating her fist against her heart in grief. When they finally lowered the coffin into the grave the women almost followed it down in their desperation not to let him go. I felt such an overwhelming sadness for his family and for the Mother Teresa children that for quite some time afterwards I would find my eyes filling with tears whenever I thought about not seeing him again. The home wouldn't seem the same without his kindly presence each night.

Eighteen months later, seeing his round, smiling face on a video, I turned to his son Gerry, who had tears dripping down his cheeks, and shared a few of those tears.

I had asked the Sisters if it would be possible to take one of their Romanian helpers with us to Britain to assist Lucien and Marian because I felt that they really needed someone who could speak their language well and who would help them to maintain their usual routines so that they would fit in again easily on their return to Bacau. I had seen with all the other children that although the nurses at the hospital were great, it was not the same as having a familiar face from home around.

'Write down the name of the girl you think would be best,' Sister Fabiana told me, 'and I will do the same.'

We both came up with the same name, Maria 'Ochelari' (Maria of the glasses), a very bright girl in her early twenties who was always asking questions about what we were doing and why. After we had spoken to her we went to see her widowed father to ask his permission for her journey, which he gave, although it was obvious he wasn't comfortable with the idea. He seemed rather set in his ways, not very considerate of his hard-working daughter's feelings in this or any other matter. He wouldn't agree to having water piped to his house because they had always fetched it from the well and he saw no reason why Maria should be any different. I noticed that when Maria pointed out to him that he had trodden mud in all over the floors that she had just finished cleaning he brushed her protests aside. 'That,' he told her, 'is what floors are for.' I knew, however, that many Romanian men of his generation were like that, and I could see that father and daughter had a tremendous love for one another, despite their disagreement about Maria's trip to Britain.

Not long before we were due to return to England I was in bed in the dormitory when Maria came round last thing to lift the children, as she always did, to try to cut down on the number of wet beds. As she went past my bed I made the same joke I always made, 'Do I have to get up, Maria, can't I stay in bed?' I noticed she didn't smile, which was unusual for her, even though she must have heard me make the same joke a hundred times. 'Are you okay, Maria?' I asked and her bottom lip began to quiver.

I took her into the washroom and she told me what was wrong. It seemed she was frightened about almost everything, from the flight itself to the responsibility of looking after the children.

'My father tells me that if one of the children dies it will be my responsibility,' she said. I assured her it wouldn't be, but I didn't think my Romanian was up to setting her mind at rest totally, so I asked Sister Fabiana to talk to her. Ultimately, Maria did come with us, nervously but willingly, Sister Fabiana having explained to Maria and her father that I would be the children's legal guardian and would take all the responsibility this entailed. Both Maria and her father were comforted by this.

The trip back to England went well partly because the airline was now used to our presence. They no longer sat us at the back of the plane in case we upset the other passengers, and they let us go straight through the airport instead of making us go round the back. Marian sat next to me and Lucien sat next to Maria, but as the plane started to taxi onto the runway Lucien became agitated and wanted to get to me. We swapped them over but as the plane gathered speed he became worse, rocking back and forth and begging me to tell the pilot to slow down. Once we had taken off he was all right but I knew we were going to have to make another stop in Romania before getting to England and would have to go through the whole thing again – worse still, we would be landing on compacted ice! Lucien, however, trusted me and was very observant. Once he saw that I wasn't showing any signs of fear he realised there was nothing to worry about – although he did keep saying, 'I will go back to the Sisters soon, won't I, Bevey?' I assured him he would. Once he knew he wasn't leaving for good Lucien became an instantly seasoned traveller, even braving a visit to the cockpit with Maria to meet the pilot.

Maria became very nervous when we landed in England because she had an ingrained fear of officialdom – the legacy of years of dictatorship. I went through Immigration with her and then she shot off because she had seen a policeman. I caught hold of her and took her over, asking the officer to come and talk to us so she could see that he didn't behave anything like a Romanian policeman. She couldn't believe how polite and softly spoken he was.

Stansted is a wonderful airport to bring handicapped people in and out of because it is so calm and friendly and so geared up for wheelchairs. As we came through Immigration we found John Hickman and Helen waiting for us. John had managed to find a brilliant van that would take wheelchairs and Helen had come up from London just to welcome the boys to England. We stopped for a cup of coffee before heading off with John for the new Mother Teresa home in Birmingham where the boys would be staying during their treatment.

We were warmly welcomed by Sister Vinetha, the Sister Superior, who had thought of everything to make their stay cosy. The home was so new that it was really still a building site and only the day before the Sisters had been painting the walls of the room which the boys and Maria were going to share. But by the time we arrived they had made it look very homely, moving beds down from another floor and filling it with pictures and toys. There was a table and chairs for them to eat at and an electric fire because the central heating had not yet been installed. They had wanted us to bring the children later, when the house was finished, but with Nigel considering retirement there was a danger that if we didn't bring the boys then they would miss their chance.

I could see that Maria was a bit intimidated by the whole experience and offered to stay with her for the first night. The Sisters found me a Z-bed which Maria insisted on taking, giving her divan up to me. She was always very respectful and courteous, even though it wasn't at all necessary. I had learnt to accept little gestures like this uncomplainingly, realising that a refusal could hurt people's feelings.

The next day John brought Patreascu up to collect me. When Patreascu walked in Maria, who had looked after him in Sister Ida's room two years beforehand, was standing at the other end of a long corridor. He still had on a heavy-duty caliper and as he limped towards her, she suddenly realised who it was and started to run, weeping hysterically. When she reached Patreascu she fell to her knees, touching, hugging and kissing him, completely beside herself.

Patreascu, whose speech was still a little indistinct, just kept patting her and saying, 'Awight, awight.' When she heard him speaking she almost fainted.

Then it was Lucien's turn. 'Patreascu Mic?' he said, unable to believe his eyes.

'Yes, Lucien,' I said, 'this is Patreascu Mic.'

'Patreascu walks?'

'That is what you will be like, Lucien,' I told him as he made Patreascu walk back and forth in front of him, staring open-mouthed in amazement.

'Patreascu speaks?' He shook his head in wonder at the miracles unfolding in front of him.

'Patreascu eats?' he said when we all sat down for lunch. He couldn't believe it!

The wonders never seemed to cease for them. When Patreascu asked to go to the toilet and then washed his hands afterwards, Maria dissolved into tears again, remembering the number of times she had had to clean up his cot or anywhere else that he had been at the moment he decided he needed to go. When he said his prayers at the beginning of the meal and helped Lucien and Marian to cross themselves it was almost too much for her.

Patreascu was desperate to use his new-found skills to help his old friends, serving them their food, testing the temperature of their drinks and buttering their bread for them. At one stage Lucien got his penis out and started playing with it. He had always had a habit of doing this and it was quite the most enormous member I have ever seen. Sister Jane was very broad-minded about her boys masturbating as long as it was not in public, although one of the other nuns was not so understanding and used to threaten to beat Lucien's erection with a wooden spoon. Patreascu's face was a picture as he saw Lucien start to unravel this gigantic thing from his trousers. His jaw dropped open and he looked from Lucien's lap down to his own with an expression which suggested that many complex new thoughts were passing through his young mind.

He immediately understood, however, that this was neither the time nor the place to proudly display one's member, whatever the size, and in the little Romanian I had taught him, he said, 'No willy out in front of Sisters, pants up and trousers zipped.' Although he was very aware of Lucien's sometimes erratic and very unusual behaviour, Patreascu seemed to want to protect him. Now that his awareness of what was accepted behaviour had developed he simply didn't want other people to ridicule his Romanian friends, some of whose behaviour was very bizarre.

Lucien had never lost the habit of using the most foul language imaginable, much of which the women carers at Ungerini had taught him in order to amuse themselves. There was a rather twee visitor at the Birmingham home who used to annoy Maria, criticising her methods and continually interfering. One morning she walked into the room and Lucien smiled broadly.

'Hallo, you hairy old vagina!' he exclaimed in Romanian and I thought Maria and I were going to die of embarrassment.

'What did he say?' the elderly visitor asked brightly, pleased at such an enthusiastic welcome.

'He was saying how nice your hair looks,' I translated and once she had left the room we collapsed in helpless giggles before trying to explain to a puzzled Lucien that he mustn't say such things to people.

When the time came for the boys to have their operations Maria got into a terrible state and so I asked Father Gerrard if he would come to sit with her while the operations went underway. I was going to be in the theatre.

Lucien was very nervous on the way in spite of the pre-meds he had been given. I always insisted the children had pre-meds, even when the anaesthetists said it wasn't necessary, because I wanted the experience to be as trauma-free as possible for them. They were given something in tablet form to relax them, and then I would insist the nurses use Emla cream, a local anaesthetic, to numb any injection sites. The children had all had such bad experiences with injections at Ungerini that the idea of the anaesthetic could be more frightening for them than the operation itself.

When it came to Marian's operation everyone had to wear goggles, double gowns and triple gloves because of the danger of catching hepatitis. It was astonishing how much bone would be flying around the theatre once the doctors got to work with their hammers and drills. Marian was eleven and had a large head due to hydrocephalus. He had club feet too, which made it very difficult for him to walk, although Nigel suspected he could have got around if he had truly wanted to. Correcting club feet is something surgeons hate to do. Vast amounts of tissue, sinews and cartilage have to be cut away to release the feet so that they can be straightened out and pinned into position, ready for walking on. In England club feet are dealt with soon after birth so an operation on a child of Marian's age is extremely rare, if not unheard of.

Lucien was fifteen, although only the size of an average seven-year-old. His legs were bent permanently in the lotus position with the bones horribly mishapen and deformed. If he was held up in a standing position his bones pointed outwards, looking as if he was wearing jodhpurs. He was on the operating table for six hours with Nigel, his surgeon son, Jonathan, and another surgeon working on him, plus a dental surgeon who was removing some of his teeth. Nigel and Jonathan and their colleague spent a long time cutting carefully through everything because the nerves and sinews would be sewn back together leaving minimal damage and the best possible chance for healing and normal function after the operation. A piece had to be cut out of the thigh bone and then the two remaining pieces of bone pulled together to form an almost straight section of bone which Nigel then plated together. The same operation had to be repeated on the other leg but to a different set of measurements. Having plated both parts of the bone together on the second leg, the lengthy process of stitching all the muscles, cartilage and tendons back together took place. It was tiring, intricate and absolutely fascinating to watch – even for one as squeamish as me.

Nigel was very concerned about the suitability of Lucien's bones for the treatment he proposed because when he'd had them X-rayed he had discovered that they did not contain any of the internal marrow that most of us have. Because he had been tied for so long in one position and had suffered rickets they had become completely solid and Nigel was worried that because they lacked marrow they would not heal properly. He was also worried that he might sever some vital nerves in trying to get to the bones. Unable ever to stop talking in moments of stress, I was constantly asking questions when I was in the theatre and most of the time Nigel would answer. At one stage he let out a strangled, 'Bev, shut up.' A few minutes later he straightened up and apologised, explaining that he had been working on a particularly fiddly section. Given that, his response was very restrained, especially after hours at the operating table.

When Lucien came round he was very distressed. It was the tooth extractions which caused him most discomfort and a lot of vomiting and nausea. I stayed with him until he was calm enough to hand over to Maria, at which stage Nigel rang up and ordered me to go downstairs. When I got to the theatre staff restroom I found that his wife, Moira, had prepared another of her lavish picnics for us all. Now the boys had survived the surgery we all

244

felt like an enormous weight had been lifted off our shoulders. There was quite a carnival atmosphere as we talked over everything that had happened. The nurses relieved Maria so that I could bring her down and she could join in, albeit rather timidly.

By Easter, there was still a long way to go until either Lucien or Marian were ready to go back home to Romania and we invited Maria and the boys home for the long weekend; it would give them a break from the hospital. With Nigel's and the Sisters' blessing they stayed three weeks in the end. Patreascu spent his whole time trying to protect them from the dangers of fires and electrical points, just as we had had to do with him when he first became mobile and curious. They could not return to the Sisters' home in Birmingham because building work was still under way and there was too much risk of infection from all the dust. During the remainder of their stay in hospital the Sisters visited them every day and Patreascu and I came up once a week together and I came up on my own again mid-week. Once they were discharged we had some lovely times every Saturday with the Sisters, Maria and the boys at the Birmingham house. I often asked Patreascu if he might prefer to do something else but he always insisted on going to Birmingham to see his friends, to help them get up and walk.

Maria 'the glasses' became a dear friend. She had always dreamed of going to London and seeing a show, so John agreed to take her for a day out, visiting *Cats*, taking a tour of the City and going out to dinner afterwards. She told me it was the most wonderful day of her life. I was awfully relieved when she came back – Marian was a terribly difficult child to cope with. He was not at all self-motivated, unlike most of the visiting children, and expected, almost demanded in his silent way, that he get the constant care a baby would, right down to not wanting even to clean his own teeth. He had big, velvety brown eyes and almost everyone fell for his idle ways. He was so big that it was virtually impossible to lift him onto a changing mattress and there was no physical reason why he couldn't use a potty and then the toilet. But life had been so hard on him he really couldn't see much point in doing anything beyond lying around, eating, sleeping or staring at the ceiling. The floor seemed very secure to him because there was nowhere for him to fall to. Persuading him to take a little exercise and gain some independence was very hard, although we did eventually get him walking to the bathroom and cleaning his own teeth, after what must have seemed to him like endless nagging. I had on several occasions had to suggest to Maria that she take Patreascu downtown for a McDonalds when I thought the strain of looking after Marian might be proving too much. It's a favourite place with both the children and their carers. The staff are always helpful – carrying trays or pushing wheelchairs – and try to make our visits special. I had been shown how much Marian was capable of when he put his mind to it by Sally Braithwaite, the physiotherapist from Brays Road School. When we were becoming particularly fed up with him she wheeled him out into the hospital car park in his chair.

'I'll show you what he can do if he has to,' she said, and set the chair rolling down a steep hill. Horrified, I was about to run after him and catch the handles but she held me back. Sure enough, after he had looked round and ascertained that no one else was going to help him, his hand shot out and stopped the chair's speeding progress as easily as if he did it all the time. Marian couldn't be more different from Lucien who was supposed to do fifteen minutes physio every hour but was so keen he would try to cram sixty-five minutes into every hour.

People used to think we were wicked for forcing Marian to get up and walk on Dr Nigel's instructions, mainly due to the theatrical protesting he was expert at. Whenever he came to our house he used to systematically collapse and go over the top of his zimmer frame, landing in a heap on the floor. We were so alarmed when he kept doing this and bruising himself that I rang Dr Nigel. 'Great!' he declared. 'That boy has an acute sense of self-preservation. He won't do anything to endanger himself. He's just making a protest. Every time he does it pick him up and he'll soon learn that he has to stay upright.'

'But he could really hurt himself,' I protested.

'I rather hope he will,' Dr Nigel replied. 'That way he will give up flinging himself about and concentrate on what he's ruddy well here for – to walk.'

We did as we were told and Nigel was right: eventually Marian stayed up and walked. He is still able to muster up sympathy by looking up at some unsuspecting person with his huge brown eyes and giving a little wail of pain and exhaustion, persuading them to carry him, but not far for he is very heavy.

Maria also came with John, Patreascu and me to the church

service at which I was accepted into the Catholic faith. I didn't tell anyone else in the family about it because I thought they might laugh at me. I had been very nervous about having to stand up in front of everyone in the church, even though there were three of us doing it. Father Sean had talked me through a practice run and assured me that he would prompt me if I went wrong. It was an exciting and special evening, the candles flickering and whole place alive with love and an exhilarating vibrance. We all sang loudly and joyfully and I felt so happy and complete that when I first took Holy Communion I thought I was going to faint. Patreascu clapped when it was my turn and called, 'That's my mum!' and everyone joined in and applauded with him.

When we got home around 10 p.m. I could see that Denise and Janet (from Abbey National), who had kindly agreed to come and look after Marian and Lucien, were very relieved to see us back. Denise and Janet had been out to Bacau so they knew what to expect, but an afternoon and evening alone with Marian and Lucien (who had been waving his willy at them all day) had proved almost more than their nerves could stand and they were exhausted.

Having decided we were all starving we discovered that Maria had never eaten Chinese food and was under the impression that they ate worms. So we ordered a take-away from the end of the road and stayed up talking into the small hours of the morning. We all felt too high to sleep.

John Hickman spent a great deal of time with the boys, ferrying them back and forth to Brays Road School each day, and I thought it would be nice for him to accompany them back to Romania and enjoy the excitement and pride that the triumphant return always engendered. He jumped at the chance.

During my October 1994 visit with the medical team, the Sisters asked if we would like to come and celebrate Mass with them at Gisteni, the Adult Institute. I was very pleased to accept because I would have the chance to see children who had transferred from Ungerini at eighteen. I had not seen them since. I was disappointed every time I visited Ungerini to find that more children had gone to Gisteni.

I had not visited Gisteni since my original trip there with the Norwegian Red Cross, but the memories were still very vivid. It had been as appalling as Ungerini, yet worse still because there were nearly five hundred adults in residence. And no running water, no light bulbs, no mattresses on the few beds and not even a blanket each! Almost as bad as the total physical and mental deprivation was the total lack of anything to do. I remembered being incredibly fearful of the noise, the screaming and so afraid that someone would hurt me.

I was pleased to find that Gisteni was better than I had remembered; there had been definite improvements but there was still a long way to go.

As we drew into the gates hundreds of the patients came rushing towards us. The Sisters helped Father Mihai set up an altar under a big tree and the patients and village people began to gather. The patients joined in the singing and praying as best they could and were very much enjoying themselves. It looked just like a scene from the Bible. Father Mihai obviously had a great affinity for the people. His services are the only recreation the patients have and a welcome influence from the outside. I wondered what would happen once the snows came – already it was almost too cold to be outside even if only for a couple of hours on a sunny day.

It is Father Mihai's dream to build a small church so that services may be held throughout the year. A friend of mine, Marcus Beale of MBA Architects has designed a simple church for Father Mihai and his unusual flock – so maybe, if God is willing, and the money comes, it will happen . . .

Later in October, Maria came up to me very coquettishly and announced that her boyfriend had asked her to marry him. She invited us to the wedding. I really wanted to go but we were running out of money by that stage and it was hard to justify the costs of so many flights to and from Britain. As I was going to be over there collecting a child before the date of the wedding my husband John very generously suggested that I stay on with John Hickman for the celebrations, and what celebrations they were. It meant being away from Patreascu for ten days which was hard, but I felt I owed it to Maria.

The Sisters dressed the big girls up for the occasions. They even managed to get Valentina to exchange her usual tomboy outfit for a dress. Everyone was wearing fur coats and make-up and looked very elegant. Maricica, who had the body of a ten-year-old and the face of an ex-boxer was also in a fur coat, with huge hoop earrings which she was very proud of. Doamna Patreascu had made flower garlands for everyone.

Just as we were ready to leave we realised that the weekly gypsy market had set up in the mud track outside the home and we weren't going to be able to get the van up to the gate. There was no way we could get the children all the way down to the van through the market stalls, so we had to go out and plead with the stall holders to move back and let the van through. Once they understood the gravity of our problem they were very helpful and cheerfully waved us off.

Maria's village is called Valea Mari and lies about twenty kilometres outside Bacau. The children sang all the way up to this scenic little hamlet with its picture-book church. When we arrived Maria, who hadn't known if I was going to be able to make it or not, was overcome with excitement. She was standing arm in arm with her husband-to-be as we drew up and shyly introduced us. He was a handsome young man, prematurely greying and with his hand resting formally inside his suit as if he were Napoleon. The Romanians are always very dignified and proper when it comes to photographs and traditional ceremonies.

After the ceremony we lost Valentina for a while, only to discover her standing between the bride and groom for the official photographs, a large grin on her face. She had exchanged her dress for some rather fancy trousers!

The reception was held in a local co-operative hall, a beautiful building with dark wood walls and floors and dozens of tables groaning under the weight of a feast which Maria's family must have been preparing for days. There were all the traditional foods of the countryside; soups, meats, rice wrapped in vine leaves, pickled tomatoes, hot chillies and bowls of raw garlic cloves. As we came in we were given glasses of Tsuika and slices of traditional bread. I don't usually drink Tsuika because it is too potent for me, but it was so cold I wanted to find some way of warming my bones.

The band, consisting of an ancient accordion, drums, saxophone, keyboard and guitar, immediately struck up the fastest music imaginable and Valentina came up and grabbed me, growling at me to come and dance with her. For a moment I held back, afraid of making people stare, then, warmed by the Tsuika and the smiles of the people around us, I melted and headed out onto the dance floor with her. The room erupted into clapping and cheering and the party was off. Everyone was so quick to start enjoying themselves and so courteous to the old people it was a joy to watch. They all seemed to be able to dance wonderfully, even the largest, most cumbersome-looking women and the most gnarled old men. They whizzed their partners around at a terrifying speed, the men whistling to one another through their teeth. The dances were a mixture of formation Latin and traditional Greek dancing. All the men wanted to dance with me.

'No, no,' I kept protesting, 'dance with her.' I indicated a very slim, pretty English woman volunteer who had come with us.

'No,' one of them shook his head. 'She looks like something left over after dinner. We want to dance with a real woman.'

'They say you are too young,' I shouted to the other woman as I was swept back out onto the floor.

After a while Maria's father wanted to go back to their home because he didn't feel well and they invited us to join them. It was a wonderfully warm, simple house and they made us very welcome, bringing out their prize jar of Nescafé and making us some powerful coffees. I felt very proud to be so much part of a community which just a few years before had seemed so alien and shocking.

CHAPTER FIFTEEN

A New Life

✻

My life has now changed completely. I no longer work at the Abbey National, my time being fully occupied with helping the Sisters with their work with the poor, the handicapped and, above all, the children of Romania, and with looking after our new son, Patreascu. To begin with I was learning as I went along, an enthusiastic amateur, but now I like to think I am wiser in the way I work. I also have a religious faith which not only means a lot to me but is a tremendous practical help too.

John and I continue to struggle through all the bureaucracy and expense involved in the adoption process (the legal costs could run up to £25,000, we are told). It cost £2,000 to have a home study conducted by the Social Services and have the authorities come up with seemingly endless petty observations, one report even saying that we weren't suitable because we were both 'morbidly obese'! My doctor wrote back asking for further explanations since he didn't understand what they meant and confessing that he found us 'plump but quite happy'. Tony Hughes, our solicitor, has been a life saver on many occasions – when the formalities seemed endless he was always positive and reassuring, and when we expressed our concern at the likely cost of the adoption process, he and his partners at Linnell's kindly waived the fees for his services.

We have even been on television! Patreascu was invited to see the *Blue Peter* studios, and spent the day with Diane-Louise Jordan, the programme's effervescent, fun-loving and kind presenter. They got on famously and have become firm friends.

We all appeared on *Hearts of Gold* – Patreascu not only took over the studio but captivated everyone too. It was as if he had been appearing on television all his life. The crew loved him and said something very special happened in the studio that evening. Everyone at the BBC was marvellous, making it a very special and memorable day for us – if somewhat of a surprise.

After struggling to master it for several months, Patreascu learnt to read. When he suddenly read a whole book to Mrs Tholen she sent him to Mrs Finkenrath, who was so thrilled she insisted he go and interrupt every class and read to them. All afternoon they told me they could hear loud cheers as he went from room to room and they were so proud of him.

Patreascu wanted to learn the trumpet at school but we were afraid the polio might have damaged his lungs too much. However, James, the trumpet teacher, told us he managed to make enough noise to stop the whole school and is now having trumpet lessons in the Annexe – as well as learning the violin.

We had always intended to take Patreascu back to visit the Sisters and see his country when we could afford it and, of course, as soon as we felt sure that the Romanian authorities would let him back out and the British let him back in. In the baking heat of the summer of 1995 it finally all came together. Some time before, I had approached a British Airways captain, Len Gruber, whom I had met on a Tarom flight, asking for a free flight for a young man the Sisters were sending over for eye operations. During a telephone chat, Len asked when I next planned to visit Romania and I told him of our dream and that we hoped it would happen next year. He asked me why I hadn't asked for free airfares for us and I admitted that I couldn't honestly say it was a matter of life and death – just that we thought it would be nice for Patreascu. Commending me for my honesty he said he would see what he could do and came back to us a few weeks later with the news that he had tickets for all three of us to travel. Things like this do not happen to us! There was only a week for us to prepare ourselves and the day before we were due to fly out we went down to the Romanian Embassy in London so that John and I could get visas.

'And where is the young man's passport?' the Consul asked.

'Actually,' I said, 'he's Romanian,' and I explained something of his story. The Consul was so impressed that we were actually taking Patreascu back to see his country and experience the culture which had previously been denied to him that he called the Ambassador, who was equally thrilled. They told us that almost no one thought to take the children back and they went out of their way to ensure that we would have no trouble with bureaucracy at the Romanian end. It was going to take a few hours for our visas to be processed and so Patreascu and I went out into Kensington Gardens. The heat was almost overpowering and the sight of the fountains was too much for Patreascu, who stripped down to his underpants and dived in, looking like Sabu the Elephant Boy. All sorts of people stopped to talk to him as he played in the water, his joyfulness infecting everyone who passed by.

The next day we flew out after only a few hours' sleep. The BA staff were marvellous and treated Patreascu like royalty. His obvious excitement and anticipation were infectious and set up a carnival atmosphere on board. Patreascu spent the whole flight helping with drinks and looking after everyone – with the flight crew's blessing.

Patreascu was received by the Romanian authorities like a returning hero. I was nervous that we would have our usual wait at Bucharest Airport while the Sisters tried to find someone to collect us – often in the past I had sat there for four hours or more, never doubting that they would come for me eventually. They had told us that Gerry, Dom Patreascu's son, would pick us up. He was a lovely man who often worked for the Sisters and whom we had asked to be one of Patreascu's godparents. To see him waiting for us, towering head and shoulders above the crowd, was wonderful because it meant we could escape the hassle of fighting our way past all the taxi drivers, money changers and unofficial porters touting for business. When he saw his godson, Gerry wept.

It was about four o'clock in the afternoon by the time we left the airport and the journey was a nightmare of traffic jams and accidents, but Patreascu was beside himself with excitement at every cow, chicken or goose that crossed the road. It was midnight by the time we reached the home and the Sisters, who always rise at 4.30 in the morning, had retired to their convent for the night. As we drew up at the high metal gates I saw a light on upstairs – someone was watching out for our arrival. As the gates were swung open we heard shouts of, 'Bevey, Patreascu, John!' and children in nightclothes spilled out onto the balconies above. I was terrified that in their rush they would hurtle headlong over the edge. As the van came through the gates they ran up and clung to the sides. The carers were joining the throng and even Bobby the dog came out barking his greetings. One of my volunteers, a tremendous girl named Heather, had stayed up to greet us too. Gerry drove slowly forward until he was eventually bogged down in a sea of bodies. We opened the doors and tried to get out as the crowd grabbed at us, kissing and cuddling and shouting their news and greetings. They threw clouds of petals over us and hung home-made garlands of flowers round our necks. They were all crying with joy at the sight of Patreascu who was wide-eyed and nervous at the noise of the onslaught.

I felt myself being carried towards the building by the crowd, my feet barely touching the ground as they insisted we come in and eat before being taken to our accommodation. I noticed Illeana standing at the back of the crowd. I had been worried that she would feel resentful at seeing us returning with Patreascu as our son. She came forward hesitantly once the crowd began to calm down and handed us a painting she had done of our house in England, the dogs and cat. She had obviously put a lot of time and trouble into it and was happy to see us, wanting to make us feel comfortable.

The Sisters had decided that it would be better if we stayed together as a family for most of the month rather than splitting us up in dormitories as usual. So they had arranged for us to move in with Tante Chiriac and her husband Gheorghe, who lived in a little peasant cottage beside the home. I had often looked out at this primitive but, picturesque smallholding on previous visits, but had never been inside.

Once we had been fed we were taken round to the dark, tiny cottage and greeted by Tante Chiriac and Gheorghe. Patreascu was very shy with this rather awe-inspiring old woman with her incredibly wizened face and hands and her gold teeth flashing in the dim light. The little wisps of hair which peeped out from under her red headscarf looked dark brown, not grey, but I knew her to be in her seventies. She wore a flowery frock and pinny. Gheorghe wore rough denim working trousers and shirt and when he took off his working cap he revealed a fine head of curly grey hair. They sweetly told us that the house was ours for as long as we wanted to stay and that they would be sleeping in their summer kitchen, which was a few yards away. Tante showed us through the three little rooms with the choice of beds set up.

We decided that Patreascu should stay with me since he was rather unsettled by his strange surroundings.

Tante then took us out into the dark to show us where the toilet was, through the grape vines, past the pigs, the fruit trees, the chickens and the dog, which seemed anxious to have a piece of our ankles. I couldn't believe it but we had forgotten to pack a torch. The loo was just an old shed with a hole in the ground with some boards to stand on and I couldn't quite imagine how Patreascu was going to manage since he only had one good leg and was therefore unable to squat! He was absolutely terrified of falling down the hole and the situation became impossible a few nights later when he got diarrhoea. It was pitch black without even any moonlight. Eventually we found the hut and I braced myself with one hand holding the side of the shed and the other holding Patreascu's gammy leg out straight, like a Cossack dancer. He squatted on his good leg, one hand gripping onto me and the other holding the shed for grim death – no way was that child going to risk falling down the hole – and we started to laugh so loud I'm sure the Sisters must have heard us in their little convent house on the other side of the wall. On the fifth visit of the night I decided the toilet was too much of an ordeal for him and let him use the garden – well away from the veg'.

When I owned up in the morning Tante told us not to give it a second thought and to let him use the garden if he ever had diarrhoea again. She was full of good advice about what he should eat and drink to get rid of the tummy bug and proceeded to throw buckets of water down everywhere, ignoring my protests that I would make good the garden.

Finally, she pumped up some ice-cold water for us to wash in and then they both retired to leave us in peace. During the night Patreascu and I were both bitten by thousands of mosquitoes. By the end of our stay we did not have a scrap of skin which hadn't been infected, while John was not bitten once.

When we woke the next morning the sun was streaming through the vines, onto bunches of ripening grapes hanging above the simple wooden table with its brightly coloured table cloth and chairs. The cottage, which had seemed so dark and scary when we arrived, now seemed like paradise. The place where we had washed ourselves the night before was now in full view of the road so we obviously couldn't wash more than our extremities there during the day, but John happily set about shaving in the cold water. A huge old enamel bowl stood on an ancient iron stand and Gheorghe held up an old mirror so that John could see what he was doing.

'Good morning,' a voice came from beside him as he concentrated on his chin and he looked up to find himself staring over the wall at Sister Fabiana, dazzling in her white and blue sari. She introduced herself and then saw Patreascu and became very emotional.

'Please,' she said, 'don't come over to our home yet. I will call you when we are ready for you.'

Patreascu remembered Sister Fabiana, describing her as Sister 'who is not brown'. She was the only non-Indian Sister before he left to come to the UK.

Tante Chiriac prepared us a breakfast of bread and salami and ice-cold water drawn straight from the well, apologising that she had no coffee and proudly showing us an empty jar which she had been given by a British volunteer some years ago but which was now simply an ornament. She and Gheorghe could only eat and drink things that they could grow or raise on their land and coffee wasn't one of them.

When Sister Fabiana called us across we could sense the excitement in the air. As we turned the corner we saw that balloons and garlands had been strung between all the buildings; the carers were all in their national costumes and there were chairs set out for a show. The children were waiting for us and then all began singing and dancing. Doamna Anna, one of the largest of the carers, bustled me inside, stripped me and insisted on cramming me into her national costume: a wrap-around skirt and white blouse, both covered with intricate embroidery, and a brightly coloured headscarf. It was a very tight squeeze indeed.

I felt ridiculous and I never know quite what to do in such situations, but I could see the children were looking forward to a party and so, tacking a sickly grin onto my face, I did my best to dance to the frantic Romanian popular folk music as the children got up to join me. The music played, carers and Sisters danced, the sun shone, the sky was blue, the garlands and balloons swayed in the gentle breeze and the neighbours poured in with little gifts of flowers and fruit. Patreascu forgot his uncertainty and got up and danced and danced. He whirled around with Illeana, his eyes alive with excitement and wonder that all this was for him, that he was so special to these people. The Sisters broke open the chocolate and the children had orange squash, a rare treat. The whole compound was alive in a celebration of Patreascu's life. I looked across to Sister Fabiana and mouthed, 'Thank you.' She just raised her eyes to heaven and mouthed back, 'Thank the Lord for Patreascu.' The whole morning was very emotional as carers who remembered Patreascu as he had been got to grips with the reality of the new Patreascu.

Eventually he spotted the toys in the playground and wandered off to amuse himself. Initially he had been too shy to leave our sides but before long we had lost sight of him. When it came to lunchtime we discovered him in with the other children eating the rice dish they had been given and trying to show Szulita that it would be better to use a spoon than to dig her fists in, gently wiping her fingers on a cloth.

All through our stay Patreascu loved to help the Sisters in their work; washing up, mopping the floor, going to market with them and helping to hand out bread and jam and milk to the poorest of the local children, who queue up in their hundreds each day for what is probably their only meal. He used to spread jam on the bread and pour the mugs of milk, smiling tenderly at each child, making sure they didn't gulp it down or spill it in their haste to quell their hunger pangs. When he worked in the soup kitchen he ladled up the soup with such an infectious smile that no one could resist smiling back. He loved all the Sisters and adored Sister Bartholomeo's smile – perhaps she reminded him of Sister Ida, the first person ever to show him kindness and to believe in him. The Sisters would even take him out with them on visits to the poor, the old and the sick. They encouraged him to be wild and free and high-spirited to show the workers how children should be when fit and healthy. When he returned to school after the holidays and the teachers asked him what his favourite thing about the trip was he said, 'Washing the chapel floor with the Sisters; it was great.'

One afternoon in August there was great excitement and the Sisters said that there was to be a concert that afternoon. Ashley and Ana-liese, now happily married, had seen a group of Romanian folk musicians play in Switzerland and had persuaded them to come to Bacau to play for the children. It was a rare treat. Seats were put out in the compound – enough to accommodate all the carers and their children, the home's neighbours and residents. Sitting in the heat of the late afternoon sun, the music was fast and exciting. Patreascu made as if to get up and I pulled his arm to get him to sit down again. Sister Fabiana whispered laughingly to me, 'Bevey, let him go, let's see what he does.'

Well, Patreascu danced and with what vigour! If only Mrs Woollard could have seen him, how proud she would have been. Patreascu twirled; he jumped; his dancing was terrific and his thin and wasted left leg did its best, splint and all, to keep up with the rest of his body. All the children clapped, loving his impromptu performance. Everyone was delighted with this spontaneous and uninhibited expression of joy. The musicians, the Sisters, the carers, the neighbours, but above all, his friends, begged him to go on.

It was very special – a tribute to enjoying life. Patreascu picked up a toy panda and began to dance with that, clowning around for the children, lost in the music, revelling in his friends' response to his comic turn. The children laughed so hard they fell onto the floor. Patreascu gently pulled them up and onto his makeshift dance floor. Felix, one boy who had laughed so much he cried, snatched the toy away and began dancing around, copying Patreascu. Soon we were all up and dancing.

It was a super afternoon with an air of jubilation – we were all one with each other, sharing something quite precious, a sense of overwhelming togetherness, and at its centre was Patreascu, full of life and love.

Patreascu soon informed us of his intention to marry Sister Fabiana at the earliest opportunity. It only took him a couple of days to pluck up the courage to propose formally. When she explained that she was already spoken for, for she was married to Christ, he was disappointed but happy, declaring Jesus to be a fine choice of husband.

I recalled my last visit when I helped Sister Bartholomeo with the soup kitchen. She had asked me to sing with the children to entertain those we were feeding. I had been reluctant until I saw the joy it brought to audience and singers. Seeing Patreascu entertaining his friends had reminded me of this. I shouldn't stop him expressing his love of life, for it proved to the locals that these formerly neglected children were capable of great joy, of having fun, just like them.

One day Sister Fabiana reprimanded me for scolding Patreascu as he was screaming at the top of his voice in the paddling pool. 'Oh, Bevey, let him enjoy himself; let him teach our children to enjoy themselves too. Let him be himself.' I was concerned that Patreascu had been teaching the children to water fight and run around screaming, but this was what the Sisters wanted – to see their children play freely, released from the restrictions of their disabilities. They wanted the children liberated from the memories of Ungerini, shown how to live life to the full, and they believed that Patreascu was the man for the job. Sister Fabiana also explained that she wanted the workers to realise that this normal childlike behaviour – even misbehaviour – was good for the children. If she was happy then I was happy too ... Even when at nine one evening, when everyone should have been settled for the night, the Sisters quietly indicated I should peep into the boys' dormitory – there were the two Luciens, Felix, Marian and Patreascu having a giant pillow fight. How we all laughed, delighted to see such natural exuberance from boys who had once been unresponsive to anything but hunger or pain.

'Patreascu is an example to everyone of what can be achieved with these children if they are made to feel loved and part of a family,' Sister Fabiana told me. 'Even the priests are amazed and cannot believe that he was once a child here. It helps them to understand why we do what we do because we believe that many other children could be helped like this.'

She has said since that after Patreascu's visit several of the carers started to take children to their homes for weekends in order to give them a little of the family experience that Patreascu had had. A school inspector called while we were visiting and spent a long time questioning Patreascu and having his school reports translated. After we left, Sister Fabiana reported that their school had been allocated more teachers. I honestly believe that taking Patreascu back for the summer has had more impact on the area than almost anything else we have done over the last few years.

After two weeks, John had to return to England because of work commitments and we were all very sad to see him go.

In the warm light of day Patreascu was no longer scared of Tante Chiriac and adored everything about the smallholding. He never tired of pumping up well water for her, feeding the chickens, preparing next year's seeds or helping her to bathe her two pet pigs each lunchtime. Tante Chiriac treated the animals as if they were her children, even though they were there to provide next year's meat supply. When one of the pigs hurt his leg she and

Patreascu would spend hours massaging it each day, and when he finally got back onto all four feet they cheered and clapped and insisted on bringing the Sisters round to view the miracle.

Each night the pigs were let out for recreation and would be waiting by the gate for Patreascu's return. Tante and Gheorghe drove a pre-war motorbike and sidecar, rumoured to have been left behind by the Nazis. Patreascu did try and persuade them to take Goitsa, Tante's favourite pig, and himself out for a spin. I am sure she would have loved to had she not been concerned the pig might get hurt!

Being there for such a glorious summer we were able to take the children on many wonderful but simple outings, where Patreascu was able to fuss around them with sun creams and hats, making sure everyone was included in the fun and got something to eat. We visited a mineral pool as dark as chocolate and viscous as the Dead Sea which I toppled into fully clothed, landing completely spreadeagled and unable to right myself. After a few seconds of polite silence, everyone collapsed laughing, me included. Once I had got used to the strange sensation of being unable to sink I started to tow the children around in the water and eventually had them all sitting on top of me as I bobbed along.

'Oh, Bevey,' Sister Bartholomeo laughed. 'The children are so lucky to have you, so many of them can ride on you at once.' I must have looked like a cruising whale.

We picnicked and walked and when, one day, the terrain became too rough for Tractor Lucien, who could still not walk and relied on his tractor to get around, Patreascu limped off to fetch a tow rope and gladly pulled him along like an ancient Egyptian slave boy. The other children are so non-judgemental of one another that Patreascu completely lost his self-consciousness about his splint and scarred leg. He cast off the long trousers he had insisted on wearing for so long, and no longer worried about covering the splint with a sock. I asked him what had made him change.

'Having a splint is a good thing, Mum,' he said. 'It helps me walk. If I hide it no children will see it and they won't know it is good and they might be frightened or embarrassed to wear one.' What he didn't realise was that not only were the children watching, but virtually the whole of Moldavia. People were able to see that wearing a splint was an indication of physical disability, not mental disability. He was helping to tear down the very real fears and beliefs of the local people which had held back the progress of handicapped children so badly in the past. Patreascu embodied the benefits of what the Sisters had been saying for years: treat the children with humanity, as you would your family – all they need to lead normal lives is a little extra assistance. The sight of Patreascu's face, shining with love and joy, which shouted out, 'Hey, I'm glad to be alive,' showed more than anything why these children are worthy of our love and our time.

One of the workers, Felicia, was to be married during our stay and we were invited out into the country to the wedding. This was even more traditional than Maria Ochelari's wedding, with the bride's family partying in one house and the groom's in another, the two sides finally coming together with a great deal of tradition and drunken theatrics. Patreascu mistakenly downed a glass of Tsuika, thinking it was water, and then went on to have four glasses of wine and water before wondering why his 'legs felt funny'. At one moment he reappeared round a corner after spending time with some local boys, rather expertly smoking a cigarette. Soon afterwards he disappeared off to groom the cows. Being allowed to milk them was the greatest treat for him. The guests were wonderful with the children, dancing with them all afternoon and evening.

During the proceedings Illeana, now nearly twenty years old, met a young shepherd boy who very formally asked me if he could dance with her. I agreed and acted like a traditional Sicilian grandmother, watching them out of the corner of my eye, but staying an extra half-hour because Illeana seemed to be having so much fun. As we were leaving in the van the boy appeared on a horse and cart with his friends. He looked very dashing as he drove up. We opened the door so that Illeana could say goodbye and he gallantly tossed in a garland of flowers. I had seen them kissing earlier and he had asked me if he could visit her. I told him she lived in an orphanage and he would have to ask the Sisters' permission.

'Did you like that boy?' I asked her once we were driving off.

'Yes,' she said, 'but I would never go out with a shepherd boy because they are too rough and drink too much.'

Illeana has blossomed so much since the surgery on her eyes, she's developed a real personality. She is still very aware of where she is and of everyone's differences, but she is much more tolerant.

She goes to school every day and then has light duties in the girls' room upstairs. She also has a Saturday job, going by herself into Bacau to clean for, and generally help, Johnny the dentist and his wife, Cecilia. This gives her some much needed independence as well as some pocket money. It is good for the children to have a break from the home and talk to ordinary Romanians living in family environments.

During our stay we went to Mass with the Sisters every morning at seven, and Patreascu served as an altar boy. In the evenings he would dance for Tante and Gheorghe, clowning around until eventually the old man fell off the bed laughing. Tante called him her 'mari schmecker' or 'big show-off boy' and when he kissed her goodnight Gheorghe would make a huge pantomime out of being jealous. One afternoon I returned to find Tante Chiriac and Patreascu curled up together, fast asleep. Gheorghe winked at me and we left them in peace to enjoy their well earned siesta.

One morning Patreascu made his way over to the home on his own and knocked on the door. Sister Fabiana let him in.

'I would like to have a meeting with you, Sister,' he announced.

'What about Mummy?' she asked.

'No,' he was adamant, 'this is between you and me.'

'Very well.' She led him to her office. 'Would you like coffee?'

Once they were sitting down with their coffees he explained his plan. 'Although I am very happy in England,' he said, 'my brother is much older than me and sometimes I am a little lonely. I would like to adopt another child from the home.'

'Who did you have in mind?' Sister asked.

'I would like to take them all but we don't have room,' he told her, 'but I think that Crenguitsa would be the best.'

'What about Emily?' Sister Fabiana asked, having been told all about his English friends.

'Emily I am going to marry. Crenguitsa would be my sister. I only have a small bedroom but we could put in bunks and she could borrow my clothes. She would need some dresses and girl's things for school because otherwise the children would tease her ...' he paused to think for a moment, '... but of course I'd punch them.'

'What about Mum and Dad?'

'They think they are too old to adopt any more children, but if we all keep praying I think it could happen.'

Though Sister Fabiana was careful not to encourage Patreascu in his plan, he didn't give it up. When we got back to England, I received a call from Mrs Finkenrath asking when the new child would be arriving at St Monica's. 'What new child?' I asked.

'Patreascu has booked a place for Crenguitsa Peberdy.'

I explained that this was not going to happen; it was all in Patreascu's mind. Mrs Finkenrath said she was disappointed as all the staff and children were looking forward to having another Patreascu in their school. We had to explain to Patreascu that we were very lucky to be getting a chance to adopt him, but that it wasn't possible for us to adopt another child because we didn't have enough money. Mrs Finkenrath remarked one day that Patreascu always looked clean and smart. Had she realised he only had one of most items and the quick turnaround necessary she would have been even more impressed. We didn't tell him that we hadn't even enough money for his adoption and that was why he had had to stop having violin and horse-riding lessons for the last eighteen months, because we didn't want to worry him.

'Also,' I told him, 'it would take a lot of work to help Crenguitsa.'

'I could help, Mum,' he insisted. 'I know what to do now.'

There is nothing physically wrong with Crenguitsa – she is a very sweet and gentle six-year-old. I can remember the day she arrived at Ungerini, terrified, her blue eyes wide with fear. Though her mental capabilities are difficult to assess at present she progressed a great deal during the summer of 1995 and is beginning to speak. Sister Fabiana is encouraging her to mix more with local children in the hope that she will improve more quickly with their example to follow. Patreascu still prays that we will adopt Crenguitsa one day or, failing that, asks Jesus to find her another family.

Patreascu's mother, Elena, has always been kept fully informed about our plans for adopting him and has always been very co-operative. John and I really wanted to meet her but decided, with the advice of the Sisters, that it might be too early for Patreascu, that it could make him very confused. So John and I, Sister Bartholomeo and Sister Marthe planned to go up into the mountains to visit her while Sister Fabiana entertained Patreascu for the day.

'If you are going out into the country,' Sister Fabiana said, 'could you take Maria to visit her family, to see if they would like her to come and stay with them sometimes?'

Maria is now seventeen years old and, checking her records, the Sisters discovered that she had arrived at Ungerini at the age of six, along with her three-year-old sister, Mihaila. At first Maria had been on our list to come to Britain for surgery. However, with the aid of calipers alone she had managed to get up and walk. Once she had overcome her fear of being upright, encouraged by the Sisters and their 'resident walking expert', Szuzannah, she had made so much progress that surgery was no longer necessary. The more she walked the stronger and straighter her legs became. At first the carers had thought me awful, making her stand, holding onto the end of the bed; then walk a little, holding onto my hands, sweating with a mixture of effort and fear. But the end result was that she was eventually able to go up and down stairs under her own steam.

Just that week Heather had, with love and encouragement, got her to take a couple of steps without crutches. Mihaila was a more serious case and was much lazier than her sister and consequently less able to do anything for herself. Maria had always sworn that she had a family but had been told at Ungerini that she was imagining it. The Sisters, however, had managed to trace them. Sister Fabiana had been tracing all the children's families to see if they could be persuaded to visit the home, or to have their children to visit them for the day or possibly even a weekend. The great risk was that if the families said no the children would have to face up to the reality of rejection once more. Sister Fabiana asked me if I thought she was right to risk this happening and I felt that if only one child could be re-united with their family this way then it would be worth it. She said she had reached the same conclusion.

All the time I had been at Ungerini I had always been puzzled by the fact that families so rarely, if ever, came to visit their children or take them out for a day. It had seemed rather shocking to me that they were willing just to dump their children in institutions and then forget about them. I was also curious to see the sort of families and homes that the girls came from. The Sisters also asked if we would look in on Shanti's mother and see if there was any chance she could have her daughter to stay sometimes. They are very keen to get as many of the children as possible spending time with their families and, of course, if everything works out happily, to be permanently reunited.

On the morning of the expedition Maria was dressed up in her best clothes, made her face up and even painted her nails a bright scarlet, and we set out in the van, with Gerry driving and two Sisters to translate. We wound further and further up into the Carpathians, bumping about on the rough tracks over terrain which would have been impassable if the weather had not been so dry. Several times we had to get out and push the van through potholes and over boulders, with Gerry asking for new directions from everyone we passed. Sister Fabiana had written to the family about Maria but had decided not to wait for a reply in case the letter had never arrived and now I could see why it might not. Eventually, after many, many hours, we reached the little hamlet where we knew the family lived. John stayed in the van with Maria, and I went to the house with the Sisters. We were all dripping with sweat as we made our way over the baked mud to the ramshackle building.

Maria's mother and father came out to meet us, surrounded by their eight children. None of them wore any shoes. They were obviously puzzled to see us and invited us in.

'Do you have a daughter called Maria?' we asked.

'We did have,' they told us, 'but we believe she is dead. When she was six, and her sister was three, the authorities decided we needed help. So they took them away. They told us that they were going to a wonderful place where they would get food and lots of gymnastika. They said that once the girls had been taught to walk they would be returned to us. We never heard another word about them. We tried writing to them but the authorities denied they existed. Eventually we found out they were at a place called Ungerini and we wrote there, but they said the girls had gone to a special school but they wouldn't say where and so we couldn't trace them.'

They showed us the letter from Ungerini and I gained another insight into the problems parents faced in tracing their children.

'This sort of thing happened all the time,' the Sisters told me. 'The authorities did not want working people to have their time taken up caring for handicapped children; they wanted them out in the fields or the factories.' I could see why so few families ever came to visit the children of Ungerini.

'Your daughters are living with us in Bacau,' the Sisters told them.

'Bacau?' Their faces lit up. 'Then we could visit them?'

'Maria is outside in our van. Would you like to ... ?' Before the Sister could finish her sentence the whole family had run outside. John opened the door when he saw them coming and, for the first time ever, Maria walked unaided across the uneven ground into her mother's arms. Even the crusty-looking old father wept to see her as she half walked and was half carried into the house. The whole family seemed to have so much love for her. John's face was full of joy, his eyes bright with tears.

When they had all calmed down a little Sister Bartholomeo asked if they would like to have Maria visit for the occasional weekend.

'No.' They were adamant and for a moment we were shocked. 'If it is at all possible, Your Worship, may she stay with us now and never leave us again?'

We hadn't planned for this eventuality! Maria had no spare clothes with her, just food the Sisters had brought for the family. Sister Bartholomeo said she felt they had been separated for so long and their joy at the reunion was so obviously sincere, that she couldn't bear to deny them this wonderful opportunity. She felt sure Sister Fabiana would not be angry. When we said yes they were overwhelmed and starting firing questions at me about how they should look after her; should they carry her around and wash her, for instance?

'Certainly not,' I told them laughingly. 'Maria must be encouraged to walk and do these things for herself. Please, Maria, don't allow your mother to run around after you.' From the adoring look she gave her mother I did not think there would be many problems.

'There is one thing,' the father said gravely. 'Everyone in this family works.'

'That's good,' I said. 'Maria will be glad to help too.'

'There will no time for this—' he pointed to the make-up '— and certainly no time for this.' He tapped on her nails. 'My wife and daughters are beautiful enough without all that.'

'That is no problem,' I laughed. 'That was just for today because it was a special occasion.'

Maria's parents asked about Mihaila and Sister Bartholomeo told them that though she was too weak to return home, they would be most welcome to visit her. I was thinking that, perhaps, in time, the Sisters would be able to get Mihaila up and walking too, and then she would also be able to go home to her family. There is a little room available for family visits – the Sisters realise that privacy is needed for parents to spend time with their children. It can be daunting to have all the children rushing at you at once. There are a few toys in the visiting room for the other children in the family to play with, and little refreshments are provided, for a lot of the families have to travel great distances to reach Bacau.

After leaving Maria we stopped for a picnic and the Sisters were in rejoicing mood. 'Doesn't it feel wonderful to be able to do these things?' they wanted to know. 'Could any amount of riches make you feel better than this?' I had to admit that I didn't think they could. I had seen another family discovering a long-lost child at Gisteni on one of my visits and I couldn't help wondering how many more of the children could go back to their families if only the family knew where they were. Many, of course, are far too irretrievably mad and institutionalised now to be able to cope in a normal family home but undoubtedly they would benefit from being visited by their relations – a little extra food or even just a hug would do them a lot of good.

A chap at Gisteni (the Adult Institute) had been taken away from his parents at seven. They had managed to stay in touch for two years but hadn't seen him for eleven years. I was on the van with his family as they took him home forever with them. His only crime, barely discernible, was to be a little simple and slow to speak and learn. What a joy it was to see their relief and their happiness and their love for each other after all that time apart. To be able to escape from such a place must seem like a miracle.

It was a different story when we visited Shanti's mother. Although she was a pleasant woman it was obvious that she was not capable of looking after a child like Shanti, even for a day. She told us that the authorities had taken all her children away from her, but she had a new baby. The house was a shambles and she had no food for the child. The Sisters had brought provisions which they gave to her.

Sister Fabiana had helped us to select some presents to take to Patreascu's mother and his older half-sister, Mirella. We had some shoes, a skipping rope and something for Mirella's hair, soap, talcum powder and cream for Elena and some chocolate for her parents. Although they knew all about the adoption they had no idea that we were arriving that day because there was no way of contacting them. Like Maria's family, they were the poorest of the poor, with no shoes. The grandfather had been to see Patreascu once at Mother Teresa's but seeing how handicapped he was had said, with sadness, it would be impossible for them to look after him. Elena was blonde, which surprised me since Patreascu was so dark, an attractive woman with troubled green eyes. She smiled a lot but still seemed sad. She was wearing a simple summer dress and her feet were covered with dust.

They told us they were ashamed to meet us because they could imagine what we thought of them for abandoning Patreascu on the first day of his life but they had genuinely believed they were sending him to a place where he would be better looked after than they could manage. 'But if you are going to ask us to have him back,' they said, 'it is impossible.'

When they realised that nothing was further from our minds they fired lots of questions at us and I promised to write once a year and to send a photograph.

'What do you tell him about us?' they wanted to know.

'That you were just too poor to be able to look after him.' They seemed comforted by this.

One day I am sure he will want to visit them and we will certainly encourage him to do that when he is ready to understand why his mother was unable to keep him and believed she was doing the right thing by him.

The interesting thing about visiting Ungerini and Gisteni when I am in Romania now is being able to see how the children who didn't get to Mother Teresa's are developing. Lazy Lazlo, for instance, now walks well and is a boisterous, good looking teenager. Wilma, the first child that I saw when I arrived at Ungerini is now at Gisteni. She always tries to look nice, wearing clothes and shoes. She grabs my arm and pushes everyone else away, hating me to kiss anyone else or shake their hands. I cannot see her ever leaving the Institute, even though she is quite good at looking after herself, because she has nowhere to go. It would be wonderful if she could get herself some sort of little job, but who would have her, who would give her that chance?

Marius was transferred to a State home for problem boys. Apparently he was reluctant to go but the Ungerini people insisted because he was becoming too difficult for them. We've never heard any more about him. Patrika is still at Ungerini and will soon transfer to Gisteni. I should think he will be all right there, although the living conditions are still appalling, because he is big and hopefully won't get picked on.

Of those who we've returned to Mother Teresa's, Bacau, Marian would still prefer to eat or lie down and sleep than actually walk, but he is far too large to be treated like a baby any more and the Sisters and carers work hard at making him do things for himself and continue doing them, pushing him to remain upright and walking.

Szuzannah still walks with crutches and probably always will. She cannot read or write, but has learned to colour in and enjoys that. She also loves to help the carer in her room to wash all the girls' clothes and sheets. They stand at one of the three sinks in the washing and drying room and wring out together. The outside drying area is up a fairly steep staircase of uneven wood but she manages to get herself up there and likes nothing better than pegging out the washing in the fresh air. The Sisters don't mind the children helping a little with household jobs, but it must never get in the way of their education and they will never allow them to be used as slaves.

Little Maria, who was one of the first children I looked after in my room, Salon One, and one of the first to go to the Sisters, now walks extraordinarily well considering her dislocated hips – albeit with a very curious gait. She has now moved to the upstairs girls' room where she has to be more independent. She is beginning to speak and still has her lovely big grin which grows even wider when I sing the old Maria songs to her.

Valentina is also still at Mother Teresa's. She has learned to read and write beautifully. She is able to do simple arithmetic and having been introduced to the joys of cooking by Denise, is employed part-time in the kitchen where she is extremely conscientious about cleanliness and a very good cook. She enjoys herself and still tends to be a trifle loud sometimes. When the Sisters traced her family they were surprised to find that they were not poor like the others but lived in a big house. They had put Valentina into Ungerini when she was nine years old because she was a bit slow. We can only imagine how that must have affected the poor girl. At first the family thought the Sisters wanted money from them for looking after her, but they explained she simply wanted to meet them. She has written to them several times and they did meet her once, but they have never made any effort to see her again and do not reply to her letters. She was so desperate to be reunited with her family and is obviously disappointed, but although she becomes depressed sometimes, she is always glad for other children like Maria who turn out to be loved after all and have returned home.

Many of the hundreds of local children whom Dr Nigel helped on his first visit are walking and independent and have not gone to Ungerini. I wish that the staff at Salt & Son in Birmingham, who sacrificed their time to make all the equipment which has helped so many of them, could see the results of their work. Also the many hospitals and others who donated wheelchairs and walking frames and much needed equipment. The children's walking and independence are the best possible and most tangible result of their tremendous generosity. Dr Nigel's equipment got the children up, and the Sisters' year-round dedicated physiotherapy kept them upright. Initially, after much coaxing, the children had consented to the physio' to please the Sisters. Then, when they began to enjoy the freedom being upright gave them, the critical point was reached – they now wanted to be up and walking for themselves!

Madam Augustina has been removed from the office of Director at Ungerini and replaced by a doctor. She has been given an administrative position and, though it must have been a blow to her self-esteem at the time, she now looks far more relaxed and happy to have been relieved of the burden of having to answer directly to the authorities. Adelina, the Chief Nurse, seems to have more responsibilities now and she has appointed Lucia to be in charge of the carers. Lucia is a strong and knowing woman, and is very keen for Ungerini and the children to look good, so the new set-up should work extremely well. Above all, the workers respect Lucia and listen to her.

I am still trying to get sponsorship for Gerry Patreascu to come to Britain and train in the construction of calipers, splints and walking aids – I am sure it will happen, if not until early 1996. I have been promised all the equipment for setting up an orthotics workshop in Bacau, so it is only a matter of time until it opens. I am also trying to get a prosthetics workshop up and running and for other Romanians, alongside Gerry, to train as prosthetics fitters and artificial limb-makers.

I was delighted to be able to help with one of the longer-term projects during 1994 – Dr Irina Tiron has been able to come to Britain for five months to supplement her studies in neonatalogy at the Birmingham Heartlands Hospital. This proved a very successful exercise and Dr Tiron is now sharing her new knowledge with her staff and colleagues at Bacau Hospital, thereby helping her many patients, drawn from the whole of Moldavia. Dr Tiron made many friends amongst her colleagues in Birmingham and I am happy to be making arrangements for some of them to travel to Romania and help out at the hospital in Bacau.

Dr Nigel has now, after a long and full career, retired. He and Moira still continue to help the children of Bacau and Moldavia and visit Mother Teresa's as part of our medical team. Their son, Jonathan, has followed in his father's surgical footsteps and is a paediatric orthopaedic surgeon – he is also showing signs of interest in travelling to Bacau to help out – taking part in Lucien's and Marian's operations must have given him a taste for it!

As for Patreascu, there are many situations in which his leg causes him huge physical problems. As there are no muscles on the left side of his leg until the hip region, he cannot lift that leg unaided and stairs are always a problem. There is no control over the left knee and it can go in any direction, making going up or down stairs potentially dangerous. However, we don't make a big thing of it – it's like having a lump of wood, albeit one that feels pain, to use as a prop to get about. He tries to run and rushes around with a sort of skipping action, but he can't go as fast as the other children at school – he's never going to be in the school football team, which is his dream, but he joins in playground games as best he can. His favourite holidays have been spent in the Lake District where, despite his handicap, he hikes across surfaces that would be ambitious for a child with two normally functioning legs. He loves the scenery, the fresh air, the waterfalls, the animals and the trees, and the freedom to roam. He falls a lot, but is immediately up and off again.

More than anything, Patreascu likes to ask a constant stream of questions on any and every subject. His mind leaps from subject to subject, leaving me trailing behind. On a recent visit to the Natural History Museum, I don't think he drew breath from ten in the morning until they closed at six. 'Why do you ask so many questions?' I asked. 'Well, Mum,' he replied, 'I have to learn and this is what children do.'

Some of his questions are surprisingly insightful. 'Mum,' he asked, 'the Sisters really love the children so much, don't they?'

'Yes, very much,' I replied.

'Then why do they send them away for adoption?'

'Well, it is because they love them, and although their home is a happy home and the Sisters are like their mother and family, the Sisters want the children to each have their own families, nans and grandads, cousins, aunts and uncles, and above all the love of their own mum and dad.'

Patreascu pondered on this for a few minutes and then said, 'Oh, it's a bit like God then, really. He loved his only son Jesus so much, but he also loved us and sent Jesus down from heaven to earth to help us, even though he loved Jesus and wanted to keep him for himself.'

One day in the spring of 1995, Patreascu and I were sitting in the car waiting for John, when he caused me really to stop and think about the last couple of years and all that has happened to me. Patreascu was watching a family of robins and telling me which was the daddy, which the mummy and who all the children were. His story was peppered with the usual quota of questions that I tried to field as he went along. I was only half listening to his happy chatter when he asked, 'Do robins cough?'

For a moment I was taken aback and then I thought about where this child had come from; how far he had travelled from such a sorrowful past, through pain and fear and struggle, and realised that Patreascu truly epitomises everything I have come to believe worthwhile. There is no such thing as a hopeless case – every child, every man and woman, rich or poor, healthy or sick, is worthy of love, worthy of a chance at life. With laughter in my voice I told him, reliably I hope, 'Well, I suppose robins do cough if they're poorly!'

More such moments came during our summer holiday in Bacau and Ungerini. These dear children, all my children at Ungerini and Mother Teresa's, Bacau, had done for me just as much as I may have done for them and they've repaid me a thousand times over. I stretched out my hand to help them – an easy move for me – and they responded to my touch with trust, a giant step for them, accustomed as they were to rejection. How hard it must have been for these children to let down their barriers, to overcome their fears, to unfold and discard the protective layers they had put up to guard against the mental and physical assaults perpetrated on them during their short, sad lives. What courage these children had – still have – I feel humbled knowing them, by the fact they have survived it all, for I am sure I would have given up the will to live. This is not my story, it is the story of the children and their struggle: they are the best possible testament to hope, never to give up.

I should like to thank Dr Judith Darmady and Mrs Felicity MacPherson of the Ungerini Orphanage Trust for giving me the opportunity to go out to Ungerini and work with the people of Romania and the children of Ungerini Irrecuperable Orphanage.

The orphanage at Ungerini continues to be supported by the Ungerini Orphanage Trust and their dedicated team of helpers.

Beverly Peberdy continues to work for the people of Romania through The Friends of Romanian Children, care of 78 Stokenchurch Place, Bradwell Common, Milton Keynes, MK13 8BY.